p. 132 - Anathema 1983
p. 162 - Mohamed

1054 -
1582 - Gregory 13
       Calendar change.
England accepted in 18C

✝

THE STRUGGLE AGAINST ECUMENISM

THE STRUGGLE AGAINST ECUMENISM

The History of the True Orthodox Church of Greece from 1924 to 1994

THE HOLY ORTHODOX CHURCH
IN NORTH AMERICA

BOSTON, MASSACHUSETTS
1998

Copyright © 1998 by the Holy Orthodox Church in North America
Boston, Massachusetts 02131
All rights reserved
Printed in the United States of America
ISBN 0-943405-09-2
Library of Congress Catalog Card Number: 98-70554

Contents

List of Illustrations	8
Preface	11
Introduction	15

PART ONE

CHAPTER I
The Introduction of the Gregorian Calendar — 23

CHAPTER II
The Beginnings of the "Resistance Movement" of the True Orthodox Christians — 39

CHAPTER III
Divisions — 57

CHAPTER IV
Recent History of the True Orthodox — 79

CHAPTER V
The Status in 1994 — 101
  1) The Synod of the Matthewites — 101
  2) The Synod of Cyprian Koutsoumbas — 102
    A. The Kallistos Schism — 102
    B. The Synod of Those in Resistance — 112
  3) The Synod of Chrysostom Kiousis — 120
  4) The Synod of Archbishop Auxentius — 125
  The Synod of Archbishop Auxentius and the Traditional Orthodox Christians in North America and Europe — 130
  The Traditional Orthodox Christians of Russia — 160
  The Current State of Affairs — 162

Epilogue — 167

PART TWO

APPENDIX A
Encyclical of the Ecumenical Patriarchate, 1920 — 177

APPENDIX B
The Barr Statement of the World Council of Churches — 181

APPENDIX C
A Letter from Metropolitan Philaret (Voznesensky) to Abbess Magdalena (Countess Grabbe), Superior of the Lesna Convent in France — 182

APPENDIX D
A Letter from Metropolitan Philaret (Voznesensky) to a Priest of the Church Abroad Concerning Father Dimitry Dudko and the Moscow Patriarchate — 196

APPENDIX E
Reflections on Metropolitan Vitaly's Nativity Epistle — 211

APPENDIX F
Monophysitism and the Orthodox Church — 216

APPENDIX G
An Encyclical on the "Summit Message" — 219

APPENDIX H
An Encyclical on the Balamand Statement — 231

APPENDIX I
Saint Joseph of Arimathea English-Speaking Orthodox Parish, Toronto, Canada: The Tenth Anniversary — 238

APPENDIX J
The Dubious Orthodoxy of Metropolitan Cyprian's Group — 243

APPENDIX K
A Letter to Stephen — 255

APPENDIX L
The First Canon of Saint Basil the Great, and Its Interpretation — 256

CONTENTS

APPENDIX M
"Sectarian" Orthodox Christians — 263

APPENDIX N
"Uncanonical" Orthodox Christians — 269

APPENDIX O
New Calendar Donatism? — 275

APPENDIX P
Our Readers Ask . . . . — 279

APPENDIX Q
Letter to Anastasia — 286

APPENDIX R
Obituary: Elder Sabbas, Monk — 288

APPENDIX S
Selective Blindness — 298

APPENDIX T
The New Martyr Catherine of Attica — 305

Chronology — 311
Bibliography — 323
Index — 334

List of Illustrations

The Chapel of Saint John the Theologian on Mount Hymettos outside Athens.	22
King Constantine and Eleftherios Venizelos in Thessalonica, 1915.	26
Ecumenical Patriarch Athenagoras performing a memorial service for Eleftherios Venizelos in 1963 at his tomb.	28
Meletios Metaxakis.	31
Archbishop Chrysostom Papadopoulos of Athens.	37
Catherine Routis, killed by the police in November of 1927.	40
The miraculous appearance of the Cross, September 14, 1925.	43
Patriarch Christopher of Alexandria.	45
The three Metropolitans who returned to the traditional Church calendar in May, 1935: Chrysostom of Florina, Germanos of Demetrias, and Chrysostom of Zakynthos.	47
Police attack the traditional Orthodox faithful who had gathered peacefully in front of the Metropoly Cathedral of Athens, June, 1935.	51
Police attack the Orthodox faithful in Metropoly Square, Athens, June 1, 1935.	52
Metropolitans Chrysostom of Florina, Germanos of Demetrias, and Germanos of the Cyclades with clergy and people for the Theophany procession, 1937.	56
Metropolitan Chrysostom of Florina in Athens, June, 1939.	58
Metropolitans Germanos of Demetrias and Chrysostom of Florina at Old Faleron, Theophany, 1938.	61
Metropolitan Germanos of the Cyclades with clergy and people gathered for Theophany.	62

ILLUSTRATIONS

Metropolitans Chrysostom of Florina, Germanos of the Cyclades, Christopher of Megaris, and Polycarp of Diavlia, 1944.	64
Metropolitans Christopher of Megaris, Chrysostom of Florina, and Polycarp of Diavlia, Theophany, 1948.	66
Theophany of the traditional Orthodox Christians, 1948.	68
Police overturn the Epitaphios of the traditional Orthodox Christians during the procession of Holy Friday, 1951, in Piraeus.	70
Archimandrite Gerasimos Skourtaniotis of the Holy Transfiguration Monastery in Kouvara, Attica, before and after being forcibly stripped of his priestly garb and shaven by the police authorities.	70
Father Nicholas Smyrlis of Kalamata, as a young priest and after being forcibly stripped of his priestly garb and shaven by the police authorities.	71
The Monastery of Hypsilos in Mytilene, to which Metropolitan Chrysostom of Florina was exiled in February of 1951.	72
Metropolitan Chrysostom at his place of exile, September 7, 1951.	72
Metropolitan Chrysostom returning from exile, July 18, 1952.	73
Procession to the burial place of Metropolitan Germanos of the Cyclades.	74
Procession with the newly reposed Metropolitan Chrysostom of Florina, September 8, 1955.	75
Metropolitan Chrysostom of Florina.	75
Father Philotheos Zervakos.	76
Metropolitan Chrysostom of Florina.	78
Archbishop Akakios Pappas.	80
The Hierarchy of the True Orthodox Christians of Greece in 1963: Chrysostom of Magnesia, Parthenios of the Cyclades, Akakios of Diavlia, Archbishop Akakios, Gerontios of Salamis, Auxentius of Gardikion.	81

Metropolitan Philaret of the Russian Church Abroad and Archbishop Auxentius of Athens, in New York in 1971.	86
Metropolitan Philaret with Bishops Kallistos of Corinth and Epiphanios of Cyprus in New York in 1971.	96
Archbishop Philotheus of Hamburg with Father Eugene Tombros, Metropolitan Kallistos, and Bishop Constantine, after Kallistos's cheirothesia at Holy Transfiguration Monastery in Brookline, Massachusetts, September 17, 1971.	96
Bishop Matthew of Bresthena.	102
Metropolitan Kallistos of Corinth.	111
Archbishop Auxentius of Athens.	124
The newly reposed Archbishop Auxentius.	128
"Forgive us, Father, for we have sinned against you. We embittered you, we slandered you..." Bishop Stephanos of Chios, of the Kiousis Synod which "deposed" Archbishop Auxentius, asking forgiveness at his funeral.	129
Metropolitan Philaret of blessed memory during a visit to the Holy Transfiguration Monastery in Boston in the early 1970's.	131
Catacomb Bishop Gury of Kazan.	161
Archbishop Auxentius of Athens.	166
Metropolitan Philaret of blessed memory, during a visit to the Holy Transfiguration Monastery in Boston.	185
Metropolitan Kallistos of Corinth and Father George (later Bishop Gregory) Grabbe at the Russian Synod headquarters in New York, in 1973.	244
The Elder Sabbas of Karyes, Mount Athos.	290
Cell at Karyes, Mount Athos.	294
Icon of the Righteous Martyrs of Mount Athos.	297
Pope John Paul II and Patriarch Demetrios in joint public prayer.	299
Icon of the New Martyr Catherine Routis.	307

Preface

FOR THE PAST SEVENTY-FIVE YEARS, the true Orthodox Christians in Greece have witnessed political opposition, intrigues, betrayals, exiles, and bloody persecutions from those erring in the Faith; duplicity, slanders, and infiltration by their enemies; and internal divisions and misunderstandings among themselves—and yet, despite all this, they have courageously stood fast in their heroic confession of the Orthodox Faith against the heresy of Ecumenism.

For the most part, their history has remained unknown to those outside Greece. Several periodicals and booklets have touched upon selective aspects of this history, but the actual documentation they provided was often scant, if not nonexistent. The most complete history of this period to date was written in 1983 by seminarian George Lardas, now a priest of the Russian Church Abroad. Much information recorded in Father George Lardas's unpublished work was drawn from the files of the Holy Transfiguration Monastery in Brookline, Massachusetts. This work has many positive attributes, though there are a number of historical errors in the matter of names and dates. The similarity of many bishops' names, as well as the difficulty in extracting information from so many diverse, and sometimes contradictory sources, accounts for this. Nonetheless, there is much of great value in Father George's work and our present history is indebted to his efforts. Even so, the actual texts of important documents and encyclicals were not included in his dissertation.

We have endeavored to fill this lack. Virtually all of the primary sources quoted in this work appear in English for the first time, and again, for virtually all of them, the complete texts are provided. This will not be easy reading for many. However, one of the purposes of this book is precisely to provide the documentation and information that we have gathered from many publications, official

Synodal files, and encyclicals. These texts speak for themselves and, in many cases, will dispel the misinformation that, regrettably, has appeared in some English-language publications that have dealt with this subject from time to time.

Readers will likely find themselves discouraged, even deeply troubled, over incidents described in this history. The bloody persecutions, personal ambitions, and internal misunderstandings have exacted a terrible toll among the traditional Orthodox Christians of Greece as regards their ecclesiastical administration, unity, and order. Indeed, one look at the *Chronology* (pp. 311-322) alone will reveal two parallel declines in the Orthodox world today: among the ecumenists and innovating jurisdictions, a visible *doctrinal* decline; among the traditional Orthodox, a relentless *administrative* decline. Here, it must be remembered that the Church has known administrative disorder before, as in the case of the fourth century Meletian schism in Antioch, in which Saints Basil the Great, Gregory the Theologian, and Gregory of Nyssa and the bishops of Asia Minor supported one candidate—Meletius; while Saint Athanasius the Great, and the bishops of Egypt and the West supported another candidate—Paulinus. Grievous as administrative disorder may be, it is of an entirely different order from apostasy from the Orthodox Catholic Faith. The first is a domestic squabble; the second is an adulterous departure from the House.

Those who would disparage the struggle of the True Orthodox Christians of Greece are often heard to say that "the old calendarists" "left the Church" over a "secondary issue," that is, over "thirteen days." This history will prove how false this statement is. Indeed, the single purpose of this account is to demonstrate the *doctrinal* nature of the struggle: the change of the calendar was only one element of a larger campaign against the Patristic Faith. To show what an essential betrayal of Orthodoxy has been brought about by the seemingly "secondary issue" of the calendar, many appendices have been provided at the end of this book.

Others, to cover their own deviations from the Orthodox Faith, will point scornfully to the divisions among "the old calendarists." Yet these divisions, distressing as they are, are not without precedent in Church history. It was mentioned above how the Orthodox Christians of Antioch had the same problem in the fourth century, and the problem was resolved over time. In the same century, here is how Saint Hilary of Poitiers described the plight of the Church:

> Since the Nicene Council, we have done nothing but rewrite creeds. While we fight about words, inquire about novelties, take advantage of ambiguities, criticize authors, fight on party questions, have difficulties in agreeing, and prepare to anathematize each other, there is scarce a man who belongs to Christ. Take, for instance, last year's creed, what alteration is there not in it already? First, we have a creed which bids us not to use the Nicene "consubstantial"; then comes another, which decrees and preaches it; next, the third excuses the word "substance," as adopted by the Fathers in their simplicity; lastly, the fourth, which instead of excusing, condemns. We determine creeds by the year or by the month, we change our own determinations, we prohibit our changes, we anathematize our prohibitions. Thus, we either condemn others in our own persons, or ourselves in the instance of others, while we bite and devour one another, and are like to be consumed one of another.
>
> (*Ad. Const.* ii 4, 5)

Those who strain out the gnat and swallow the camel, dismissing the True Orthodox Christians because of merely human failings yet excusing the heretical activities of the "official" Orthodox jurisdictions, might well bring to mind Winston Churchill's criticism of democracy—the worst form of government except for all the others. Certainly, when one considers the open betrayal of the Orthodox Faith that one witnesses in the official statements and actions of bishops and clergy of "World Orthodoxy," the divisions among the true Orthodox Christians, though lamentable, are truly "the secondary issue."

We are indebted to the many clergy and lay people who contributed their insights in the preparation of this volume, and to the others who, through their generous contributions, have made its publication possible. To both the former and the latter, we offer special acknowledgments and our heartfelt gratitude. Among them are Father John and Presbytera Valerie Bockman; Father Neketas Palassis; Father Christos Constantinou; Father Seraphim Johnson; Father Constantine Parr; the fathers of Holy Transfiguration Monastery in Brookline, Massachusetts; the mothers of Holy Nativity Convent, also in Brookline; Neil and Helen Galarneau; Helen Keegan; Margo Koutlas; Constantine Angelos; Peregrina Skotdal; Michael and Philothei Gombos; and many others. Without their suggestions and assistance, this work could not have been completed.

In all the vicissitudes they have experienced during the twentieth century, the true Orthodox Christians can find comfort in the words of Saint Basil the Great, written in that period of Church history known as "the Golden Age":

> A Church pure and untouched by the harshness of our times is not easily found and from now on rarely to be seen—a Church that has preserved the apostolic doctrine unadulterated and inviolate! . . . Beloved brethren, we are small and humble, but we have not accommodated our faith according to changing events.
>
> (*To the Evaisenians, Letter 251*)

If Saint Basil could write this in the "Golden Age," the Orthodox Christians of today, despite their failings, may say the same: we have not compromised our Faith just to be in step with the times. If there have been human failings, they will be overcome, as they have been overcome in the past. "But," says the holy Psalmist, "the truth of the Lord abideth forever" (Psalm 116:2), even as the One, Holy, Catholic, and Apostolic Church—no matter how great or small it may be—will abide forever. The Church has known times far worse than ours, and yet it prevailed, precisely because it is the Body of Christ.

With these thoughts, therefore, we have dedicated this book to all those faithful who labored with steadfast devotion and great sacrifice to hand down to us, the unworthy children of most worthy forefathers and mothers, the priceless heritage of the Apostolic Faith.

May their memory be eternal! Amen.

Introduction

THE ONE, HOLY, CATHOLIC, AND APOSTOLIC CHURCH of Christ our Saviour has, throughout its history, always been and ever will be one in its faith and in its teaching of the truths of the holy Gospel. It has upheld these truths without change, without deviation, and with fear of God.

This unanimity of faith and teaching has been observed with reverence and honor by the entire Church dispersed throughout the world, beginning with the holy Apostles and their immediate successors, the Apostolic Fathers; through the Apologists, the holy and God-bearing Fathers; down to the Confessors and Martyrs of our own times.

The Apostles, those eyewitnesses and disciples of the teaching of the incarnate Word of God, became unerring beacons from the illumination that was bestowed upon them by the Holy Spirit on the day of Pentecost. Thenceforth, preserved by divine grace, they were not inclined to the evils of conceit and false reasoning from which the sicknesses of heresy and spiritual delusion spring forth.

When a controversy arose concerning the observance of the rite of circumcision by pagan converts to Christianity, the Apostles of Christ came together in council in Jerusalem, under the presidency of the first bishop of the Holy City, Saint James the Brother of God, and with one accord they decreed that circumcision was superfluous, for "in Christ, neither circumcision availeth any thing, nor uncircumcision, but faith which worketh by love" (Gal. 5:6).

In this spirit of conciliarity and mutual love, the Church of Christ upheld its unanimity of faith. So long as the variances that appeared among the local churches pertained only to administrative and liturgical questions, no need was felt for the convocation of a general council, since these issues were of secondary importance and therefore of local concern.

But as time passed, it became necessary for the Church to

confront serious deviations from "the Faith which was once delivered unto the Saints" (Jude 3). The primary cause for these dissensions was the inclination of the mind of fallen man to enter into the innermost and ineffable mysteries of the Godhead, to subject them to the scrutiny of its finite and narrow perception, and to interpret them according to carnal human reason.

Hence, when these speculative discussions began to insinuate themselves into the unchanging doctrines of the Faith, and into the teaching of the nature of the God-man, our Lord and Saviour Jesus Christ, the convocation of a general—an ecumenical—council became necessary.

In this First Great Council, at which 318 Fathers of the Universal Church gathered, the pernicious heresy of Arius was refuted and condemned. Arius had taught that Christ, one of the Persons of the All-holy Trinity, was not true God, of one essence with the Father, but rather that He was a creature, essentially no different from us.

Hence, at this Council, the first articles of the holy Creed—the "Symbol of Faith"—were set forth, and herein the Church proclaimed the Apostolic teaching that our Saviour, Jesus Christ, is "the Son of God, the Only-begotten, begotten of the Father before all ages; Light of Light, true God of true God; begotten, not made; being of one essence with the Father; by Whom all things were made . . ."

In its *Synodal Letter*, the First Ecumenical Council also decreed that all the Churches of Christ throughout the world should honor the holy feast of Pascha according to the same reckoning, so that all might celebrate the great triumph of Christ's Resurrection on the same day, and that the Church's oneness might thus be made manifest to all. Henceforth, then, the day of Pascha was to be observed after the Jewish Passover, on the first Sunday following the first full moon after the spring equinox according to the Julian calendar, which was also the basis for this particular Paschal Canon. All the other moveable feasts and the Gospel lections for the entire liturgical year were to be determined according to this reference point.

A few years after the First Ecumenical Council, the Church had to deal with the heresy that arose concerning the Person of the Holy Spirit, Who proceeds from the Father alone, and "Who with the Father and the Son together is worshipped and glorified." This was proclaimed at the Second Ecumenical Council, which condemned Macedonius, the Archbishop of Constantinople who taught against the divinity of the Holy Spirit. The definition of this Council, therefore, together with the teaching that the Church is One, Holy, Catholic, and Apostolic; that there is but one Baptism, that of the One Church; and that Orthodox Christians await "the resurrection of the dead and the life of the age to come" completed and sealed the Creed, the Symbol of our Faith, to which there can never be any addition, subtraction, or alteration.

In the centuries that followed, false teachings arose concerning Christ's two natures and two wills, and also regarding the doctrinal and pastoral imperative of proclaiming the reality of His Incarnation by means of the holy icons. The appearance of these un-Apostolic teachings became the occasion for five more Ecumenical Councils to be convened to refute and condemn these innovations. Again, still later, controversies arose over the false teaching called the "Filioque," the matter of papal authority, and the Latin doctrine of "created grace." All these innovations were dealt with in the various local, general, and Pan-Orthodox Councils that met under illustrious churchmen, such as Saint Photius the Great, Saint Gregory Palamas, and the Ecumenical Patriarch Jeremias II, who was called "the Illustrious."

The Universal Church, the Holy Orthodox Church, continues, and will continue forever, to be one. To be sure, "Christendom"—not the Church of Christ—has splintered into various sects and denominations, especially in the West. The One, Holy, Catholic, and Apostolic Church itself, however, remains inviolate and true to its divine origins.

It is by Divine Providence that the Church has maintained its unity of doctrine and life down to our own times. By following faithfully in the footsteps of the holy Fathers who gathered in the holy Ecumenical Councils, the ancient local Councils, and the great Pan-Orthodox Councils of subsequent centuries, the Church unwaveringly upheld the Apostolic principles of the Christian Faith. By this faithfulness, the Church was preserved in peace and, to a great degree, was spared the great upheavals, the inquisitions, the decades of bloody and remorseless warfare and persecutions that swept like incessant tidal waves over the papal and protestant West. Certainly, much of the Church of Christ suffered under the Tartar or Moslem yoke, but this became the occasion not of division, but of glory for the Body of Christ, in that so many of its faithful sons and daughters gained the everlasting crowns of martyrdom in their confession of the one and true Apostolic Faith.

But with the arrival of the twentieth century, a cataclysmic upheaval struck the Church.

This upheaval came in the form of a terrible and twofold blow: the appearance of militant atheism under the guise of communist ideology and the emergence of syncretistic Ecumenism.

In Russia, where atheistic communism made its foremost and most powerful appearance, a number of the hierarchy and clergy of the local church succumbed to the brutal dictates of the communist government, and, alas, became party to the savage and barbaric persecution of the Orthodox flock, for whom Christ shed His precious Blood. Thus, many clergy, monastics, and lay people went underground, into the catacombs, as it were. This Catacomb Church of Russia provided many millions of holy new martyrs for the Church of Christ—more martyrs, indeed, than all the previous centuries together had given to the Church.

In contrast, the malignancy of Ecumenism entered into the hearts and minds of some Orthodox churchmen in a more subtle and devious manner. It began with what appeared to be a purely local innovation of minor significance. But it proved to be—as many understood immediately—the vanguard of a much more deadly contagion.

This small alteration took place in Greece on March 10, 1924. The people who implemented it called it "a correction of the calendar," but in fact it was only the first step of an eleven-point program that had already been determined upon and had in view the union of Orthodoxy and heresy.

✝

DEDICATED

TO THE MANY THOUSANDS OF THE TRUE
ORTHODOX CHRISTIANS OF GREECE WHO
SUFFERED RIDICULE, PERSECUTION,
EXILE, AND MARTYRDOM ITSELF
FOR THE SAKE OF THE FAITH
OF THE ONE, HOLY,
CATHOLIC, AND
APOSTOLIC
CHURCH

✝

THE STRUGGLE AGAINST ECUMENISM

PART ONE

The History of the True Orthodox Church of Greece from 1924 to 1994

> They who audaciously changed the church calendar in our days, assuredly did not take into account the gravity [of the Church's conciliar decrees and anathemas], and for the sake of astronomy they paid no heed at all to the venerable tradition and spirit of the Church; and though occupying themselves with ecclesiastical matters, they used science only as a pretense to conceal the innovating inclinations that possessed them.
>
> Christopher, Metropolitan of Leontopolis,
later Patriarch of Alexandria
(*Calendar Issues*, 1925)

The Chapel of Saint John the Theologian on Mount Hymettos outside Athens.

A year and a half after the introduction of the Gregorian Calendar in Greece, a miraculous Cross of light—like that which had appeared to Saint Constantine the Great, and again over the city of Jerusalem in 351—appeared in the sight of over two thousand witnesses above this chapel, where the True Orthodox Christians had gathered on the night of the Feast of the Exaltation of the Cross, September 14, 1925, according to the traditional ecclesiastical calendar.

According to one tradition, when Saints Basil the Great and Gregory the Theologian were fellow students at the University of Athens, it was here that they resorted together to struggle in asceticism.

CHAPTER I

The Introduction of the Gregorian Calendar

SINCE 1924, Christians in Greece who remain devoted to the Faith and traditions of the Orthodox Church have been commonly called "Old Calendarists" because of their adherence to the traditional liturgical calendar used by the Orthodox Church for the past 1600 years. Yet for them the point of contention is not the adoption of the Gregorian calendar alone, but the syncretism and secularism represented by the Ecumenical movement, which has gained momentum over the last seventy years—and especially the last thirty—and was the real motive for introducing the Gregorian calendar. The essence of the Ecumenical movement is the belief that the unity of the One, Holy, Catholic, and Apostolic Church has been fragmented, and that all denominations are somehow part of the Body of Christ.[1] This is entirely at variance with what the Church of Christ has always believed and taught.

In January of 1920, the Church of Constantinople under Patriarchal *locum tenens*, Metropolitan Dorotheos of Prusa, and ten other metropolitans published an Encyclical entitled "To the Churches of Christ Wheresoever They Might Be," addressing the denominations outside the Holy Orthodox Church as "fellow heirs and partakers of the same promise of God in Jesus Christ." The title of this Encyclical already presupposed that the Church was not one; its intent was to open an ecumenical dialogue with all the different heterodox bodies on an equal footing. The first item in this agenda proposed the adoption of a common festal calendar so that all the "Churches" could celebrate the great Christian feasts simultaneously. There followed a list of other proposals that would serve to heal the divisions among the churches. Here, in part, is the text of this Encyclical:

[1] See Appendix G, page 219.

After the essential re-establishment of sincerity and confidence among the churches, we think that, above all, love should be rekindled and strengthened among the churches, so that they should no more consider one another as strangers and foreigners, but as kinsmen, and as being a part of the household of Christ and "fellow heirs, and formed of the same body and partakers of the same promise of God in Jesus Christ" (Eph. 3:6).

For if the different churches are inspired by love, and place it before everything else in their deliberations and relations among themselves, instead of increasing and widening the existing dissensions, they should be enabled to reduce and diminish them. By stirring up a right brotherly interest in the condition, the well-being, and the stability of the other churches; by readiness to take an interest in what is happening in those churches and to obtain a better knowledge of them; and by willingness to offer mutual aid and help, many good things will be achieved for the glory and the benefit both of themselves and of the entire Christian body. In our opinion, such a friendship and kindly disposition towards each other can be shown and demonstrated particularly in the following ways:

1) through the adoption by all the churches of one single calendar so that the great Christian feasts may be everywhere celebrated simultaneously;

2) through the exchange of fraternal letters on the occasion of the great feasts of the ecclesiastical year, as is the custom, and on other special occasions;

3) through more fraternal relations between the representatives of the different churches;

4) through establishing relations between the theological schools and the representatives of theological science, and the exchange of theological and ecclesiastical periodicals and works published by each church;

5) through sending young men from one church to the schools of other churches for their studies;

6) through the convocation of pan-Christian assemblies for the examination of matters of common interest to all the churches;

7) through the dispassionate and more historical examination

of the dogmatic differences from a scholarly point of view and by dissertations;

8) through mutual respect for the practices and customs of the various churches;

9) through reciprocal granting of houses of prayer and cemeteries for funerals and burials of the adherents of other confessions who have died in foreign lands;

10) through the implementation of common rules by the different confessions concerning the question of mixed marriages;

11) through a reciprocal and voluntary support of the churches in the realm of religious edification, philanthropy and other such activities.[2]

This Encyclical was a reflection of the "revolutionary Church reforms" envisioned by Eleftherios Venizelos and Meletios Metaxakis, the churchman who was the chief protagonist in implementing these reforms.

More deserves to be said concerning both Venizelos and Metaxakis.

Venizelos (1864-1936) was a very prominent and energetic politician who played a major role in unifying his native island of Crete with the Greek nation, and later, as Prime Minister of Greece, in expanding his nation's territory at the expense of the dying Ottoman Empire. His programs were called "revolutionary" primarily because of his clashes with the sovereigns of Greece which eventually turned to complete opposition to them and led him, during the First World War, to establish a rival government in Thessalonica with French and British support. Through his liberal political party, he ultimately sought the complete abolition of the royalist government. His reforms, however, were not only political, but extended into religious life as well. These reforms had been in preparation for a considerable time. As early as November 10, 1916, Andrew Michalakopoulos, a minister in the "revolutionary" Greek government, wrote a letter to Venizelos.

---

[2] *The Dogmatic and Symbolic Monuments of the Orthodox Catholic Church*, Vol. II, John Karmiris, Graz, Austria, 1968, pp. 958-959 (in Greek). See Appendix A, pp. 177-181, for the entire text.

King Constantine and Eleftherios Venizelos in Thessalonica, 1915.

In this letter, which reveals the long-range program that these two politicians had for the Church, and how Meletios Metaxakis fit into these plans, Michalakopoulos wrote:

> Mr. President, I told you a long time ago in the Council of Ministers that after we had brought to a successful conclusion the national struggle that you have undertaken, it would be necessary, for the good of the country, for you to take care of another, equally important, struggle, that of modernizing our religious affairs.... To head this truly revolutionary reform, you will need a far-seeing Hierarch, one almost like you in politics. You have one: We are speaking about the hierarch from

Cyprus [Meletios Metaxakis]. Under your guidance, *he will become the Venizelos of the Church of Greece* [emphasis added].

Once the political revolution has removed Archbishop Prokopios of Athens and those like him, what are the elements that will require reform in intellectual and monastic circles, when there will have been put in place an ecclesiastical Hierarchy and a universal Synod, or perhaps only a Greek Synod...?

Michalakopoulos goes on to outline what reforms will be needed:

a) Abolition of the Fasts ("Nobody keeps the Fasts, except those who have nothing to eat").
b) Modernization of the ceremonies and Liturgies ("two or three hymns... during a half-hour period" is all that is necessary).
c) Priests educated in "special schools" (so that they can speak "in an intelligible way" about "love of one's country" and "the political duties of their listeners").
d) Abolition of the different Feasts (they are "only an excuse for idleness").
e) Abolition of the monasteries ("Their lands will pass into the hands of the peasants...").

And, he continues, "Of course, all the foregoing is just a very small part of the program. Many other things will need to be reformed...." Elsewhere in the letter Michalakopoulos complains "... unfortunately, it is not possible to make the idea of holiness disappear;" however, through the publication of appropriate books, and with "the collaboration of good Church and lay writers,.... the word 'holy' will disappear."[3]

The first hint of a "calendar change," however, came in January, 1919, when Venizelos was Prime Minister and Meletios Metaxakis was Archbishop of Athens.

---

[3] D. Gatopoulos, *Andreas Michalakopoulos, 1875–1938*, Athens, Elevtheroudakis, 1947, pp. 90–93. A work in Greek based exclusively on the private archives of the statesman who would subsequently become President of the Council. Quoted in *The Old Calendarists and the Rise of Religious Conservatism in Greece*, by Dimitri Kitsikis, pp. 9–11, St. Gregory Palamas Monastery, Etna, California.

Ecumenical Patriarch Athenagoras performing a memorial service for Eleftherios Venizelos in 1963 at his tomb (above) and kneeling in prayer (below).

Who was this Metaxakis? An excellent study written by Bishop Photios of Triaditsa contains the following important information about this high-ranking Freemason, deeply imbued with universalistic beliefs and attitudes:[4]

> [Meletios Metaxakis'] name in the world was Emmanuel. He was born on September 21, 1870 in the village of Parsas on the island of Crete. He entered the Seminary of the Holy Cross in Jerusalem in 1889. He was tonsured with the name Meletios and ordained a hierodeacon in 1892. He completed the theological courses at Holy Cross and was assigned as secretary to the Holy Synod in Jerusalem by Patriarch Damianos in 1900. Meletios was evicted from the Holy Land by Patriarch Damianos, along with the then administrator Chrysostom, later Archbishop of Athens, in 1908 for "activity against the Holy Sepulchre."[5]

In "Famous Freemasons," Alexander Zervoudakis writes that, during a visit to Cyprus in 1909, Metaxakis and two other clergymen (one of whom was Metropolitan Basil of Anchialos, an official representative of the Ecumenical Patriarchate) were initiated into the Masonic Lodge.[6] In 1910, Metaxakis became Metropolitan of Kition in Cyprus. Driven by a "violent, impetuous, and caviling spirit," as Zervoudakis—his admirer—records, Metaxakis sought to become Ecumenical Patriarch in 1912. Failing in this, he turned his attention again to Cyprus.[7] Failing there also, he abandoned his flock and went to Greece where, with the support of Venizelos, he became Archbishop of Athens in 1918. But when Venizelos lost the next election, Metaxakis likewise was ousted from his see.

---

[4] See "The 70th Anniversary of the Pan-Orthodox Congress in Constantinople," *Orthodox Life*, Jan.–Feb., 1994.

[5] Batistatos, D., *Proceedings and Decisions of the Pan-Orthodox Council in Constantinople, May 10–June 8, 1923*, Athens, 1982 (in Greek).

[6] "Famous Freemasons," by Alexander I. Zervoudakis, in the official publication *Masonic Bulletin*, Number 71, Jan.-Feb., 1967 (in Greek).

[7] In *Studies on the History of the Church of Cyprus, 4th–20th Centuries*, Benedict Englezakis describes how Metaxakis attempted, unsuccessfully, to assume the position of Archbishop of Cyprus in 1916, but a "decisive part in his failure was played by his being suspected of modernism, his unconcealed admiration for Venizelos, and his authoritarian character" (Vaparoum, Ashgate Publishing Limited, Aldershot, Hampshire, Great Britain, 1995, p. 440).

Bishop Photios of Triaditsa continues:

> ... In February 1921 Meletios visited the United States. On December 17, 1921, the Greek Ambassador in Washington, D.C. sent a message to the prefect at Thessalonica stating that Meletios "vested, took part in an Anglican service, knelt in prayer with Anglicans, venerated their Holy Table, gave a sermon, and later blessed those present."[8]

This came to the attention of the Holy Synod of the Church of Greece, which formed a commission to investigate Metaxakis in November of 1921.[9] But, as Bishop Photios of Triaditsa notes:

> While the investigation was proceeding against Metaxakis, he was unexpectedly elected Patriarch of Constantinople. Nonetheless, the Holy Synod of the Church of Greece deposed Meletios Metaxakis on December 29, 1921 for a series of infractions against canon law and for causing a schism.[10] In spite of this decision, Meletios Metaxakis was enthroned as the Ecumenical Patriarch on January 24, 1922. Under intense political pressure, Meletios' deposition was uncanonically lifted on September 24, 1922. Political circles around Venizelos and the Anglican Church had been involved in Meletios' election as Patriarch.[11] Metropolitan Germanos (Karavangeis) of the Holy Synod of Constantinople wrote of these events, "My election in 1921 to the Ecumenical Throne was unquestioned. Of the seventeen votes cast, sixteen were in my favor. Then one of my lay friends offered me £10,000 if I would forfeit my election in favor of Meletios Metaxakis. Naturally I refused his offer, displeased and disgusted. At the same time, one night a delegation of three men unexpectedly visited me from the "National Defense League" and began to earnestly entreat me to forfeit my candidacy in favor of Meletios Metaxakis. The delegates said that Meletios could bring $100,000 for the Patriarchate and, since he had very friendly relations with Protestant bishops in England and America, could be useful in [Greece's] international causes. Therefore, international interests demanded that Meletios be

---

[8] Delimpasis, A.D., *Pascha of the Lord, Creation, Renewal, and Apostasy*, Athens, 1985, p. 661 (in Greek).
[9] *Ibid.*   [10] *Ibid.*   [11] Batistatos, D., *op.cit.*, page d.

Meletios Metaxakis.

elected Patriarch. Such was also the will of Eleftherios Venizelos. I thought over this proposal all night. Economic chaos reigned in the Patriarchate. The government in Athens had stopped sending subsidies, and there were no other sources of income. Regular salaries had not been paid for nine months. The charitable organizations of the Patriarchate were in a critical financial state. For these reasons and for the good of the people [or so thought the deceived hierarch] I accepted the offer . . ."[12] Thus, to everyone's amazement, the next day, November 25, 1921, Meletios Metaxakis became Patriarch of Constantinople.

[12] See Delimpasis, A. D., *op.cit.*, p. 662.

The uncanonical nature of his election became evident when, two days before the election, November 23, 1921, there was a proposal made by the Synod of Constantinople to postpone the election on canonical grounds. The majority of the members voted to accept this proposal. At the same time, on the very day of the election, the bishops who had voted to postpone the election were replaced by other bishops. This move allowed the election of Meletios as Patriarch. Consequently, the majority of bishops of the Patriarchate of Constantinople who had been circumvented met in Thessalonica. They announced that, "the election of Meletios Metaxakis was done in open violation of the holy canons," and proposed to undertake, "a valid and canonical election of the Patriarch of Constantinople." In spite of this, Meletios was confirmed on the Patriarchal Throne.[13]

Under pressure from Meletios, the Patriarchate of Constantinople accepted the validity of Anglican orders in 1922 ... Then in 1923 Meletios initiated the "Pan-Orthodox" Congress (May 10–June 8).

The Orthodox populace was not happy with the results of this "Pan-Orthodox" Congress, and in mid-June an attack was made on the Patriarchal premises. In her article, "The Julian Calendar," Ludmilla Perepiolkina provides a graphic description of Metaxakis' hasty departure from Constantinople: "Meletios IV was forced to go into retirement in connection with the extreme indignation of the Orthodox population of Constantinople; the Greeks wrecked the premises of his patriarchate and 'subjected him to assault and battery.'"[14] Bishop Photios continues:

On July 1, 1923, on the pretext of illness and the need for medical treatment, Meletios left Constantinople. On September 20, 1923, under pressure from the Greek government and through the intervention of Archbishop Chrysostom of Athens, Meletios resigned as Patriarch.

In Alexandria, with the support of Anglican clergymen, and under pressure from the British government (this was still the time of the British mandate in Egypt), the Egyptian government con-

---

[13] *Ibid.*, p. 663.
[14] "The Julian Calendar," (*Orthodox Life*, No. 5, 1995, p. 26).

INTRODUCTION OF THE GREGORIAN CALENDAR 33

firmed Metaxakis as Patriarch in May of 1926. Bishop Photios concludes his account of Metaxakis:

> As Patriarch, "at the cost of disapproval and division," Meletios instituted the new calendar in the Alexandrian Patriarchate.[15] While still Patriarch of Constantinople he established ties with the [Soviet-sponsored] "Living Church." The synod of the "Living Church," on the occasion of the election of Meletios as Patriarch of Alexandria, wrote: "The Holy Synod [*sic*] recalls with sincere best wishes the moral support which Your Beatitude showed us while you were yet Patriarch of Constantinople by entering into communion with us as the only rightful ruling organ of the Russian Orthodox Church."[16]
>
> Finally, although critically ill, Meletios offered himself as a candidate for Patriarch of Jerusalem, but no election took place. Metropolitan Methodios Kondostanos wrote: "This exile from the Holy Land, from Kition, from Athens, from Constantinople, Meletios Metaxakis—an unstable, restless, power-hungry spirit, an evil demon—had no qualms about grabbing for the Throne of Jerusalem even from Alexandria in his desire to further himself."[17] Meletios Metaxakis died on July 28, 1935, and was buried in Cairo.

According to Archbishop Athenagoras of Thyateira and Great Britain, who was present then as an archdeacon and eye-witness, Metaxakis was given a full Masonic funeral.

As Ecumenical Patriarch, Metaxakis presided over the ten sessions of the aforementioned "Pan-Orthodox" Congress of 1923. During the course of this Congress, a prelate of the Anglican Church, Charles Gore, the Bishop of Oxford, was present at the invitation of Metaxakis. He was asked to sit at the Ecumenical Patriarch's right side, and to participate in the sessions. Among the proposals adopted by this Congress were a change in the Paschalion and in the festal calendar to coincide with that used in the West, a reduction of fasts and church services, the abolition

---

[15] See *The Church Herald*, No. 13, 1929, p. 152 (in Bulgarian).
[16] Buevsky, A., *The Patriarch of Constantinople, Meletios IV, and the Russian Orthodox Church*, 1953, No. 3, p. 36 (in Russian).
[17] Quoted from Batistatos, D., *op.cit.*, p. e.

of the proscription against the marriage of clergy after ordination, and the abolition of special clerical garb.

It is noteworthy that only three national Churches were represented in the Congress—Greece, Romania, and Serbia; Alexandria, Antioch, and Jerusalem were not. Metaxakis and his Synod adopted the above-mentioned resolutions in disregard of the Pan-Orthodox Councils of 1583, 1587, and 1593, which had condemned the use of the Gregorian calendar for liturgical use in the Orthodox Church. The use of the Gregorian calendar for liturgical purposes had been synodically condemned on many other occasions also—specifically by Patriarch Dositheos of Jerusalem in 1670, Ecumenical Patriarch Agathangelos in 1827, Ecumenical Patriarch Anthimos in 1895, the Holy Synod of the Church of Constantinople in 1902 and 1904; the Holy Synods of Russia, of Jerusalem, of Greece, and of Romania, each independently, in 1903; the Holy Synod of Greece again in 1919; and the Holy Synod of the Patriarchate of Alexandria in 1924.

The Churches of Constantinople, Greece, and Romania—the only ones that accepted the calendar innovation right away—broke their liturgical unity with the other local Orthodox Churches only in order to celebrate with the heterodox. In other words, the calendar change was adopted for the very reason it had previously been condemned by the three Pan-Orthodox Councils of the sixteenth century: Uniatism. It was, in fact, the fulfillment of the first proposal of the Ecumenical Patriarchate's 1920 "Encyclical to the Churches of Christ Wheresoever They Might Be."

Metaxakis' dishonest tactics are also worthy of note. As Perepiolkina points out, "The methods which Meletios IV (Metaxakis) used in introducing the new style [calendar] merit special attention. Thus, in his letter to Archbishop Seraphim of Finland, dated 10 July, 1923, Meletios tells a manifest lie, by affirming that the new style was accepted according to popular demand and a consensus of the Orthodox Churches."[18]

Some years before these developments, in 1918, Archimandrite Chrysostom Papadopoulos wrote an article that appeared in

---

[18] Perepiolkina, *op.cit.*, p. 26.

the church periodical *Church Herald* (Ἐκκλησιαστικὸς Κήρυξ). This article rejected the calendar reform, basing its conclusions on the decisions of the Pan-Orthodox Councils of the sixteenth century.[19] In 1919, Papadopoulos wrote another study on behalf of the Church of Greece rejecting the change of the calendar on the basis of all previous tradition. Yet, despite all this, when he became Archbishop of Athens, Chrysostom Papadopoulos changed the calendar in the Church of Greece in 1924. This came about under pressure from the Greek government.

The new Revolutionary Government of Colonel Nicholas Plastiras, says one study, "did not find Archbishop Theokletos suitable to their purposes," and it arbitrarily replaced him with Archimandrite Chrysostom Papadopoulos on February 25, 1923. On December 14 of that year, the Revolutionary Government abolished the old charter under which the Church of Greece had operated for seventy years and established a new charter whereby the Governing Synod of five bishops was abolished and the sole governing body became the full Synod of Bishops called once a year. Meanwhile, the day to day affairs of church administration were left in the hands of the archbishop, to be ratified each year at the annual Synod. Moreover, the government reserved the right to transfer or retire bishops on the grounds of 'suitability.'

"It was under these conditions that a general Synod of the Church of Greece was held on December 24–30, 1923, at which the dictator Plastiras, the Prime Minister of the Revolution, Gonatas, and the Minister of Religious Affairs and Education, A. Stratigopoulos, were present. The Minister of Religious Affairs

---

[19] Here, in part, is what Papadopoulos wrote: "The letter of Patriarch Jeremias II [1572–1584, 1586–1595] indicates in an excellent manner the position which the Orthodox Church immediately took against the Gregorian modification of the calendar. The Church considered it yet another of the many innovations of Old Rome, a universal scandal, and an arbitrary affront to the traditions of the Church. The reform of the calendar is not only a matter of astronomy but also pertains to the Church, because it is related to the celebration of the Feast of Pascha. Hence, the Pope had no right to reform the calendar, [but by doing so, he] proved that he esteems himself superior to the Ecumenical Councils. Consequently, the Orthodox Church has not been in favor of the reform of the calendar" (Archimandrite Chrysostom Papadopoulos, *Church Herald*, #143, 1918).

underscored the necessity of agreement between the civil and religious calendars."[20]

Colonel Plastiras made his agenda known to the bishops in no uncertain terms:

> The Revolution requests you then, my respected hierarchs, to leave all personal preference to one side and proceed to purge the Church ... The Revolution hopes that a useful work for the new generation will result from your labors, and it will reckon itself happy to see the rebirth of the Church set in motion .... Consequently, it would not have you limit yourselves to the ancestral Canons, but to proceed to radical measures.[21]

Seminarian George Lardas recorded the following information in his unpublished history:

> Archbishop Chrysostom Papadopoulos obtained from the Synod a resolution giving him the authority to make a change in the calendar, if the rest of the Orthodox Churches complied with the decision of the Congress of 1923 and with the approval of the Ecumenical Patriarchate. In fact no other Orthodox Church was seriously contemplating such a change, including the Ecumenical Patriarchate, for Patriarch Meletios was driven from Constantinople by his own flock at the end of the Congress of 1923. He was succeeded by Patriarch Gregory who was preoccupied with putting the Church of Constantinople in order after the exchange of populations between Greece and Turkey. Archbishop Chrysostom obtained this resolution on the condition that he supply the Greek Synod with proof in the form of written evidence that the various local Churches had approved the new calendar at the "Pan-Orthodox" Congress earlier that year. He failed to produce the evidence.
>
> For the next two months, Archbishop Chrysostom conducted correspondence with Ecumenical Patriarch Gregory trying to persuade him to accept the new calendar, but Patriarch Gregory

---

[20] From an unpublished paper on the history of the Old Calendar movement prepared by George Lardas, Holy Trinity Seminary, Jordanville, NY, 1983, pp. 15–16.

[21] Archimandrite Theokletos A. Strangas, Ἐκκλησίας Ἑλλάδος Ἱστορία, ἐκ πηγῶν ἀψευδῶν, 1817–1967 [History of the Church of Greece, from Reliable Sources], Vol. 2, Athens, 1970, p. 1181, quoted in *The Old Calendarists and the Rise of Religious Conservatism in Greece*, p. 18.

*Archbishop Chrysostom Papadopoulos of Athens
(of the new calendar Church).*

hesitated, asking letters from the other Orthodox Churches. Archbishop Chrysostom had already decided the matter, that the change should take place on March 10/23, 1924. As that date approached and nothing was forthcoming from Constantinople, Archbishop Chrysostom used the offices of the Greek Ministry of Foreign Affairs to put pressure on Patriarch Gregory. He requested that the Ministry inform the Eastern Churches that the Church of Greece was putting into effect the "decision" of the Ecumenical Patriarchate to reform the calendar, and to inform the Patriarchate in particular that this had already been decided by the Church of Greece. The letter was dated March 4, 1924. It is no secret that the Ecumenical Patriarchate is dependent on the Greek state for [financial] support and can hardly oppose its wishes. The calendar change took place on March 10/23, 1924 as planned. It was announced by an encyclical signed only by Archbishop Chrysostom on behalf of the Synod of the Church of Greece only seven days before the change. It was disseminated by telegraph to the various newspapers and was published that Sunday, March 3/16, 1924.

The immediate reaction of the other local Churches was strongly negative. The Patriarch of Jerusalem emphasized that the new calendar was unacceptable to his Church because of the dangers of Latin proselytism at the Holy Places. The Patriarchate of Antioch saw it as a danger to the unity of the Church. Only the Churches of Constantinople and Romania accepted the change.

The strongest opposition to the calendar change was on the part of Patriarch Photios of Alexandria. He called a local Synod in Alexandria in which it was decided that there was absolutely no necessity to change the calendar, and having consulted with Patriarch Gregory of Antioch, Patriarch Damianos of Jerusalem, and Archbishop Cyril of Cyprus, it was decided that there should be no change. The Synod expressed sorrow and pain that such a thing should be considered at all and [declared] that this change was a danger to the unity of the Orthodox faithful not only in Greece but everywhere.[22]

However, even the Patriarchate of Alexandria finally succumbed. The circumstances that brought this about are as follows:

After the Constantinopolitan Congress of 1923, which accepted the new calendar, Ecumenical Patriarch Meletios Metaxakis—as mentioned above—had to flee for his life from his angry flock because of his innovations and also because of the political and military reversals Greece suffered at the hands of Kemal Ataturk's military forces in Asia Minor in 1924. He came finally to Alexandria in 1926 where, with political support, he succeeded Patriarch Photios, who had strongly objected to the change of the calendar. Not dissuaded by his predecessor's confession, Metaxakis introduced the new calendar there. The Patriarchate of Alexandria, nonetheless, remained in sympathy with the traditional Orthodox Christians of Greece, especially when Patriarch Christopher (1939-1966), the former Metropolitan of Leontopolis in Egypt, was raised to the throne of Alexandria. However, Patriarch Christopher, because of pressure from the Greek government, was unable to restore the traditional church calendar to the Patriarchate of Alexandria. The Greek government's "revolutionary reforms" and concerns over the unity of "the Greek diaspora" apparently had precedence over the Church's unity and its conciliar decisions.

[22] Lardas, *op.cit.*, pp. 16-17.

CHAPTER II

The Beginnings of the "Resistance Movement" of the True Orthodox Christians

WHEN THE NEW CALENDAR was first introduced in Greece in 1924, virtually all of the clergy submitted. Only the fathers on Mount Athos and some of the pious lay people refused to comply. A lay "Orthodox Association" was formed to retain the traditional calendar. Soon two priests in the area of Athens returned to the traditional calendar and aligned themselves with the Orthodox laity, and more clergy joined later. On Mount Athos, a "Sacred Union of Zealot Monks" was formed. That same year the "Orthodox Association" was reorganized under the name of "The Greek Religious Community of True Orthodox Christians."[1] From the very beginning, this movement was violently persecuted by the police authorities at the behest of Archbishop Chrysostom Papadopoulos. In one instance, after a Liturgy celebrated on the Feast of the Holy Archangels on November 8, 1927, the faithful who were leaving a church at Mandra of Attica were assaulted by the police. Two women were hospitalized, one with a gunshot injury and the other with head injuries from a clubbing by police when she tried to protect the priest. This woman, Catherine Routis, the young mother of two children, died a week later on November 15.[2]

On April 24, 1926, the State Church of Greece issued a very harsh encyclical (Protocol Number 2398/2203) directed against the traditional Orthodox Christians. The encyclical states:

---

[1] Lardas, *op. cit.*, p. 18. See also *Papa Nicholas Planas, the Simple Shepherd of the Simple Sheep*, by the Nun Martha, translated by the Holy Transfiguration Monastery, Boston, 1981, pp. 101-102.

[2] See Appendix T, pp. 305-310.

Catherine Routis, killed by the police in November of 1927. Attacks on the faithful such as the one from which she died were always carried out at the behest of the new calendar Archbishop of Athens, Chrysostom Papadopoulos.

They separate themselves from the Church and cut themselves off from the Body of Christ, drawing upon themselves condemnation and excommunication, not knowing, or perhaps forgetting, that he who does not hear the Church is "as the heathen man and the publican" (Matt. 18:17) .... The decisions of the Church are absolutely obligatory; he who does not obey them no longer belongs to her; *he is deprived of the means of divine grace; he is separated and cut off from her, and is liable to eternal torment* [emphasis added].

This, from a church body which only two years before had itself trampled upon "the decisions of the Church"! Recognizing the non-Orthodox as "fellow heirs of God in Jesus Christ" apparently presented no problems. But being an "old calendarist" meant one had no share in that heritage and was "as the heathen man and the publican," and was "deprived of the means of divine grace."

Despite this persecution of the faithful, the forced closure and demolition of their places of worship by the authorities, and the official decree that the traditional Orthodox Christians were "deprived of the means of divine grace," by 1930 there were about eight hundred chapters of the True Orthodox Christians in existence throughout Greece. They continued to submit appeals to the new calendar Synod of the Church of Greece in 1929 and 1933, pointing out the condemnation of the Gregorian calendar by three Pan-Orthodox Councils. They called for a return to the traditional calendar in order to avoid schism in the Church of Greece.[3] Furthermore, even many clergy who had submitted to the government's decree strenuously protested the change.

On the night of the Feast of the Exaltation of the Cross, September 14, 1925, according to the traditional ecclesiastical calendar, the True Orthodox Christians were given spiritual strength by the miraculous appearance of the Cross over the Chapel of Saint John the Theologian on Mount Hymettos outside Athens. Over two thousand people witnessed the vision, including the police sent to disband the vigil service and arrest the priest. The vision made a profound impression on everyone, and the faithful—including the now-converted police—continued the service without interruption.[4]

To commemorate and make known this awesome miracle, the traditional Orthodox Christians published the following text with the accompanying illustration:

[3] Lardas, *op.cit.*, p. 19.
[4] *Papa Nicholas Planas*, pp. 113-119.

THE APPEARANCE IN THE SKY OF THE VENERABLE CROSS ACCORDING TO THE OLD CALENDAR

At about midnight on September 13–14, 1925, above the chapel of Saint John the Theologian in Athens.

According to accurate reports by eye-witnesses and a large number of police officers.

The scene as it appeared when viewed from a distance of 200 meters from the northeast.

The announcement of the council of the Orthodox, published on September 14/27, 1925.

The "Association of the Orthodox," a recognized group following the Old Ecclesiastical Calendar, in which it remains steadfast since it regards the introduction of the Gregorian calendar as anti-religious and anti-canonical, celebrated today, September 14 according to the traditional ecclesiastical calendar, the feast of the Exaltation of the Venerable Cross. Because of this feast, more than two thousand members of the association had gathered since 9 o'clock yesterday evening at the country chapel of Saint John the Theologian, where a Vigil was celebrated. Naturally, this gathering of the faithful did not escape the attention of the police authorities, who came to observe the service at 11 p.m., "for the sake of order," as they affirmed.

However, whatever their mission was, a few minutes after their arrival, for reasons which are superior to every human order of authority, they were involuntarily forced to be numbered among the multitudes of the faithful, who were already so numerous they could not fit even in the courtyard of the church. It was 11:30 before midnight when, directly above the church and in a direction from east to west, there appeared a bright white cross; its illumination fell only on the area of the church and on the multitude of the faithful attending the service. It completely overpowered the shining of the stars, while at the same time it illuminated the church and courtyard as though an electrical spotlight were directed toward them. The horizontal line of this Heavenly Cross inclined toward the right, and on the lower part of its perpendicular line a smaller cross was

BEGINNINGS OF THE RESISTANCE MOVEMENT

The miraculous appearance of the Cross, September 14, 1925.

formed by another smaller horizontal bar. This heavenly sign was visible continuously for a half an hour and it then began to fade away little by little.

What followed the appearance of this heavenly sign cannot be described by human speech. With one mouth and one heart, all the people at the Vigil fell to their knees and cried out with emotion and began to chant and glorify the Lord. The police authorities forgot their original mission and found again in the depth of their hearts the faith of their childhood years. That entire place was transformed into a corner of some other world that is beyond this earth. Everyone was overcome by an ineffable and sacred emotion; everyone wept. The Vigil continued and finished around 4 a.m., at which time that whole torrent of people began coming back to the city, and everywhere narrated this miracle which had taken place in the night, and which overwhelmed everyone with emotion.

Perhaps there will be some who will not believe, who will doubt the event; perhaps there will be people who, thinking themselves wise, will seek to explain the phenomenon as an illusion, or who will strive to dismiss it by some other contrived arguments. However, both lines of reasoning are overturned, if we take into consideration that that which appeared was not a momentary bright fleeting vision, but a phenomenon which was visible continuously for a half an hour and longer, which more than two thousand people saw and marvelled at. It is fortunate also that among those who saw and were awestruck by this heavenly and radiant Cross there were included members of the police authorities. Therefore both the Church and the State have an obligation to examine and verify the event on an official level.

However, aside from this, we believe that the appearance of this Heavenly Cross on the day of the feast of the Exaltation of the Cross according to the old calendar, constitutes yet another confirmation from God concerning the rightness of the beliefs of those who follow this calendar; it also provides from Heaven a helpful admonition to those directing ecclesiastical matters today, so that they might reconsider their anti-canonical decision concerning the unilateral introduction of the Gregorian calendar; for by this decision, they have separated themselves from the greater part of Orthodoxy.

The Administrative Committee of the Association of the Orthodox:

Pericles Getouris, Secretary
Constantine Berlis
Andrew Vaporidis
Alexander Simionidis
John Sideris
Constantine Kotsiaftopoulos
Haralambos Mavroyiannis

Patriarch Christopher of Alexandria.

In 1925, Metropolitan Christopher of Leontopolis, who became Patriarch of Alexandria in 1939, published a detailed study entitled *Calendar Issues* (Ἡμερολογικά).

In this study, Metropolitan Christopher condemned the calendar change in no uncertain terms, and, among other things, wrote the following:

> They who audaciously changed the church calendar in our days, assuredly did not take into account the gravity [of the Church's conciliar decrees and anathemas], and for the sake of astronomy they paid no heed at all to the venerable tradition and spirit of the Church; and though occupying themselves with ecclesiasti-

cal matters, they used science *only as a pretense to conceal the innovating inclinations that possessed them* [emphasis added].[5]

Metropolitan Germanos of Demetrias protested the introduction of the new calendar and did not allow it to be introduced into his diocese until 1928, and then only under extreme pressure from the Greek government. In October of 1933, Metropolitans Basil of Dryinopolis, Germanos of Demetrias, Irenaeos of Cassandria, and Basil of Drama submitted a statement to the new calendar Synod of the Church of Greece, urging a return to the traditional calendar. What was the response of the majority of the new calendar bishops? The four hierarchs were threatened with deposition.[6]

Although there were eleven bishops of the new calendar State Church who deeply sympathized with and supported the heroic confession of the True Orthodox in Greece, most were deterred by fear of persecution and the loss of their income from the government.[7] In May of 1935, however, Metropolitans Germanos of Demetrias, Chrysostom of Florina, and Chrysostom of Zakynthos (who was accepted by the first two by the laying-on of hands, since he had been consecrated after the calendar change), seeing that their pleas to the Synod went unheeded, announced that from henceforth they would take up the pastoral care of the traditional Orthodox Christians and would form the Synod of the True Orthodox Christians of the Church of Greece.

On May 13, 1935, in the presence of some 25,000 faithful, Metropolitans Germanos of Demetrias, Chrysostom of Florina, and Chrysostom of Zakynthos consecrated the first of four new bishops for the True Orthodox Church in Greece: Germanos of the Cyclades Islands. On subsequent days, the following were consecrated: Christopher of Megaris, Polycarp of Diavlia, and

[5] *Calendar Issues,* Metropolitan Christopher of Leontopolis, 1925, p. 8 (in Greek).

[6] *Memorandum,* Metropolitan Chrysostom of Florina, 1945, p. 23 (in Greek).

[7] The names of the eleven Metropolitans and their sees are: Iakovos of Mytilene, Germanos of Demetrias, Anthony of Patras, Gregory of Halkis, Athanasios of Syros, Agathangelos of Thera, Basil of Dryinopolis, Irenaeos of Cassandria, Chrysostom of Florina, Basil of Drama, and Sophronios of Eleftheropolis.

The three Metropolitans who returned to the traditional Church calendar in May, 1935. From left to right: Chrysostom of Florina, Germanos of Demetrias, and Chrysostom of Zakynthos.

Matthew, as a suffragan (not ruling) Bishop of Bresthena. These seven bishops had Germanos of Demetrias as their president. Metropolitan Germanos had been first in seniority after Archbishop Chrysostom Papadopoulos of the State Church. Metropolitan Chrysostom of Florina was one of the most erudite and respected hierarchs of the Church of Greece.

Two days after these episcopal ordinations, the three senior hierarchs addressed the following document to the hierarchy of the State Church:

TO THE HOLY SYNOD OF THE CHURCH OF GREECE[8]

... It is known to the [new calendar] hierarchy of Greece that, from the very beginning, we set ourselves in opposition to your

---

[8] *Memorandum*, Metropolitan Chrysostom of Florina, pp. 27–29.

opinion concerning the matter of bringing the Church's calendar into accord with the civil [new] calendar. And though at first we also conformed ourselves to the majority decision of the hierarchs and implemented the new calendar in our dioceses, we did this for two reasons: first, so that we might avoid the resulting ecclesiastical schism, and second, we were always lulled by the hope that the hierarchy, seeking to avoid the division of the faithful, would of its own good will return to the ancient ecclesiastical calendar of the feasts out of love for the faithful, for whom Christ died, even if it meant that the hierarchy had to sacrifice its own personal desire for honor.

Now, however, after the passage of a decade, seeing, on the one hand, that a division in the Church has not been avoided and has been created—even without us—by a numerous segment of the Orthodox people of Greece, who with sacred zeal remain faithful to the festal calendar handed down to us by the Fathers; and on the other hand, seeing that the hierarchy has no intention of returning to the path of the Orthodox calendar, from which it strayed, we now believe that the reasons for which we also followed the new church calendar—for reasons of ecclesiastical economy—are deficient.

Wherefore, fulfilling the duty of our conscience, and led by a desire for the unity of all the Orthodox Greek Christians upon the foundation of the [ecclesiastical] calendar and Orthodox tradition, we come forth to make the following known to the governing Holy Synod:

Whereas the governing hierarchy of Greece, at the inspiration and suggestion of its president, His Beatitude [Chrysostom Papadopoulos], unilaterally and uncanonically introduced into the Church the Gregorian calendar, despite the decrees of the Holy Seven Ecumenical Councils and the ancient practice of the Orthodox Church;

Whereas the governing hierarchy of Greece, by introducing the Gregorian calendar into our divine worship without the consent of all the Orthodox Churches, broke thereby the universal Orthodox Church's unity in the celebration of the feasts and divided the Christians into two opposing parties on account of the calendar;

Whereas the governing hierarchy of Greece, by implementing the new calendar, set at nought the divine and sacred canons that govern what pertains to our divine worship, especially in regard to the Fast of the Holy Apostles, which is oftentimes completely done away with (as it is, for example, this year);

Whereas the governing hierarchy of Greece, regardless of how much it insists that it left the canon concerning Pascha untouched and that it celebrates Pascha according to the old calendar, [nevertheless] by implementing the Gregorian calendar unilaterally, could not avoid indirectly violating this [canon] also when it changed the festal calendar of the annual cycle of the lections of the Sunday Gospels, the fasts, and the other Church services, which are inextricably bound with the canon that was instituted by the First Ecumenical Council;

Whereas the governing hierarchy of Greece, by its unilateral and anti-canonical introduction of the Gregorian calendar, has rent asunder the unity that the universal Orthodox Church possesses in her divine worship as regards the celebration of the feasts, and has divided the Christians into two opposing parties because of the calendar, and has indirectly violated also the doctrine of the Symbol of Faith concerning the "One, Holy, Catholic, and Apostolic Church";

Whereas, finally, because of all the above-mentioned reasons, the governing hierarchy of Greece has, in spirit, torn and walled itself off from the sacred canons and the entire Body of Orthodoxy, and potentially and in essence [δυνάμει καὶ κατ' οὐσίαν] declared itself schismatic, according to the determination of the committee of experts in canon law, theologians, and professors of the University [of Athens] who were assigned to study the calendar question (one of the committee members at that time being His Beatitude, the Archbishop of Athens, who was a Professor of History in our national University):

Therefore, in submitting the protest which we have incorporated herein, we declare that we henceforth sever every relation and ecclesiastical communion with [the new calendar hierarchy of Greece] since it remains in the calendar innovation, and we assume the spiritual leadership and ecclesiastical pastorship of the Orthodox Greek people, who have remained faithful to the

Julian calendar of our fathers. In bringing this to the attention of the governing hierarchy, we cherish good hopes that it will perceive the great responsibility it has in the eyes of God, of the Orthodox Church, and of the nation, which it divided needlessly into two opposing religious parties, and that it will review its decision regarding the church calendar, and will be moved of its own good will to restore in the Church the traditional festal calendar, while the government retains the new calendar, according to the Royal Decree of 1923, and thereby remove the scandal that has been created and also restore the peace of the Church.

We greet you with a fraternal embrace.

Athens,	✝ Germanos of Demetrias
May 15, 1935	✝ Chrysostom of Florina
	✝ Chrysostom, Metropolitan of Zakynthos

In another statement addressed to the faithful of the True Orthodox Church, the three bishops declared the following:

> The papal calendar is an innovation of false doctrine, since it is in opposition to many canons of *The Rudder* of the Church, and even [in opposition] to the teaching of the One, Holy, Catholic, and Apostolic Church, since it has broken its unity into old calendarists and new calendarists . . . The Church in Greece has now been torn from the trunk of the Church of the Holy Fathers and the Seven Ecumenical Councils, and has become schismatic. According to the First Canon of Saint Basil the Great,[9] it has lost grace, and has died since it no longer partakes of grace, and it has been severed from the Body of the Church, and has henceforth cast aside the struggles of ancient holy Fathers who preserved the Faith intact for so many centuries.[10]

These actions and declarations of the traditionalist Synod of Bishops provoked the intense wrath of the State Church and government authorities. As a result, the seven bishops were immediately arrested by the government at the instigation of the

---

[9] See Appendix L, pp. 256-262.

[10] *The Causes and Reasons for the Division of the True Orthodox Christians into Separate Jurisdictions,* Hieromonk Amphilochios Tambouras, Larisa, 1975, pp. 8-9 (in Greek).

At the order of Chrysostom Papadopoulos, new calendar Archbishop of Athens, police attack the traditional Orthodox faithful who had gathered peacefully in front of the Metropoly Cathedral of Athens, June, 1935.

State Church and brought to ecclesiastical trial in June of 1935, on charges of causing division and disturbance by organizing "unlawful assemblies," and of showing contempt for the "legal" and "canonical" church.

During this trial, which took place in the Metropolitan Cathedral of Athens, a large crowd led by forty priests and sixty monastics gathered quietly in the square in front of the cathedral to chant the Supplicatory Canon to the Mother of God. This orderly assembly was assaulted by the police and dispersed with fire-hoses and clubs, and over 100 were injured (one of whom was the future Archbishop Auxentius).

The result of this trial was announced on June 15, 1935. Three of the bishops—Germanos of Demetrias, Chrysostom of Florina, and Germanos of the Cyclades Islands—were banished; Matthew

Police attack the Orthodox faithful in Metropoly Square, Athens, June 1, 1935. The young monk Auxentius (later Archbishop) was in this multitude.

of Bresthena, on account of illness, was confined to his monastery; Chrysostom of Zakynthos, Polycarp of Diavlia, and Christopher of Megaris recanted and returned to the State Church.

Before the hierarchs were sent off to their places of exile and imprisonment, they were able to address their flock with one last *Pastoral Encyclical*. Since the new calendarists refused to end their schism or to recognize the holy Mysteries of the True Orthodox Christians (while, nonetheless, recognizing the sacraments and priestly orders of the non-Orthodox), the Synod of Bishops of the True Orthodox Church of Greece published their *Pastoral Encyclical*, stating officially that the new calendar State Church was in schism and that its mysteries were invalid—that is to say, they simply affirmed what Chrysostom Papadopoulos himself had said only one year before he became Archbishop and changed the calendar.[11] Here is the text of the *Pastoral Encyclical* of the Holy Synod of the traditional Orthodox Christians:

PASTORAL ENCYCLICAL TO THE ORTHODOX GREEK PEOPLE[12]

Unjustly condemned by the schismatic Synod to deposition and a five-year imprisonment in monasteries, and seized by force by the government (which has become the executory arm of the [new calendar] Archdiocese, which by a mere word has placed itself above the divine canons, the [Church's] Charter, and the Constitution of Greece) because we had the courage and the spiritual strength to raise the glorious and venerable banner of Orthodoxy, we consider it our pastoral duty before we depart [for prison] to direct the following admonitions to you that adhere to the Orthodox festal calendar of our fathers:

While faithfully following the Apostle's admonition, "Stand fast and hold the traditions which ye have been taught, whether by word, or by our letter," do not cease from struggling

---

[11] In his Report to the Committee of the Department of Religion, dated January 16, 1923, the then Archimandrite Chrysostom Papadopoulos wrote: "No Orthodox autocephalous Church can separate itself from the rest and accept the new calendar without becoming schismatic in the eyes of the others."

[12] *Ta Patria* (Τὰ Πάτρια), Vol. 1, No. 1, 1976, pp. 20–23.

by every lawful and Christian means for the strengthening and triumph of our sacred struggle, which looks to the restoration of the patristic and Orthodox festal calendar within the Church; only this can re-establish the diminished Orthodox authority of the Greek Church and bring back the peace and unity of the Orthodox Greek people.

By the judgments which the Lord knows, the majority of the hierarchy of the Greek Church, under the influence and initiative of its president, has placed the blot of schism upon what up until now had been its pure and truly Orthodox countenance, when it rejected the Orthodox festal calendar—which has been consecrated by the Seven Ecumenical Councils and ratified by the age-long practice of the Orthodox Eastern Church—and replaced it with the papal calendar.

Of course, this schism of the Orthodox Greek people was created by the majority of the hierarchy, which forgot its sacred and national mission and the old Greek [revolutionary] slogan: "Fight for Orthodoxy and for Greek liberty," and which, without the agreement of all the Orthodox Churches, introduced the papal festal calendar into our divine worship, thereby dividing not only the Orthodox Churches, but also the Orthodox Christians into two opposing camps.

In assuming the pastorship of the Orthodox Greek populace that follows the Orthodox festal calendar of our fathers, and being conscious of the oath of faith that we took that we would keep all that we have received from the Seven Ecumenical Councils, we abjure every innovation and cannot but proclaim as schismatic the State Church, which has accepted the papal festal calendar which has been described by Pan-Orthodox Councils as an innovation of the heretics and as an arbitrary trampling underfoot of the divine and sacred canons of the ecclesiastical traditions.

On account of this, we counsel all who follow the Orthodox festal calendar to have no spiritual communion with the schismatic Church and its schismatic ministers, from whom the grace of the All-holy Spirit has departed, since they have set at nought the resolutions of the Fathers of the Seven Ecumenical Councils and all the Pan-Orthodox Councils that condemned the Gregorian festal calendar. The fact that the Schismatic

Church does not have grace and the Holy Spirit is confirmed by Saint Basil the Great, who says: "Even though the schismatics have not erred in doctrines, yet because Christ is the Head of the Body of the Church according to the divine Apostle, and from Him are all the members quickened and receive spiritual increase, the [schismatics] have been torn from the consonance of the members of the Body and no longer have the grace of the Holy Spirit abiding with them. And how, indeed, can they impart to others that which they have not?"

While the Schismatic Church imposes oppressive and intolerable measures in order to violate our Orthodox conscience, we exhort you to endure all things and to preserve the Orthodox heritage intact and unstained, even as we received it from our pious Fathers, having us as luminous and fortifying examples, seeing we were not afraid—even in the waning years of our lives—to withstand with boldness and dignity the bigoted and medieval measures of our exile and imprisonment in monasteries, as it were in prisons.

Esteeming this as honor and glory and joy, according to the Apostle, who enjoins us to rejoice and boast in our sufferings in behalf of Christ, we counsel you also to have endurance and persistence in these griefs, and afflictions, and evils, and outrages to which you will be subjected by a Church that is schismatic; and ever hope in God, Who will not permit that you be tried above what you are able to endure, and Who, in His infinite and unfathomable long-suffering, will be well-pleased to enlighten those who, out of innocence, have been led astray and follow the papal festal calendar; and in the end may He grant you the triumph of Orthodoxy and the unity of those who bear the name of Christ, the Orthodox Greek people, for whom we struggle to the glory of Christ, Whose grace and infinite mercy be with you all.

June 21, 1935 ✠ Germanos of Demetrias
✠ Chrysostom of Florina
✠ Germanos of the Cyclades Islands

Later in 1935, with the installation of Prime Minister George Kondylis, who (ironically, as it turned out) found this religious persecution politically embarrassing, the four bishops were released and allowed to return to Athens.[13] Metropolitans Germanos of Demetrias, Chrysostom of Florina, Germanos of the Cyclades Islands, and Matthew, Bishop of Bresthena, now constituted the Synod of the True Orthodox Church in Greece.

[13] The irony derives from the fact that when the Precious Cross appeared in the heavens on September 13–14, 1925, over the Chapel of Saint John the Theologian on Mount Hymettos (see pp. 41–44), it was this same George Kondylis who, as a government minister at the time, sent the police to arrest Fr. John Floros, the priest who was serving at the Vigil when the Cross appeared.

Metropolitans Chrysostom of Florina, Germanos of Demetrias, and Germanos of the Cyclades with clergy and people for the Theophany procession, 1937.

CHAPTER III

Divisions

IN 1937, Metropolitan Chrysostom of Florina, in a personal letter to Bishop Germanos of the Cyclades Islands, set forth the opinion that the State Church was in "potential schism."

It is evident from this letter that Metropolitan Chrysostom was attempting to deal with what—especially in the early years—had become a complex state of affairs. There were contradictory elements in the calendar dispute that caused considerable confusion in the ranks of the True Orthodox as to how they should address these issues. The primary cause of this confusion was the ambivalence of the new calendar bishops themselves.

On the one hand, it was clear that in itself the change of the calendar was *not* a direct change of doctrine, although it did violate the Church's oneness by disrupting its liturgical unity. On the other, it was equally clear—as the Ecumenical Patriarchate's Encyclical of 1920 affirmed—that the calendar change was only "step one" in the rapprochement with the heterodox denominations. This *was* a doctrinal issue. Furthermore, although the new calendar Synod of Greece had, by majority vote, adopted and issued an encyclical in April of 1926 declaring that the traditional Orthodox Christians and their mysteries were "bereft of the means of divine grace," and although the Ecumenical Patriarchate in its notorious Encyclical of 1920 had recognized the heterodox denominations as "Churches of Christ" and "fellow heirs of God," there was, nonetheless, a sizable number of new calendar hierarchs who rejected these theological innovations and supported the Church's traditional teaching. Also, although there were new calendar bishops in Greece who viciously persecuted the traditional Orthodox clergy and lay people, and desecrated their churches and even the Holy Mysteries, there were also new calendar bishops

Metropolitan Chrysostom of Florina in Athens, June, 1939.

who sympathized with, supported, and assisted the True Orthodox Christians. Finally, whereas the Pan-Orthodox Councils of the sixteenth century had placed under anathema anyone who would change the calendar and the Paschalion (the method of reckoning the date of Pascha each year), the new calendar Synod of Greece had indeed, on the one hand, adopted the change of the calendar, but, on the other, had avoided tampering with the Paschalion, which had been instituted by the First Ecumenical Council and which, they said, was alone binding on all Orthodox.[1]

In view of these unprecedented developments, it became evident—to Metropolitan Chrysostom of Florina, at least—that there was no clear answer except "wait and see," and because of this, he modified and softened his original position. In addition, he initially had sincere and, as it appeared to him, justified hopes that

---

[1] The Synod of the Church of Romania, under the leadership of Patriarch Myron Cristea, a former Uniate, decided to change the Paschalion also. This immediately resulted in bloody riots in the streets; whereupon the Synod reversed its decree on the Paschalion and retained only the calendar change. The Church of Finland, which is under the jurisdiction of the Ecumenical Patriarchate, decided to change both the church calendar and the traditional Paschalion, thereby completely adopting the usage of the Protestant and Roman Catholic denominations in this matter.

a Pan-Orthodox Council of all the other local churches would soon convene to condemn, once again, these innovations and put a stop to them, and that the Ecumenical Patriarchate and the Church of Greece would soon return to the traditional calendar. Furthermore, a number of government officials and ministers promised to support the traditional Orthodox Christians' call for an end to the calendar innovation. Alas, subsequent events demonstrated that Metropolitan Chrysostom's hopes were in vain.

In November of 1937, however, when these issues were still very much alive, Metropolitan Chrysostom wrote a very lengthy personal letter to Bishop Germanos of the Cyclades Islands. In many ways, this letter was quite harsh. Initially, Bishop Germanos had been of one mind with Metropolitan Chrysostom in the matter of how new calendarists should be received—that is, simply by confession of faith and not by holy chrismation. However, Bishop Germanos changed his position and adopted that of Bishop Matthew of Bresthena—that is, that all new calendarists should be received by holy chrismation since, according to the strict interpretation of the canons that deal with schism, grace had departed from the innovating State Church. Bishop Germanos's change of policy deeply wounded Metropolitan Chrysostom, and prompted his letter, dated November 9, 1937, in which he set forth his thoughts on these issues.[2] His opinion can be summed up in the following extracts:

> This separation on the part of His Beatitude [Chrysostom Papadopoulos] and the hierarchy that followed him gives us the right to express our personal and completely private opinion that His Beatitude and the hierarchy with him—in view of the fact that they have knowingly broken the unity of the universal Orthodox Church as regards the simultaneous celebration [of the feasts] and the simultaneous observance of the fasts—have potentially, but not actually, fallen from divine grace, since they have fallen under the curses and the anathemas which the divine Fathers of the Seventh Ecumenical Council placed upon those

[2] *The Calendar Schism—Potential or Actual?*, Fr. Theodoretos Mavros, ed., 1973 (in Greek).

who set at nought the traditions and removed the everlasting boundaries which our fathers have established.

However, His Beatitude and the bishops who are of one mind with him will fall away from divine grace and become aliens to the Orthodox spirit of the Mysteries in actuality only when they are proclaimed as such and as actual schismatics by a Pan-Orthodox Council, which alone has this right, according to the laws of the Eastern Orthodox Church.

And he ends his letter with the following assurances:

... With the might of Christ, we shall soon raise [the banner of Orthodoxy] on the Orthodox citadel of the Ecumenical Patriarchate and the Church of Greece. Yes, Your Grace, if the luminous dayspring of Orthodoxy's triumph has begun to dawn with rose-colored hues, this, with the might of Christ, is due to the Orthodox, and Christian, and truly hierarchical position we have maintained *vis-à-vis* the State Church and the Nation, not even fearing to raise our hierarchical stature against the violence wrought against us; [we endured this] so that we might not forsake and betray the glorious and venerable banner of Orthodoxy and of the Orthodox faith and confession....

The triumph of Orthodoxy shall soon be celebrated by all in the Metropoly of the Church of Greece by the might of Christ and the truly Orthodox and patriotic desire of our God-preserved King, and the leader of the Greek Government, who has accomplished great deeds, and all the true Orthodox Greeks shall justly receive the crown of joy and glory ...

✠ Chrysostom, former Metropolitan of Florina

While deploring Bishop Germanos's opposition to him, Metropolitan Chrysostom wished to point out in this letter that he felt it was unwise at this time (1937) to apply the full strictness of the canons that would normally apply to those in schism. Because of the confusion that prevailed at that time in church life, he still had high hopes—as his letter reveals—that a Pan-Orthodox Council would convene soon and that the State Church would return to the ecclesiastical calendar, since some bishops of the State Church sympathized with the traditional Orthodox Christians and there

Metropolitans Germanos of Demetrias and Chrysostom of Florina at Old Faleron, Theophany, 1938.

was evidence, as well, that the Greek government was reconsidering its stance.

It is noteworthy that Metropolitan Chrysostom here emphasizes that, in the year 1937, he was expressing his "personal and completely private opinion" concerning the status of the new calendar Church. Thirteen years later, in 1950, not in a personal and private letter, but in an official Encyclical, together with his entire Holy Synod, he will amend this purely personal opinion (see pp. 66-69, and pp. 113-116). Since Metropolitan Chrysostom acknowledged in this letter that the new calendar hierarchy had "fallen under the curses and anathemas which the divine Fathers of the Seventh Ecumenical Council placed upon those who set at nought the traditions and removed the everlasting boundaries which our fathers have established," one could ask: why would

Metropolitan Germanos of the Cyclades with clergy and people gathered for Theophany.

another Council be necessary? Were not the decisions of the previous Ecumenical and Pan-Orthodox Councils binding? A Pan-Orthodox Council did not ratify the adoption of the Gregorian calendar. Why, then, would another Council be needed to condemn what had already been condemned repeatedly?

Although the President of the Synod, Germanos of Demetrias, agreed with Metropolitan Chrysostom's view, Bishops Germanos of the Cyclades and Matthew of Bresthena viewed it as a betrayal. The latter two were of the opinion that, from the moment of the change of the calendar in 1924, the State Church was in schism and therefore the canons that apply to schism should be applied with all strictness—meaning that the new calendar mysteries became devoid of grace the moment the State Church adopted the Gregorian calendar. Hence, they separated themselves from Metropolitans Chrysostom and Germanos over this issue. Later, Bishops Matthew and Germanos of the Cyclades disagreed over yet some other issue and separated from each other.[3]

---

[3] Lardas, *op.cit.*, p. 22.

As a result of these divisions, the followers of Metropolitan Chrysostom of Florina (who were in the great majority) came to be known as "Florinites," and those who followed Bishop Matthew came to be called "Matthewites." In considering this division between the traditional Orthodox Christians, we must remember that there were bishops in the new calendar Synod of Greece who supported them and might be won over by patience and mildness, as indeed happened later, in 1944, when two Metropolitans—Christopher of Christianopolis (formerly of Megaris) and Polycarp of Diavlia—returned again to the traditional Orthodox. But there were also State Church bishops who were ruthless persecutors—bishops who would not stop even at physical violence and sacrilege—whose actions cried out for stern measures.[4] This difference affected the traditional Orthodox so that parties were formed according to how each one felt these contradictory circumstances should be dealt with.

In 1943, during the Nazi occupation of Greece, Metropolitan Germanos of Demetrias died, leaving Metropolitan Chrysostom by himself.[5] However, in 1944, Christopher of Christianopolis (formerly of Megaris) and Polycarp of Diavlia, two of the bishops who had been consecrated in 1935 by Chrysostom of Florina and Germanos of Demetrias and had subsequently recanted and rejoined the State Church because of persecution, returned again to the True Orthodox Church of Metropolitan Chrysostom. In addition, Germanos of the Cyclades, who had separated from Metropolitan Chrysostom, was again meeting with him at this time, seeking to resolve their differences. These developments appeared to lend support at that time to Metropolitan Chrysostom's manner of dealing with the new calendar schism.

[4] See, for example, Appendix M, p. 267, and Appendix T, pp. 305-310.

[5] Metropolitan Germanos was buried with honors by the new calendar bishops, who claimed that he had submitted a petition shortly before his death, asking to be received again into the State Church. In the book *The Agony in the Garden of Gethsemane* (p. 144), however, author Stavros Karamitsos states that many discounted this claim of the new calendarists as spurious. However, under the circumstances of the Nazi Occupation, it was impossible to take any action to clarify the matter.

Metropolitans Germanos of the Cyclades, Chrysostom of Florina, Christopher of Megaris, and Polycarp of Diavlia, 1944.

Meanwhile, Bishop Matthew, now alone, eventually despaired of finding bishops who shared his own views. Hence, in violation of the First Apostolic Canon he consecrated, single-handedly, four new bishops in August of 1948. The bishops' names and titles were Spyridon of Trimythus, Andrew of Patras, Demetrios of Thessalonica, and Kallistos of Corinth. One of these bishops, the saintly Spyridon of Trimythus, spent the last years of his life in seclusion, refusing to celebrate as a hierarch because he had repented of being consecrated in this completely uncanonical way. These unlawful consecrations were a blow to many of Bishop Matthew's supporters; and many clergy, monastics, and laity left him, since they were unable to accept his uncanonical course of action. They argued: "How can we censure others for not keeping the holy canons, when we ourselves violate basic canons concerning the consecration of bishops?" Although Bishop Matthew's integrity, personal virtue, and asceticism were admitted by all, his course of action only widened the division between the "Matthewites" and "Florinites."

In January of 1950, Metropolitan Germanos of the Cyclades, who had been imprisoned for ordaining priests, was released and was once again united with Metropolitan Chrysostom of Florina, to the great joy of the faithful.

The "Florinites" and the "Matthewites" made many attempts at reconciliation, but all were unsuccessful.[6] Stavros Karamitsos, a theologian and author of the book *The Agony in the Garden of Gethsemane,* describes as an eye-witness the two instances in which Metropolitan Chrysostom of Florina personally attempted to meet with Bishop Matthew. Unfortunately, on both occasions—the first, which had been planned to take place on January 19, 1950, at the Matthewite Convent in Keratea at the invitation of Bishop Spyridon of Trimythus, and the second, which actually did take place at the Athens Metochion of the Keratea Convent—the abbess and senior nuns of that convent, at the prompting of the

---

[6] Many have questioned the role that certain prominent clergymen played in both the Florinite and Matthewite jurisdictions. In the latter, one notable priest had an ecclesiology that could be very flexible (during a pilgrimage to the Holy Land, Syria, and Mount Sinai, he celebrated at several shrines, and—contrary to his jurisdiction's principles—commemorated the names of the local innovating hierarchs. He expressed regret over these incidents, but many felt that his apologies were more from expediency than sincerity). The fact that he was always at the center of every effort to *thwart* the re-unification of the traditional Orthodox Christians of Greece; his long and unexplained disappearances and absences; the fact that, during the bloody persecutions of 1950-1955, he alone among the traditionalist clergy was able to go about his business unhindered, fully dressed as a clergyman, and well known for what he was to the government authorities, while all the other traditional clergy had to hide for fear of their lives, raised suspicions in the eyes of many regarding his relations with the new calendar Church and State. When once asked about this, his answers were evasive. The same fears were expressed concerning a certain person who became a bishop in the Synod of Archbishop Auxentius. After his tonsure as a monk, he was inducted into the Greek military service, in which he served as an officer. He often worked in assignments which involved the Greek secret service. More important, his ecclesiastical career was marked by a behavior that was consistently divisive and disruptive. For example, despite Archbishop Auxentius's efforts, this hierarch, by his influence in the Archdiocese's finances, was able to prevent the establishment of a seminary for the education and training of the future traditionalist clergy.

From left to right: Metropolitans Christopher of Megaris, Chrysostom of Florina, and Polycarp of Diavlia, Theophany, 1948.

Matthewite protopresbyter, Eugene Tombros, intervened and would not allow Metropolitan Chrysostom to speak with Bishop Matthew. On the second occasion, in May of 1950, when Bishop Matthew was on his deathbed and had been unconscious for three days, Metropolitan Chrysostom arrived at Bishop Matthew's quarters and approached his bedside. Standing at his side, Metropolitan Chrysostom bowed down and quietly asked him, "My holy brother, how are you feeling?" To the astonishment of all present, Bishop Matthew regained consciousness and opened his eyes. When he saw the Metropolitan, he sought to sit up out of deference and began to whisper something faintly. At that very moment, the Abbess Mariam of the Convent of Keratea entered the room with several other sisters and demanded that all the visitors leave. Only a few days later, on May 14, 1950, Bishop Matthew died, and the two hierarchs were never again to meet in this life.

On May 26, 1950—some twenty-six years after the calendar innovation—seeing that the new calendarists showed no signs of changing direction despite the many appeals addressed to the Holy Synod of the State Church, Metropolitan Chrysostom of Florina and the other bishops of his Synod, published an encyclical, in which they said that the time had arrived to apply more strictly the canons that deal with schism. Henceforth, in accordance with the First Canon of Saint Basil the Great, the mysteries of the State Church were to be considered invalid and those who belonged to the State Church were to be received into the True Orthodox Church by holy chrismation. The encyclical was signed by Metropolitan Chrysostom of Florina, who was now presiding bishop of the Synod of the True Orthodox Church, as well as by Metropolitans Germanos of the Cyclades, Christopher of Christianopolis (formerly of Megaris), and Polycarp of Diavlia. The text of this encyclical is as follows:

TO THE MOST REVEREND PRIESTS OF OUR MOST HOLY CHURCH OF THE TRUE ORTHODOX CHRISTIANS IN GREECE[7]

May 26, 1950
Protocol Number 13
Beloved Children in the Lord,

Grace and peace be unto you from God, and prayer and blessing from us.

Taking into consideration reports that some of our most pious priests are negligent in fulfilling the duties on the basis of the canons and the confession [of faith] we made in the year of Salvation, 1935, the Sacred Synod of our Most Holy Church undertakes to remind all of the following:

In the year of Salvation, 1935, we proclaimed the Church of the innovating new calendarists schismatic; we reiterate this proclamation once again and, consequently, we enjoin that the First Canon of Saint Basil the Great be applied, given that the mysteries celebrated by the new calendarists are—since they are schismatics—deprived of sanctifying grace.

---

[7] *Thus Do We Believe, Thus Do We Speak* (Οὕτω Φρονοῦμεν, Οὕτω Λαλοῦμεν), a pamphlet published by the Church of the True Orthodox Christians of Greece, Athens, 1974, pp. 5–7.

Theophany of the traditional Orthodox Christians, 1948.

Hence, you must not receive any new calendarists into the bosom of our Most Holy Church, nor, as a consequence, minister unto them without their having previously made a confession [of faith], whereby they condemn the innovation of the new calendarists and proclaim their Church as schismatic. Those who have been baptized by the innovators should be chrismated with holy chrism of Orthodox provenance, which also we have in sufficiency.

On this occasion we direct this final appeal to all True Orthodox Christians, inviting them paternally to unite with us. The furtherance of our struggle for the piety of our Fathers demands this and is the fervent desire of all of us.

In extending this invitation to you, we do away with the stumbling-blocks that were created through our responsibility, and to this end we revoke and repudiate whatever was written or spoken by us from 1937 until today, either in sermons, pronouncements, publications, or encyclicals, and whatever was incompatible with or contrary to the principles of the Eastern Orthodox Church of Christ and our sacred struggle in behalf of Orthodoxy, as it was proclaimed in the encyclical published by the Sacred Synod in the year 1935, without any addition or omission, including even the technical phrase "potentially and in actuality" [δυνάμει καὶ ἐνεργείᾳ].[8]

These things do we affirm this final time for the sake of the scandalized Christians, whose spiritual salvation we desire; and on this occasion we [again] proclaim that all of us must preserve intact even to the end of our days the confession we made in 1935, invoking God's mercy for every deviation.

Wherefore, let us stand well.

With fervent prayers,
The Sacred Synod.

The President
✠ Chrysostom, formerly Metropolitan of Florina

> The Members
> ✠ Germanos, Metropolitan of the Cyclades Islands
> ✠ Christopher, Metropolitan of Christianopolis
> ✠ Polycarp, Metropolitan of Diavlia

The reaction of Archbishop Spyridon of the State Church was immediate. The most violent and ruthless persecution of the True Orthodox Church now broke out and lasted for five years (1950–1955).

"In a memorandum to the Greek government in June of 1950, Archbishop Spyridon Vlahos stated that Old Calendarism was more dangerous to the nation than any propaganda, and more dangerous even than Communism [!], and that the Old Calendar movement was just as much a vanguard of pan-Slavism as Communism, and was part of an attempt to enslave the Greek nation. He suggested that the State abolish all Old Calendarist societies and make Old Calendarism equivalent to rebellion (treason); furthermore he proposed [that the government institute] ... police surveillance and deportation of monastics to Mount Athos, and that the baptisms and weddings [of the traditional Orthodox] not be recognized by the State as valid. In comparing Old Calendarism with communism and identifying it with pan-Slavism, Archbishop Spyridon was playing on fears of communism and the bitter memories arising out of the [Greek] civil war of 1945–1949.

---

[8] See also pp. 49, 57-63, 113-120, 256-262, and 268.

Police overturn the Epitaphios of the traditional Orthodox Christians during the procession of Holy Friday, 1951, in Piraeus.

Archimandrite Gerasimos Skourtaniotis of the Holy Transfiguration Monastery in Kouvara, Attica, before and after being forcibly stripped of his priestly garb and shaven by the police authorities.

Father Nicholas Smyrlis of Kalamata, as a young priest (left) and after being forcibly stripped of his priestly garb and shaven by the police authorities during the persecutions of the early fifties.

"On January 3, 1951, the Cabinet of Ministers of the Greek Government enacted a decree (No. 45) of persecution of the True Orthodox Christians by the State."[9]

Hence, the churches of the traditional Christians were closed, confiscated, or demolished. During Holy and Great Friday, the Epitaphios processions of the faithful were broken up by the police and the Epitaphios's were overturned and thrown to the ground. The clergy and monks were hauled into police stations where they were forcibly shaved and stripped of their clerical garb. Holy Tables were overturned, the holy Mysteries desecrated.

This persecution was motivated only by malice against the traditional Orthodox Christians for their confession of faith: the churches, clergy, and faithful of the heterodox denominations throughout Greece remained safe and sound.

[9] Lardas, *op.cit.*, p. 24.

The Monastery of Hypsilos in Mytilene, to which Metropolitan Chrysostom of Florina was exiled in February of 1951.

Metropolitan Chrysostom at his place of exile, September 7, 1951.

Metropolitan Chrysostom of Florina returning from exile, July 18, 1952.

"On the first of February, 1951, Metropolitan Chrysostom of Florina, who was in hiding, was discovered, arrested, and exiled. He was eighty-two years old at the time. Metropolitan Germanos of the Cyclades, who also was in hiding, reposed during this period. The civil and church authorities refused permission for a church funeral for Metropolitan Germanos, nor would they allow any priest to serve even a memorial service. Hence, he was buried by laymen. Many traditional Orthodox clergy who came to the burial were arrested.

"In February of 1954, Metropolitans Christopher and Polycarp, despairing of the future of the True Orthodox Church under such persecutions, again capitulated and returned to the State Church."[10]

As a result of this, Chrysostom of Florina remained alone as the head of the larger group of the True Orthodox Church until his death. Several candidates for the episcopacy were presented to him. Bishop Nikolaj (Velimirovic) of the Serbian Church, who was then residing in the United States, offered to help him consecrate new bishops. However, although he could have done so had he

---

[10] *Ibid.*, p. 25.

Procession to the burial place of Metropolitan Germanos of the Cyclades. The authorities refused to allow a funeral service, or even a memorial service, to be performed for him. He was buried by laymen.

chosen, Metropolitan Chrysostom declined to consecrate any of the candidates. In answer to the pleas of his flock for bishops, he directed that they come to terms with the bishops Matthew had consecrated and have them somehow regularized according to the canons. While matters stood thus, a full five years after his Encyclical of 1950, Metropolitan Chrysostom reposed on September 7, 1955.

On September 25, 1955, in the Patriarchal Church of Saint Sabbas the Sanctified in Alexandria, Egypt, Patriarch Christopher of Alexandria presided at a solemn memorial service for the repose of the soul of Metropolitan Chrysostom of Florina. Three years later, his grave at the Convent of the Dormition of the Theotokos in Parnitha, Attica was opened and his remains were found to be fragrant. In fact, the fragrance was so strong that lay workers came to ask what the source was of this sweet aroma that had filled the entire surrounding area.

Some clergy of the State Church lodged protests with their bishops and tried to mediate between the State Church and the

Procession with the newly reposed Metropolitan Chrysostom of Florina, September 8, 1955.

Metropolitan Chrysostom of Florina.

Father Philotheos Zervakos.

traditional Orthodox Christians. Father Philotheos Zervakos, abbot of the Monastery of the Life-giving Spring in Longovarda on the island of Paros, was one such prominent clergyman of the new calendar State Church of Greece. Since he had been involved in church matters virtually since the turn of the century, he had a first-hand knowledge and experience of all that had come to pass during this period. Like many others, he attempted repeatedly to convince the hierarchy of the State Church to return to the traditional church calendar, but like the others, he failed. Though he enjoyed widespread respect in Greece as a spiritual father, the new calendar hierarchy ignored his admonitions. His efforts, noble but futile, might serve as an example today for those who hope that they can "work from within" the framework of a hierarchy that is enmeshed in heresy and stubbornly committed to innovation. The following excerpt from a pamphlet written by Father Philotheos Zervakos, although it omits many important facts, gives a clear example of his thoughts on the calendar issue and the persecution against the True Orthodox Christians.

The Fruit Borne by the New Calendar in the Orthodox Church of Greece[11]

The introduction of the new calendar into the Orthodox Church of Greece brought about its division, and though it had been one [Church] since its foundation, this act divided it into two Churches: that of the old calendarists and that of the new calendarists. This division expelled the feeling of love from many and also from the two Churches [*sic*]. Most of the fanatical new calendarists, thinking that in adopting the new calendar they had seen the true light and found the true faith, heaped insults upon the old calendarists, deriding them as ignorant, bumpkins, fanatics, backward, schismatics, "acephalites" [i.e., having no patriarch or hierarchy]. But many of the old calendarists addressed the new calendarists with the same insults and more. They called them new calendarists, impious, unbelievers, atheists, Masons, accursed, Franks, excommunicated, anathematized by all the Saints and all the Holy and Ecumenical Councils, and some of them would not cease from continuously anathematizing the new calendarists. Since the new calendarists had the government authorities on their side, they persecuted the old calendarists, exiling, cursing, torturing, and imprisoning them, and coercing them by force, threats and persecutions to accept the new calendar. But they accomplished nothing. Why? Because they did not consider wisely, prudently, and justly that the old calendarists did well in not accepting the unlawful and anti-canonical introduction of the new papal calendar; for the holy and God-bearing Fathers had decreed that the Paschalion and the festal calendar should remain unchanged forever. Consequently, the old calendarists upheld the one patristic tradition which the 318 God-bearing Fathers enacted, and which the [later] Six Ecumenical Councils ratified, and which myriads of Saints kept unshaken

---

[11] From *The New, Papal Calendar and Its Fruits,* by Archimandrite Philotheos Zervakos, pp. 8-9, Thessalonica, undated. The entire booklet is forty pages long.

for some 1600 years. If some of the old calendarists, out of fanaticism, undiscerning zeal and ignorance fell into extremes, reckless arrogance, or even errors, *the cause for this was the unlawful and anti-canonical introduction of the new papal calendar and the rejection of the patristic festal calendar* [emphasis added].

Metropolitan Chrysostom of Florina ✢ *September 7, 1955.*

CHAPTER IV

Recent History of the True Orthodox

AFTER THE DEATH of the blessed Metropolitan Chrysostom, his flock was without bishops. For various reasons—but primarily because of Bishop Matthew's uncanonical consecrations—they could not reconcile themselves to Matthew's Synod. For the time being the affairs of the True Orthodox Church were managed by a twelve-member ecclesiastical commission. Some of the bishops of the State Church—such as Metropolitan Evlogios of Korytsa—seemed sympathetic and interested in assisting the traditionalist movement, but nothing actually came to pass. In November of 1958, Patriarch Christopher of Alexandria also interceded for the True Orthodox before the Greek government and State Church, but to no avail.[1]

In December of 1960, Archimandrite Akakios Pappas traveled to the United States to petition the Russian Orthodox Church Abroad to consecrate bishops for the True Orthodox Church. This was not the first time the True Orthodox Christians had petitioned the Russian Church Abroad to consecrate bishops. Metropolitan Anastasy of the Russian Church Abroad, well known for his extreme caution, decided that there was no need to get involved with any haste. However, Archbishop Seraphim of Chicago (who had received the monastic tonsure on the Holy Mountain and was acquainted with the zealot movement there) and Bishop Theophilus Ionescu of Detroit agreed to consecrate Archimandrite Akakios, who received the title "Bishop of Talantion" (in Greece). One major complication here was that Bishop Theophilus, though affiliated with the Russian Church Abroad, used the new calendar. Furthermore, this consecration was done without the blessing and knowledge of Metropolitan Anastasy or the Synod of the Russian

---

[1] Lardas, *op. cit.*, p. 26.

Archbishop Akakios Pappas.

Church Abroad. In addition, because of the uncanonical circumstances under which his consecration had taken place, Bishop Akakios would not reveal what bishops had consecrated him, nor would he present any certificate of consecration. Hence, suspicions arose on all sides.

Later, in 1962, Archbishop Leonty of Chile of the Russian Church Abroad traveled to Greece and, together with Archbishop Akakios, consecrated Parthenios of the Cyclades, Auxentius of Gardikion, and Chrysostom of Magnesia. These consecrations also were done without the knowledge or blessing of the Synod of the Russian Church Abroad. Subsequent to these events, Archimandrite Akakios (the nephew of Archbishop Akakios Pappas of Talantion) was consecrated for the diocese of Diavlia, and Archimandrite Gerontios was consecrated bishop for Salamis. It should

The Hierarchy of the True Orthodox Christians of Greece in 1963. From left to right: Chrysostom of Magnesia, Parthenios of the Cyclades, Akakios of Diavlia, Archbishop Akakios, Gerontios of Salamis, Auxentius of Gardikion.

be noted that the above-mentioned Archimandrite Auxentius—like many other Matthewite priest-monks and monastics—had left the Synod of Bishop Matthew in protest over Matthew's consecration of bishops by himself alone. The True Orthodox Church now had a Synod of six bishops, with Archbishop Akakios of Talantion as their head.

On the sixth of December, 1963, Metropolitan Parthenios of the Cyclades reposed, followed soon after by Archbishop Akakios in the same month of the same year. Bishop Auxentius of Gardikion was then elected Archbishop.

As a result of these developments, the Matthewites, in their turn, now condemned the uncanonical nature of the consecrations of the Florinite bishops. Each side was quick to blame the other for not observing the holy canons, while at the same time justifying its own side's canonical deficiencies as *economia*. The truth is that, according to proper canonical order, both sides had flawed episcopal consecrations.

The seriousness of this matter and the controversy it engendered both in Greece and abroad prompted the Synod of Archbishop Auxentius to appeal to Metropolitan Philaret of the Russian Church Abroad in 1969. Upon consulting with clergy of Greek background who were under the omophorion of the Russian Church Abroad and hearing their positive reports concerning the character of Archbishop Auxentius, Metropolitan Philaret presented the petition of the True Orthodox Christians of Greece to his Holy Synod, where the matter was discussed.

Thus, on December 18, 1969, Metropolitan Philaret and the entire Synod of the Russian Church Abroad officially ratified and recognized the consecrations of the True Orthodox Church in Greece of the Florinite jurisdiction; thereby, they accepted the Synod of Archbishop Auxentius as a sister church and declared that full ecclesiastical communion should be established. The text of this decision is as follows:[2]

18/31 December, 1969

To His Beatitude Auxentius,
Archbishop of the Church of the
True Orthodox Christians of Greece

Your Beatitude,

Your Beatitude's fraternal letter of 25 November, 1969, was read by us at a meeting of our Synod today.

The many trials which the Orthodox Church has endured from the beginning of its history are especially great in our evil times, and, consequently, this especially requires unity among those who are truly devoted to the Faith of the Fathers. With these sentiments we wish to inform you that the Synod of Bishops of the Russian Orthodox Church Abroad recognizes the validity of the episcopal ordinations of your predecessor of blessed memory, the reposed Archbishop Akakios, and the consequent ordinations of your Holy Church. Hence, taking

[2] Reproduced photographically in *Thus Do We Believe, Thus Do We Speak*, p. 12.

into account also various other circumstances, our hierarchical Synod esteems your hierarchy as brothers in Christ in full communion with us.

May the blessing of God rest upon all the clergy and faithful of your Church, especially during the coming days of the Nativity in the flesh of our Lord and Saviour Jesus Christ.

The President of the Synod of Bishops
☦ Metropolitan Philaret

> The Members:
> ☦ Nikon, Archbishop of Washington and Florida
> ☦ Seraphim, Archbishop of Chicago and Detroit
> ☦ Vitaly, Archbishop of Montreal and Canada
> ☦ Anthony, Archbishop of Los Angeles and Texas
> ☦ Averky, Archbishop of Syracuse and Trinity
> ☦ Anthony, Archbishop of Western America and San Francisco
> ☦ Sabbas, Bishop of Edmonton
> ☦ Nectary, Bishop of Seattle
> ☦ Andrew, Bishop of Rockland
> ☦ Laurus, Bishop of Manhattan

One author in Greece offers what is, perhaps, the best evaluation of the entire matter regarding the consecration of Archimandrite Akakios Pappas to the episcopacy.

> The pharisaism of the defenders of new calendarism and Ecumenism reaches its apogee when it concerns itself with the consecration of the contemporary old calendar bishops. The agreement of all ecumenistic bishops with Masonic syncretism does not bother them; nor does the fact that most of the new calendar bishops in Greece today are simoniacs and adulterer bishops.[3] Even the question of transferring one bishop from one diocese to another, which at other times unsettled them, does not appear to impress them any longer. One matter alone appears completely unacceptable to them—that the old calendar

---

[3] Adulterers in the sense that they have taken dioceses belonging to other bishops.

bishop (Akakios Pappas) was consecrated by two bishops. They rend their clothes and shout, "'What further need have we of witnesses?' (Matt. 26:65); the consecration of a bishop by two bishops is uncanonical!"[4] "Woe unto you, scribes and Pharisees, hypocrites! For ye pay tithes of mint and anise and cumin, and have omitted the weightier matters of the law, judgment, mercy and faith ... ye blind guides which strain out the gnat, and swallow a camel!" (Matt. 23:23-24).

By using the same method and by applying exactness, one can prove that all the bishops of Greece are uncanonical. If there were irregularities in the consecrations of some old calendarists, these were dictated by the persecutions they were enduring at the hands of the ecumenists and the unavoidable necessity of the times, and they were later corrected. What necessity, however, dictates the terrible and unforgivable uncanonicities in the consecrations of the ecumenist bishops? Besides, as long as they themselves later accept the doctrinal substantiality of the old calendar ordinations (inasmuch as the new calendarists say that the uncanonicity of a consecration is one issue and its doctrinal substantiality is another), why do they continue to discuss the canonicity of the old calendar consecrations? Even if out of necessity and because of the persecutions, the old calendarists made some mistakes in their consecrations, nonetheless, they preserved the Faith. The ecumenists, however, violate both the Faith and the canons and are the last who have the right to speak about the violation of the canons. People who consecrate bishops, despite the fact that the laity in the church are shouting "Unworthy!" and while those standing outside are scornfully hooting both the consecrators and the ones being consecrated, must have much effrontery in order to judge the consecrations of the traditional Orthodox Christians.

It is true that the episcopal consecrations of the True Orthodox Christians, all performed under conditions of duress, confusion,

---

[4] The consecration of a bishop by two bishops is not uncanonical, provided there is synodal approval for it. The First Canon of the Holy Apostles, adopted and ratified by subsequent Ecumenical Councils, is explicit: "Let a bishop be ordained by two or three bishops" (provided—as later Councils stipulated—that the local Synod of Bishops has accepted and approved of the consecration).

and persecution, were, from a strict canonical standpoint, flawed. In such troubled times, as Church history shows, because of unavoidable circumstances, irregularities do occur. Had it not been for the decision of a greater synod which examined and regularized these consecrations, as the Russian Synod Abroad did in 1969 for the Florinites and in 1971 for the Matthewites, the consecrations would have remained deficient and flawed. Our author continues:

> Later, we observe that another hierarch of the Russian Synod Abroad (Archbishop Leonty of Chile) travelled to Greece and, together with Akakios, consecrated the rest of the bishops of the True Orthodox Church of Greece. The agreement of the Russian Church Abroad for the consecration of the Greek old calendar hierarchs is shown by the subsequent (*ex post facto*) official recognition of them by the whole Synod of the Russian Church in diaspora in December of 1969.
>
> "The consecration of the True Orthodox Bishops of Greece," say the ecumenists, "was performed by bishops of America, an action that is prohibited by the canons." "The Holy Synod of the Church of Greece," they write, "is prohibited from consecrating a bishop or another clergyman for the Church of Cyprus, or of Crete, Serbia, Bulgaria, etc." We agree that this is indeed prohibited when the Churches of Crete, of Cyprus, of Serbia, of Bulgaria, etc., are *Orthodox* in all things. If, however, it were supposed that the Church of Cyprus had become heretical, would it continue to be prohibited by the canons for the Church of Greece to consecrate one or two bishops for the few remaining Orthodox of Cyprus? Would it not be criminal negligence if she did not perform such consecrations? If the festal calendar had not been changed in Greece; if the innovating bishops had not taken the road of Ecumenism; if Greece, for example, had remained truly Orthodox; then, indeed, the consecration of Greek bishops by the Russian hierarchy in America would have to be considered extra-jurisdictional, and therefore uncanonical. Now, however, not only are they not uncanonical, not only can they not be considered extra-jurisdictional, but to the contrary, they are unto salvation. In this manner was the remnant of grace—the chosen people of the old calendarists—preserved in Greece. Like Israel of old, in spite of all their provincialism and

Metropolitan Philaret of the Russian Church Abroad and Archbishop Auxentius of Athens. This photograph was taken at the headquarters of the Russian Synod in New York at the time of Archbishop Auxentius's visit in 1971.

failings, they serve as a bridge of truth upon which all who still worship God in spirit and *in truth* will tread in order to cross the raging torrent of the present trial of Ecumenism.

"By 1973, the Auxentian Synod had ten bishops, 123 churches in Greece, thirty-nine monasteries and convents, several charitable organizations, numerous periodicals, and most of the traditional Orthodox faithful in Greece."[5]

[5] Lardas, *op.cit.*, p. 30.

✳ ✳ ✳

OTHER RELATED EVENTS

In 1971, two bishops representing the Matthewite Synod, Kallistos of Corinth and Epiphanios of Kition of Cyprus, came to the United States and visited Holy Transfiguration Monastery in Boston. They also visited various other establishments of the Russian Church Abroad, including Holy Trinity Monastery in Jordanville, New York, where they met the late Archbishop Averky. The same two Matthewite bishops, with their Chancellor, Father Eugene Tombros, returned again later in 1971 on behalf of their Synod to petition the Russian Church Abroad to regularize their consecrations under whatever conditions the Synod of the Russian Church Abroad should impose. The text of their petition was as follows:[6]

> To His Beatitude
> The Most Eminent Metropolitan Philaret,
> President of the Sacred Synod of the Bishops
> of the Russian Church Outside Russia, in New York
>
> Rejoice in Christ Jesus, our true God.
>
> The Synodal Committee of the Church of the True Orthodox Christians of Greece (jurisdiction of the late Archbishop Matthew) has been empowered by our Holy Synod's Decree, number 736, of September 12, 1971, to enter into a full discussion with your Holy Synod concerning the sacred struggle for Orthodoxy. With reference to the matter of our consecrations (the consecrations of a bishop by one bishop) we make known to your Holy and Sacred Synod the following:
>
> From the year 1937 until August 1948 we continually sought to bring about a union, salutary to our sacred struggle in Greece.
>
> Likewise we continually and uninterruptedly sought by representatives, by personal meetings, and by encyclicals, for union and for the consecration of bishops from the hierarchs of that time: Chrysostom, former bishop of Florina, and Germanos of the Cyclades. The people not only desired to see shepherds,

---

[6] From the files of Holy Transfiguration Monastery, Brookline, Mass.

but there was a great need in the Church for the existence of a hierarchy, namely consecrations, ordinations, and prayers of absolution. But Bishop Chrysostom as president stood immovable, granting neither union [*sic*] nor ordinations.

Having given up hope, therefore, we turned to bishops of other nationalities and jurisdictions. The response was in the negative. And the flocks, both in Greece and abroad, were aroused, and they constrained us by petitions, by letters, and by representatives, persistently and beseechingly seeking shepherds and consecrations of bishops. At that time, and under such circumstances of necessity, we decided to perform the consecrations.

As is well known, in the ancient Church, these acts—insofar as they are in accord with canonical injunctions—bring us to the sure conclusion that a consecration of a bishop by one bishop is canonical and necessary under these circumstances. Consequently, a bishop consecrated under such circumstances cannot be considered uncanonical, and therefore, invalidly consecrated—unless, of course, other factors enter into the picture, which would invalidate the consecrations, such as a consecration outside of the church building itself, simony, etc.

Furthermore, by condescension and *economia*, any doubt that might exist concerning the canonicity of such consecrations is dispelled, especially when it is shown that they were performed in a time of persecution when no other bishop was to be found, as mentioned above.

Consequently, it can be clearly understood that a consecration of a bishop by one bishop is—because of the situation that existed—permitted and therefore lawful, because it does not go beyond the limits foreseen by the Church's usage of *economia*.

Wherefore, in view of this, we submit our present petition unto Your Holy and Sacred Synod, and we are ready to accept its every decision based, always, upon the divine and sacred Canons.

New York, September 1971.

   The Synodical Committee
     ✠ Kallistos, Metropolitan of Corinth, president
     ✠ Epiphanios, Metropolitan of Kition
     ✠ Eugene Tombros, protopresbyter.

In a Resolution dated September 15, 1971 (Protocol No. 16–II), the Synod of Metropolitan Philaret agreed to this regularization by the rite of *cheirothesia*—the "laying-on of hands"—with the condition that the two Matthewite bishops, on their return to Greece, perform the rite of laying-on of hands on all the other Matthewite hierarchs, and that the bishops, in turn, perform this rite for all their clergy. Another condition was that the Matthewite Synod make peace and unite with the Synod of Archbishop Auxentius. The full text of this Resolution is as follows:[7]

RESOLUTION OF THE COUNCIL OF BISHOPS OF THE RUSSIAN ORTHODOX CHURCH OUTSIDE OF RUSSIA

15/28 September 1971
Protocol Number 16–II

In their address to the Synod, Metropolitans Kallistos and Epiphanios explained that after a number of parishes in Greece decided not to accept the new calendar because they regarded it as a violation of Orthodoxy, they painstakingly sought for a means whereby bishops might be consecrated [for them] in a canonical manner. Only after all their efforts were unsuccessful did Bishop Matthew decide to perform the consecration alone. Appealing to the Synod to consider their situation, the aforementioned Bishops—in their own name and in the name of their brethren—express their willingness to accept any canonical decision which the Synod will find fit to pronounce.

Earlier, in an address to the Synod on August 29, 1971, Archbishop Auxentius requested the Synod of Bishops of the Russian Orthodox Church Outside of Russia to express its judgment regarding how clergymen from the old calendar group of the "Matthewites" (i.e., Old Calendar Greeks who are led by bishops originating from the consecration performed by one bishop) should be accepted.

The history [of this matter] is as follows:

When the Church in Greece in 1924 declared that it accepted the new calendar, discontent arose and several groups were formed which did not accept that reform. However, they were not united.

[7] From the files of Holy Transfiguration Monastery, Brookline, Mass.

In 1935 three bishops, who at that time belonged to the State Church (Germanos of Demetrias, Chrysostom of Florina, and Chrysostom of Zakynthos) joined the movement [of the traditional Orthodox Christians]. They immediately proceeded to consecrate four more bishops: Germanos of the Cyclades Islands, Christopher of Christianopolis, Polycarp of Diavlia, and Matthew of Bresthena.

However those bishops soon developed disagreements [among themselves] and their Synod dissolved. Three bishops abandoned the movement. Germanos of Demetrias died [in 1943]. Only Polycarp of Diavlia and Matthew of Bresthena were left, whereas Chrysostom of Florina separated from them and remained alone.[8] In 1948, Bishop Matthew, convinced that under conditions of persecution no other means existed to maintain a truly Orthodox Greek hierarchy, proceeded alone to perform consecrations of bishops. It is impossible for us to clearly decide how far it could have been possible for him at the time to secure the assistance of Bishop Polycarp or Bishop Chrysostom in performing the first consecration. In any case, from this consecration performed by him alone proceeded the so-called "Matthewite" hierarchy, which was not recognized by the other part of the old calendarists headed later by Archbishop Akakios, and now by his successor, Archbishop Auxentius.

It seems that in Greece there are two opinions regarding the possible means of accepting into communion the bishops and clergymen from the group presently represented by Metropolitan Kallistos and Metropolitan Epiphanios [of the Matthewites]. As often happens in such cases, the Synod is faced by the confrontation of two principles: *exactness* and *economia.*

Before deciding which point of view should prevail in this case, one must decide if it is at all necessary to apply one of these two principles; or, to be more exact, cannot the principle

---

[8] This paragraph contains a number of errors in the matter of dates. Because of the persecutions, Polycarp of Diavlia recanted and returned to the State Church in 1935, only to return again in 1944 to rejoin Metropolitan Chrysostom of Florina. In 1954, he again recanted and returned to the State Church because of the persecutions. Metropolitan Chrysostom of Florina "remained alone" ultimately only in 1954.

of *economia* extend so far as to recognize the Matthew consecrations as valid in general. In other words, one must consider the validity of episcopal consecrations by one bishop.

In the *Apostolic Constitutions* there is an indication that, in general, a consecration performed by one bishop is not recognized as valid. A consecration of a bishop should be performed by three bishops and, in the case of necessity, by two. However, there is a clause that, in case of persecution, an exception may be made if the participation of a second bishop is impossible. It is pointed out that in the history of the Church there were some—truly very few—precedents for such consecrations. However, in these cases either they were usually preceded by canonical elections or else they were recognized as valid after a subsequent decision of a Council. Such cases were known also in Greece during the war for liberation, when communication with Constantinople broke down. In 1825, Bishop Gabriel of Zarna consecrated three bishops. Later those consecrations were recognized as valid by a Council in 1834. However, his consecration of Prokopios as Bishop of Andrubis in 1832 was considered unjustified by the circumstances and, hence, not valid, and he himself was deposed because of it. Later both bishops, Gabriel and Prokopios, were pardoned after their repentance and were reinstated as bishops. It is to be noted that Christopher, the late Patriarch of Alexandria, accepted in their orders clergymen ordained by bishops of the Matthew succession. In Russia, there is the case of Bishop Ioasaph, who was consecrated for Alaska by one bishop, but he drowned before he could begin to rule the diocese. He was canonically elected to his See, and the Synod appointed two bishops to perform the consecration, but one of them was unable to be there owing to obstacles beyond his control.

But if we find that in history consecrations performed by one bishop did occur, one should keep in mind that not every precedent is worthy of being repeated. It is safer to follow more authoritative Church regulations.

One may not rely excessively on the *Apostolic Constitutions*, since the Fathers of the Sixth Ecumenical Council ruled that the *Constitutions*, as transmitted by Clement, should be "cleansed of matter that was 'contrary to piety,'" so as the better to make sure of the edification and security of the most Christian flock" (Canon 2).

Meanwhile, the undisputed canons clearly indicate that the consecration of bishops should be performed by three or, in the last resort, by two bishops. "A bishop must be consecrated by two or three bishops" rules the First Apostolic Canon. Canon Four of the First Ecumenical Council says the same: "It is proper indeed that a bishop be installed by all the bishops of the province. But if such a thing is difficult, either because of the urgency of circumstances, or because of the distance to be travelled, at least three should gather together and, with the votes of those who are absent and who agree with the election by letter, they should then perform the consecration." The same rule is repeated in Canon Three of the Seventh Ecumenical Council. Thus, these canons also indicate that the whole episcopate should participate in the election of a bishop, and that his consecration should be performed by at least two bishops. This is so because the consecration of a bishop is not the concern of only one bishop, but is an act of the whole hierarchy; it is performed by it synodically, and in no case is it a matter of one bishop unilaterally. There is an attempt to approve the consecration performed by one bishop because of the existing persecutions. However, one must keep in mind that if the requirement of two bishops for a consecration is indicated in the Apostolic Canons (which also originated in the years of persecution), then the clause in the *Apostolic Constitutions* which permits *in extremis* a consecration of a bishop by one bishop, must be regarded as belonging to provisions which were not approved by the Council in Trullo.

The requirement that at least two bishops perform the consecration has yet another explanation. According to the words of the Apostle Paul, "the less is blessed by the better" (Heb. 7:7). It is quite clear that this principle is observed when a bishop ordains a priest. But for a [consecration of a] bishop—one bishop is not "the better." For him, "the better" is a synod of bishops. Therefore, the consecration of a bishop by one bishop distorts the Orthodox principle of the ecclesiastical hierarchy.

Consequently, although the zeal of the followers of Bishop

Matthew in preserving the Church tradition and Church calendar is laudable, and although the bishops originating from his consecration are not to be reproached in anything except the order of the consecration, many preferred to remain without a bishop rather than be subject to them until a hierarchy appeared, which, obviously, for them combined the zeal of observing the ecclesiastical tradition with the consecration performed by canonical bishops.

Every consecration performed without observing the canons is already essentially invalid, even if it is performed by canonically consecrated bishops. Canon Four of the Second Ecumenical Council, for instance, did not depose Maximus the Cynic for his misdeeds, but declared his consecration invalid. Even though it was performed by canonical bishops, it was performed in violation of the canons. This refers also to the ordination of priests. In his letter to the *chorepiscopoi*, Saint Basil the Great writes that those who were irregularly ordained to the priesthood should be deposed. He closes the canon with the words: "He whom you have admitted to the service without our consent and approval will be a layman" (Canon 89). This important principle is expressed even more clearly in Canon Six of the First Ecumenical Council: "The Great Council has determined that whoever was consecrated bishop without the [local] metropolitan's approval, must not be a bishop."

Only the Roman Catholic Church, distorting the very idea of the bestowal of grace within the Church, recognizes as valid every ordination performed by canonically consecrated bishops, even if it is otherwise uncanonical. According to them, the granting of the grace is indissolubly connected with the properly-pronounced formula of consecration, which acts as a validation, independent of its being done unilaterally, or not in fulfillment of the will of the Church. Such a doctrine is foreign to the Orthodox Church. It is therefore understandable that the consecration of Archbishop Akakios and the consecrations which followed it raised doubts in many until it was confirmed and legalized by a decision of the Synod [on December 18, 1969].

However, by way of *economia*, an illegal act receives the force of a sacrament without being performed anew. Saint Basil the Great, in his First Canon, writes concerning the Cathari that they were deprived of the gifts of the Holy Spirit because they were schismatics. However, by *economia* he permits their acceptance into communion without a new baptism. Also, Canon Eight of the First Ecumenical Council says concerning them: "As for those who call themselves Cathari [i.e. "pure"] and who claim to be adherents of the Catholic and Apostolic Church, it has seemed right to the Holy and Great Council that when they have received the laying-on of hands, they may remain in the clergy."

There is some difference of opinion in regard to understanding the phrase "laying-on of hands" in that Canon. Aristenos understands it in the sense of chrismation. His opinion is repeated by Bishop John of Smolensk. However, it seems that a more authoritative explanation was given by Saint Tarasius at the Seventh Ecumenical Council. When someone asked how one should understand the words "laying-on of hands" in Canon Eight of the First Ecumenical Council, the Saint explained that the word "consecration" [*cheirotonía*] is not used here, but another one [*cheirothetoúmenoi*],[9] and that this [latter] term means only a blessing. One can agree with Bishop Nicholas Milosh that, on the basis of Saint Tarasius's authoritative interpretation, "the meaning of these words in that Nicene Canon is that, when Novatian clergymen were accepted from schism into the Orthodox Church, the assigned bishop or priest must lay his hands on them, as is done in the mystery of repentance, and that he must read the appropriate prayer [over them], thereby reconciling them with the Church." The same procedure was applied in the Church of Carthage, according to Canon Seventy-nine [Canon Seventy-seven in the Greek edition of *The Rudder*], when the Donatists, much more embittered schismatics than the Novatians and the Cathari, were accepted. It is permitted in regard to

---

[9] *Editors' Note:* From *cheirothetéo*, which, in fact, has several connotations. It can mean "to lay hands on," "to bless," "to ordain." In some Church writers, the terms *cheirotonía* (to ordain, or to consecrate a bishop) and *cheirothetéo* (to lay hands on) are used interchangeably.

them, because of "the great need, for the peace and prosperity of the Church, that those Donatists who were clergymen and who by good advice had desired to return to Catholic unity, should be treated according to the will and judgment of each Catholic bishop who governs the Church in that place; and, if it seemed good for Christian peace, they should be received with their honors," notes the Canon, "as it is clear was done in the former times of this same dissension."

From what was said in the beginning of this Resolution, it is evident that the old calendarists headed by the hierarchy proceeding from Matthew's consecration can hardly be compared with such schismatics as the Donatists or the Novatians. They have not sinned against Orthodoxy in their doctrines; but in their efforts to protect it, they violated the hierarchical order when an episcopal consecration was performed by Bishop Matthew alone. A simple recognition of their orders could bring scandal as a direct violation of canons: the First Apostolic Canon, Canon Four of the First Ecumenical Council, and Canon Three of the Seventh Ecumenical Council. However, it is evident from the other examples mentioned that there is full reason to apply *economia* to them, in accordance with Canon Eight of the First Ecumenical Council and Canon Seventy-nine of Carthage.

Taking into consideration all the aforesaid, as well as the desire expressed by Archbishop Auxentius that the union of all people devoted to true Orthodoxy be achieved, the Synod of Bishops resolves:

1. To acknowledge the possibility of fulfilling the petition of Metropolitans Kallistos and Epiphanios. To that end, two bishops must perform the laying-on of hands over them. They, in turn, must subsequently perform the same over their brethren, and all bishops [must perform the same rite] over the priests;

2. To oblige Metropolitans Kallistos and Epiphanios, as well as their brethren, to take all possible steps to unite their hierarchy, clergy, and people with those who are headed by His Beatitude, Archbishop Auxentius;

3. To inform His Beatitude, Archbishop Auxentius, concerning the aforesaid [decisions];

Metropolitan Philaret with Bishops Kallistos of Corinth and Epiphanios of Cyprus in New York in 1971.

Archbishop Philotheus of Hamburg (center) with (from left) Father Eugene Tombros, Metropolitan Kallistos, and Bishop Constantine, after Kallistos's cheirothesia *at Holy Transfiguration Monastery in Brookline, Massachusetts, September 17, 1971.*

4. To delegate the Most Reverend Archbishop Philotheus and Bishop Constantine to fulfill the provision of paragraph one of this Resolution at Transfiguration Monastery in Boston.

For the Council of Bishops,

☩ Bishop Laurus of Manhattan,
Secretary to the Synod

Metropolitans Kallistos and Epiphanios and Chancellor Eugene Tombros agreed to these conditions and, on September 17/30 and September 18/October 1, 1971, during the Divine Liturgies, the two hierarchs received the laying-on of hands at Holy Transfiguration Monastery. Archbishop Philotheus of Hamburg and Bishop Constantine of Brisbane of the Russian Church Abroad officiated at these services and confirmed the act of the rite of laying-on of hands with the following signed document:[10]

ACT

In fulfillment of the Sobor's decree dated 15/28 September, 1971, we read the prayers with the laying-on of our hands upon His Grace Kallistos, Metropolitan of Corinth, on September 17/30, 1971, and on September 18/October 1 of the same year upon His Grace Epiphanios, Metropolitan of Kition, in the Monastery of the Transfiguration in Brookline, Mass.

After this we celebrated the Divine Liturgy with them.

Brookline, Mass.
Date: Sept. 18, 1971

SIGNATURES:
☩ Archbishop Philotheus
☩ Bishop Constantine

WITNESSES:
Archimandrite Kalliopios
Archimandrite Panteleimon
Hieromonk Haralambos

Unfortunately, the conditions laid down by the Russian Church Abroad and agreed to by the Matthewite representatives were only partially implemented in Greece. The Matthewite Synod agreed to the first condition (that the rite of *cheirothesia* be performed over their bishops), but refused to comply with the second (that the

[10] From the files of Holy Transfiguration Monastery, Brookline, Mass.

same rite be performed over their priests and deacons), though a number of their clergy persistently requested it.[11] In a privately published memorandum, dated March 17, 1977, Metropolitan Epiphanios of Cyprus—and also Metropolitan Kallistos of Corinth, in private memoranda and open letters which he wrote—rebuked their fellow Matthewite bishops and clergy for showing bad faith and for bearing the burden of guilt in the breakdown of their negotiations with the Florinites and the souring of their relations with the Church Abroad. Thus, the union that the Russian Church Abroad had desired for all the True Orthodox Christians in Greece was not achieved. Furthermore, relations eventually soured between the Matthewite bishops and the Russian Church Abroad over what was considered by the Matthewites as canonical infractions; hence, the Matthewites severed their relations with the Russian Church Abroad on February 20, 1976. They claimed—falsely—that the Russian Church Abroad accepted the Matthewite "confession of faith" (see page 101) in September, 1971, and that it was only under this condition that they accepted to have their uncanonical episcopal ordinations corrected—which correction they later repudiated officially (see, for example, *Herald of the True Orthodox*, March, 1984, pp. 102-3). This means that their bishops have reverted to their previous irregular and uncanonical status (since they were consecrated by only one bishop, Matthew).

In 1974, because of the marked increase of modernism and the heresy of Ecumenism within the State Church of Greece and the other ecumenistic jurisdictions of "World Orthodoxy," Archbishop Auxentius's Synod issued an encyclical that reaffirmed the earlier Encyclical of May 26, 1950. The clergy were reminded that the State Church was in schism and that the First Canon of Saint Basil was to be applied according to strictness, that is, that the mysteries of the State Church could not be considered valid, and that those who wished to enter into communion with the True Orthodox Church were to be received by holy chrismation. The full text of this Encyclical follows:[12]

---

[11] *Thus Do We Believe, Thus Do We Speak*, pp. 22-23.   [12] *Ibid*, pp. 9-10.

TO THE SACRED CLERGY OF OUR CHURCH

Athens, June 5, 1974
Protocol Number 1191

Most Righteous and Reverend Ministers of the Most High:

Grace, mercy and peace be unto you from God, and prayer and blessing from us.

By means of this present Encyclical we address ourselves to you, bringing to your remembrance an imperative duty which should distinguish your course of action, in obedience to whatsoever was delivered unto us from of old by the God-bearing Fathers.

Thus, we enjoin you yet once again to limit your ministrations only to the members of our Church, lest you set a stumblingblock before the brethren and, as ones who do not believe those things that are professed by us, draw upon yourselves the criticism of the common people.

The celebration of a Mystery and the giving of Holy Communion to new calendarists was forbidden from the time that the schism created by the State Church began. Therefore, it is necessary that you uphold this position without deviation, in obedience to the understanding of all that has been handed down to us in the Church. Should any from the new calendar desire to enter our ranks, it is absolutely necessary that they make a confession of Faith in regard to all that has been transmitted unto us by our God-bearing Fathers, and that they renounce and condemn every heresy and innovation, among which is the new calendar in the Greek Church, which became schismatic from its acceptance thereof in 1924 until the present, according to the very confession of the innovator, Archbishop Chrysostom Papadopoulos, and, as a consequence, its mysteries are deprived of sanctifying grace.

Also, regarding those who have been baptized in the aforementioned Church and have not returned to piety, it is necessary that, according to the First Canon of Saint Basil the Great, they be re-chrismated with holy chrism of canonical provenance.

As a consequence of the above, we enjoin that, in conformance with the holy and sacred canons, you henceforth cease any sacramental ministration you might have tendered anyone coming from the New Calendar Church, unless the above-mentioned procedure is first implemented, since, otherwise, the sanctions predetermined by the sacred canons will be imposed upon those who transgress it.[13]

<table>
<tr><td>The President</td><td>The Sacred Synod</td></tr>
<tr><td>✠ Archbishop Auxentius</td><td>✠ Akakios of Diavlia and Attica</td></tr>
<tr><td></td><td>✠ Gerontios of Piraeus and Salamina</td></tr>
<tr><td></td><td>✠ Paisios of Euripus and Euboea</td></tr>
<tr><td></td><td>✠ Chrysostom of Thessalonica</td></tr>
<tr><td></td><td>✠ Kallinikos of Thavmakos</td></tr>
<tr><td></td><td>✠ Akakios of Canada</td></tr>
<tr><td></td><td>✠ Gabriel of the Cyclades Islands</td></tr>
<tr><td></td><td>✠ Anthony of Megaris</td></tr>
</table>

It is to the credit of the authorities of the Greek government that, despite the sharp protests of the new calendar State Church, the true Orthodox Christians finally began to receive legal recognition and protection, sporadically at first, but more consistently with the passage of time. This recognition was first affirmed in the city of Piraeus in 1947, when the baptisms and weddings of the traditional Orthodox Christians were recognized. In 1980, the Supreme Court of Greece[14] (Decisions 378 and 379) decreed that traditional Orthodox Christians are neither schismatics nor heretics. More recently, the Greek government has also offered various benefits (for example, free medical insurance) to the True Orthodox clergy. However, there is considerable reluctance to accept these favors, since Orthodox Christians have come to learn that the "protecting hand" of the government can often be quite oppressive.

---

[13] The original text of this Encyclical has the following footnote: "The present Encyclical was ready to be issued on April 4, 1973. It has been postponed until now awaiting His Eminence, Bishop Peter of Astoria, who, though invited repeatedly to endorse the Encyclical, refused to do so. On this account, in its meeting of June 5, 1974, the Holy Synod struck him from its membership and removed him from the exarchate of the True Orthodox Christians of America."

[14] In Modern Greek this court of justice is still referred to as *Areopagos* ("Mars Hill"). See Acts 17:19, 22.

CHAPTER V

The Status in 1994

WE WILL NOW EXAMINE briefly the particular histories and the theological positions of the old calendar jurisdictions in Greece in the following order:

1) The Synod of the Matthewites
2) The Synod of Cyprian Koutsoumbas
   A. The Kallistos Schism
   B. The Synod of Those in Resistance
3) The Synod of Chrysostom Kiousis
4) The Synod of Archbishop Auxentius

1) *The Synod of the Matthewites*

We have already discussed the history and theological position of the Matthewite jurisdiction, now headed by Archbishop Andrew. They have taken the position that, with the change of the church calendar, all grace departed from the State Church in 1924. Metropolitan Kallistos of Corinth, at that time a prominent member of the Matthewite Synod, used to demonstrate this element of its "confession of faith" by going to a light switch and turning it off, thus graphically illustrating his Synod's views.[1]

Recently, the Matthewite jurisdiction has seen its unity sorely tested by a sharp controversy that threatens to separate them into two factions. Despite the decrees of ancient Church councils and the witness of Church Fathers, Archbishop Andrew's Synod issued two Encyclicals defending Renaissance-style "icons" of God the Father (which, as can be historically documented, are of Roman Catholic origin), while at the same time "correcting the theological errors" found in icons that, in fact, are fully traditional

---

[1] See also pp. 109-110 and 114-115 below.

Bishop Matthew of Bresthena.

and Orthodox.² Also, they continue to justify Matthew's single-handed "consecrations." Though their petition to the Church Abroad in 1971 admitted that there were other Orthodox bishops in Greece (see pp. 87-88), it did not elaborate on why Chrysostom of Florina was unwilling to consecrate more bishops of Matthew's mentality. Finally, their repudiation of the Church Abroad's correction of their irregular acts (though this correction was initially hailed by them—see, for example, *Thus Do We Believe, Thus Do We Speak*, p. 19) puts their canonical status in question at present.

2) *The Synod of Cyprian (Koutsoumbas)*

A. *The Kallistos Schism*

Before discussing the Synod of Bishop Cyprian, it is needful first to examine the short-lived "Kallistos Schism."³

---

² The Encyclicals were dated January 23, 1992 (Protocol Number 2566), and February 26, 1993 (Protocol Number 2660).

³ See the Special Supplement to the *Orthodox Christian Witness*, Vol. XVIII, No. 12, *Latest Developments in the Church of the Genuine Orthodox Christians of Greece (The Schism of the "Kallistos" Group)*.

In February of 1979, two bishops of the Auxentius (i.e., Florinite) group—Metropolitans Kallistos[4] (formerly of the Matthewite Synod) and Anthony of Megaris—in league with a group of archimandrites, broke away from the Synod of Archbishop Auxentius and proceeded to consecrate a new group of bishops secretly.

The motives of these bishops were not matters of faith, but purely ethical and moral concerns, as they themselves affirmed.[5] In the very first days of the schism, the two bishops consecrated eight bishops from among the aforementioned archimandrites, and thus created a new Synod, made up of ten bishops (Kallistos, Anthony, Cyprian, Maximos, Kallinikos, Matthew, Germanos, Kalliopios, Mercurios, and another Kallinikos), and they named their movement "The Greek Church of the Genuine Orthodox Christians."

The protagonists in this schism—aware that there was no canonical justification for this action in the prevailing circumstances—claimed that Archbishop Auxentius had given "tacit encouragement and agreement" and that the consecrations were "at Archbishop Auxentius's request."[6] When apprised of the above statements, however, Archbishop Auxentius categorically denied them. In fact, he and his Holy Synod immediately deposed Kallis-

---

[4] Metropolitan Kallistos left the Matthewite Synod and joined the Synod of Auxentius in June of 1977 in protest over what he considered the Matthewite Synod's lack of good faith in the effort at reconciliation with the Holy Synod of Archbishop Auxentius.

[5] See, for example, their official publication, *Guardians of Orthodoxy* (Vol. 1, March 1979, pp. 1–2 [in Greek]). The new group was asked to provide concrete evidence to back up their accusations. Archbishop Auxentius publicly demanded that they prove these allegations and had them subpoenaed for defamation and slander (*Voice of Orthodoxy*, March–April, 1979, pp. 13–14; August, 1979, p. 10; September, 1979, p. 9 [in Greek]).

[6] *The Old Calendar Orthodox Church of Greece*, Bishop Chrysostom, Etna, California, Third Edition, 1991, p. 20. In a recent edition of *An Apostolic and Patristic Voice* (Jan.–March, 1997, issue #3 [in Greek]), however, the editor, Metropolitan Kallinikos of the Dodecanese, admits that these consecrations were indeed performed secretly and without Archbishop Auxentius's knowledge (and hence, without even a canonical election of the candidates). Since Metropolitan Kallinikos was one of those who were uncanonically consecrated at that time, he has first-hand information of these events, which he describes quite candidly in the above-cited periodical.

tos, Anthony and all the others who took part in this action, and demoted them to the rank of unordained monks. Since some members of the original Kallistos group deny to this day that this penalty was ever imposed, it is important for the sake of historical truth to present the substantiating documentation. The Holy Synod passed two resolutions condemning these secret consecrations. The text of these resolutions is as follows:[7]

MINUTES OF THE FIRST RESOLUTION

In Petroupolis of Attica, on this day, the 14th of February, 1979, it being a Tuesday, at six o'clock in the evening, in the residence of the chief hierarch [Archbishop Auxentius], the Holy Synod of the True Orthodox Christians of Greece assembled, comprised of the President, His Beatitude, the Archbishop, kyr Auxentius, and the members, Their Eminences, the Metropolitans kyr Gerontios of Piraeus and Salamina, and kyr Kallinikos of Phthiotis and Thavmakos; [the Holy Synod met] at the invitation of its President in order to formulate a position on the sedition brought about by its members, Kallistos of Corinth and Anthony of Megaris, who illegally severed themselves from the body [of the Holy Synod] and high-handedly undertook to consecrate bishops. Upon discussing this matter at length, on the basis of the holy canons of the One, Holy, Catholic, and Apostolic Church of Christ, [the Holy Synod] unanimously decreed and imposed upon the two seditious Metropolitans the punishment of deposition, as the holy canons themselves enjoin. [The Holy Synod decrees] that this decision be released and published straightway in the Athenian press. Since there was no time to convoke the assembly of the clergy, upon deliberation, because of the gravity of this event, it decided this very day to consecrate new bishops for [the Holy Synod's] restoration and replenishment. Various points of view were exchanged and proposed by all the holy hierarchs, and the archimandrites listed below were elected [for the episcopacy]: 1) Paisios Phinokaliotis; 2) Gerasimos Vrakas; 3) Euthymios Orphanos; 4) Theophilos Tsirbas; 5) Athanasios Postalas; 6) Athanasios Haralambidis;

---

[7] From the files of the Holy Synod of the True Orthodox Church of Greece.

7) Stephen Tsikouras; 8) Maximos Vallianatos; 9) Paisios Loulourgas; 10) Justin Kulutouros.

The following were elected and consecrated in accordance with all the forms of our Holy Orthodox Church in the following order:

1) Euthymios Orphanos was consecrated Bishop of Stavropolis by the three first-ranking hierarchs, His Beatitude [the Archbishop], [Gerontios] the Metropolitan of Piraeus and Salamina, and [Kallinikos] the Metropolitan of Phthiotis and Thavmakos,

2) Then, Theophilos Tsirbas, Bishop of Christianopolis
3) Paisios Loulourgas, Bishop of Gardikion, for America
4) Athanasios Postalas, Bishop of Platamon
5) Stephen Tsikouras, Bishop of Kardamyllae
6) Maximos Vallianatos, Bishop of the Seven Islands
7) Gerasimos Vrakas, Bishop of Talantion
8) Athanasios Haralambidis, Bishop of Grevena
9) Paisios Phinokaliotis, Bishop of Aegina
10) Justin Kulutouros, Bishop of Marathon

for the purpose of shepherding the people well, and in response to the desire of many that this Holy Synod be strengthened in order to resolve the serious issues that concern the sacred struggle. There being no other matter for discussion, the present [minutes] are endorsed as follows:

The President   The Members
✠ Auxentius of Athens   ✠ Gerontios of Piraeus and Salamina
                                  ✠ Kallinikos of Phthiotis and Thavmakos

MINUTES OF THE SECOND RESOLUTION

In Athens, on this day, the 27th of February, 1979, it being a Monday, at ten o'clock in the morning, in the offices on 32 Kaningos Street, at the invitation of His Beatitude [Archbishop Auxentius], the Holy Synod of the Church of the True Orthodox Christians of Greece met in order to resolve various issues concerning our sacred struggle. Present were:

1) His Beatitude, kyr Auxentius, the President
2) His Eminence, kyr Gerontios of Piraeus and Salamina
3) His Eminence, kyr Kallinikos of Phthiotis and Thavmakos

4) His Eminence, kyr Euthymios of Stavropolis
5) His Eminence, kyr Theophilos of Christianopolis
6) His Eminence, kyr Paisios [Loulourgas] of Gardikion
7) His Eminence, kyr Athanasios of Platamon
8) His Eminence, kyr Stephen of Kardamyllae
9) His Eminence, kyr Maximos of the Seven Islands
10) His Eminence, kyr Gerasimos of Talantion
11) His Eminence, kyr Athanasios of Grevena
12) His Eminence, kyr Paisios [Phinokaliotis] of Aegina
13) His Eminence, kyr Justin of Marathon.

After the opening prayer, the minutes of the First Resolution [of February 14, 1979] were read and ratified. The holy President [of the Synod] set forth the matter of the deposed Kallistos of Corinth and Anthony of Megaris, who illegally consecrated the Archimandrites Germanos Athanasiou, Kalliopios Giannakoulopoulos, Kallinikos Sarantopoulos, Matthew Langis, Cyprian Koutsoumbas, Maximos Tsitsimbakos, Kallinikos Karaphylakis, and Mercurios Kaloskamis, and [described] also their generally deceitful maneuvers.

The holy President [of the Synod] voiced his prayers for the strengthening of the new bishops, as well as for the cooperation and agreement of all the members for the progress of the struggle. He also discussed and analyzed the various events which had taken place in our Church.

The President of the Holy Synod said that the abovementioned hierarchs, Kallistos and Anthony, who were deposed by us because of their unlawfulness during the first ten days of February of 1979, had secretly undertaken to consecrate to the episcopacy certain glory-hungry archimandrites at the Sacred Monastery of Saints Cyprian and Justina in Fili of Attica, outside of their dioceses [παρ' ἐνορίαν], that is, within his [the Archbishop's] eparchy, without their having been previously elected by at least three bishops and without the necessary consent of the chief hierarch, and without the assent of the bishops to whom the ordained were subject, as the divine and holy canons specifically enjoin; and then they subsequently proclaimed themselves to be a Synod. In their document, sent to His Beatitude on March 3, 1979 (n.s.) by a judicial bailiff, and dated February 1/14, 1979, and addressed to His Beatitude and the ruling Holy Synod, they make known that they have proceeded to perform episcopal consecrations and have formed a Synod under the presidency of Kallistos of Corinth, and they renounce the ruling Holy Synod of our Church.

At the end, when the President of the Holy Synod had read this document, he presented the endorsement and approval of the decree of [their] deposition, as well as the declaration of the uncanonical nature and invalidity of the episcopal consecrations:

Whereas, through their aforesaid document, they fully admit the accusations [against them] and shamelessly confess their guilt, and proclaim with a superfluity of presumption and audacity that they renounce the ruling Holy Synod, so that there is no need for them to make a defence for themselves;[8]

Whereas their actions, as may be clearly deduced from their *own* document, record varied and extremely serious transgressions, especially that of conspiracy, factionalism, and the establishment of unlawful assemblies and schism, as well as of the performance of consecrations without a previous vote by at least three bishops for the candidates to be consecrated, and without the necessary consent of the chief hierarch, in another's diocese (outside of their own episcopal jurisdiction), without the permission of the local bishop, and without even the opinion of the bishops to whom those consecrated were subject;

Whereas, the above-mentioned transgressions were foreseen by the divine and sacred canons: the 31st and 35th of the Holy Apostles, the 18th of the Fourth Ecumenical Council, the 1st of Saint Basil, the 15th, 13th, 19th and 22nd of Antioch, the 34th of the Quinisext Council, the 6th of Gangra, the 15th of the Council of Sardica, and the 13th of the Council in Carthage, which specify that they who enact such things are deposed, and the consecrations performed by them are invalid;

---

[8] This reveals another curious aspect of this schism. On the one hand, the perpetrators appealed to Archbishop Auxentius's authority when they were performing their consecrations (see footnote 6, p. 103), but on the other hand they refused to acknowledge the Archbishop's authority when he and his synod deposed them for these uncanonical and secret acts.

Whereas, upon consultation and deliberation together, the Holy Synod concluded that it is necessary that the deposition decided upon be approved and ratified as canonical and valid, and that the consecrations be proclaimed invalid, in that they are uncanonical, which they themselves in essence confess;

Whereas, their renunciation of the Holy Synod is bereft of canonical value and legal consequence, since it was enacted by violators of the sacred canons—indeed, by those who are conspirators, factionalists, establishers of unlawful assemblies, and schismatics, and who are subject to this [Holy Synod's] jurisdiction, their ruling authority—these individuals, however, since they are such, cannot any longer have a position of any sort whatsoever, nor any relation to the body of our martyric Church, and it is necessary that they be severed therefrom, as insubmissive members, and be renounced, with the cessation of every communion with them:

WHEREFORE

It Decrees Unanimously

—To approve and ratify the Holy Synod's condemnatory Resolution of February 1/14, 1979, deposing both those who performed the consecrations—Constantine Macris [Kallistos of Corinth] and Anthony Thanasis [Anthony of Megaris]—and those who were consecrated by them: Germanos Athanasiou, Kalliopios Giannakoulopoulos, Kallinikos Sarantopoulos, Matthew Langis, Cyprian Koutsoumbas, Maximos Tsitsimbakos, Kallinikos Karaphylakis, and Mercurios Kaloskamis;

—To declare invalid the consecrations that were performed;

—And to denounce the deposed [clergymen] and sever them from the body of our Holy Church as conspirators, factionalists, establishers of unlawful assemblies, and schismatics, and to have no communion whatsoever with them any longer.

It is necessary that an encyclical be published in the periodical *Voice of Orthodoxy*[9] in order to inform the Christ-named flock of our Church.

---

[9] The Encyclical, protocol #1420, dated March 2, 1979, appeared in the *Voice of Orthodoxy*, No. 759 (in Greek).

There being no other subject for discussion, the present [Resolution] is signed by the following:

The President	The Members
✠ Auxentius of Athens	✠ Athanasios of Acharnae and New Ionia
	✠ Theophilos of Patras and the Peloponnesus
	✠ Gerasimos of Talantion
	✠ Justin of Marathon and Euboea
	✠ Euthymios of Stavropolis
	✠ Athanasios of Larisa
	✠ Maximos of Cephalonia and the Seven Islands
	✠ [signature not clear]

In May of 1979, three bishops of the "Kallistos Schism"—Metropolitans Kallistos, Kalliopios, and Matthew—visited Holy Transfiguration Monastery in Brookline, Massachusetts. Several of the Monastery's senior fathers met with the said bishops, who opened the conversation with the words:

"Holy fathers, we have come to visit you so that you might express your congratulations for what we have done."

To this, the monastery's abbot replied, "As regards what you have done, we feel we must express not our congratulations, but our condolences."

"Your condolences! Surely you cannot mean that!"

"Of course we do. As if there were not enough factions in Greece, you have just now added one more. Furthermore, how can we offer our congratulations when we know for certain that, among other things, you do not all share the same confession of faith?"

"My beloved little Father," replied Metropolitan Kallistos, "of course we all share the same confession of faith. How can you say that? Before the consecrations, all the candidates affirmed that since 1924 the innovators created a schism and that there is no grace in their mysteries."

To this, the abbot replied, "Just now, in a recent issue of the publication of the Monastery of Fili, they say something to the contrary."

At this, Metropolitan Kallistos turned to Bishop Kalliopios and said, "Make a note of this so that when we go back, we can look into it."

The abbot then said, "Your Eminence, you don't have to go very far to ascertain this. There are three of you here. We know that you yourself believe that there has been no sanctifying grace in the mysteries of the new calendarists since 1924, and we know that Bishop Kalliopios believes the same as you do. But does Bishop Matthew here agree?"

"Of course he agrees, my beloved Father," replied Metropolitan Kallistos.

Then, turning to Bishop Matthew, the abbot of the monastery asked,

"Your Eminence, do you believe that there is no grace in the mysteries of the new calendarists?"

"Well, according to the Letter of 1937, written by Metropolitan Chrysostom of Florina...,"

"Your Eminence, excuse me, please forget about Metropolitan Chrysostom's letter of 1937," interjected the abbot. "Metropolitan Chrysostom wrote that letter and later, in 1950, retracted it. What do *you* say, right now, here in the presence of all of us? Do the new calendarists have grace, yes or no—as the Matthewites would say—black or white, yea or nay?"

The bishop would not respond.

Whereupon, the abbot turned to Metropolitan Kallistos and said, "Do you see now, Your Eminence, that you do not all have the same confession of faith?"

This became evident in a very short span of time. From 1979 until 1984, various important developments took place within the Kallistos group. Three of the new "bishops" (i.e., Maximos, Germanos, and Kallinikos) repented of their uncanonical consecrations, and were received into the Synod of Archbishop Auxentius. One of them reposed (Mercurios). Their president (Kallistos) separated himself from the rest over matters of faith;

Metropolitan Kallistos of Corinth.

however, he did not return to Archbishop Auxentius. Until his death in September of 1986, he remained alone, under no one, and in communion with no one. Those that remained (Anthony—who was their president for a short time—Cyprian, Kallinikos, Matthew, and Kalliopios) maintained an external unity, but did not agree among themselves as regards their confession of faith.

In 1984, for example, Bishop Cyprian was castigated by a new calendar periodical because, though he claimed to be a bishop of the traditional Orthodox Christians, "he accepted hundreds of new calendarists at his monastery and churches," and because "he has joint prayers with them," "gives them the mysteries and divine Communion," and "allows those who come to confession to him to receive the immaculate mysteries in new calendar churches."[10] In reply to these public accusations about his confession of faith, Bishop Cyprian called this public notice "a personal attack," and maintained that it was a matter of "pastoral discretion," which

---

[10] *Orthodoxos Typos*, January 20, 1984, p. 3 (in Greek).

"concerns [him] alone."[11] When he was accused again for not answering the charges or for not repudiating the above-mentioned accusations, and when, in addition, the title of "Ecumenist" was bestowed on him,[12] his answer was a repetition of the first—that these charges were "purely personal attacks."[13]

B. *The Synod of Those in Resistance*

In 1984, Bishop Cyprian finally broke with his former colleagues and formed his own Synod, the "Synod of Those In Resistance." His concelebrant in forming this new Synod was a certain John of Sardinia. Regarding John of Sardinia, Father Theodoretos, editor of the periodical *Hagiorites,* wrote the following in a letter in August, 1985:

> John of Sardinia ... was a Capuchin monk [who] became a priest under the jurisdiction of the Moscow Patriarchate, without first being baptized, however.[14] Later he abandoned Moscow and was consecrated bishop by the heretical Nestorians! Subsequently, he thought of the True Orthodox Christians of Greece, and approached the Kallistites [i.e., the bishops with Metropolitan Kallistos]. From here on, his new ministry begins ... Allow me to explain myself.
>
> When the Kallistites decided to receive [John of Sardinia] into their bosom, they desired—naturally—to baptize him, since he was lacking Orthodox baptism. This, however, was not at all pleasing to kyr Cyprian, who desired that he should be received without baptism! Since his co-workers disagreed with him, he did not attend the baptismal service.
>
> Now, according to the sacred canons, John could in no wise be permitted to serve even as a deacon, since he had apostatized and joined the heretical Nestorians.
>
> It is with this bishop, twice-consecrated by heretics and by schismatics, that Cyprian now co-operates, and with whom he has formed his "Sacred Synod of Those in Resistance."

---

[11] The entire text of the epistle is in his monastery's periodical *Agios Kyprianos* (Feb.–March, 1984, pp. 288–291 [in Greek]).

[12] *Orthodoxos Typos,* March 16, 1984, p. 3.

[13] *Agios Kyprianos, loc. cit.,* p. 304.   [14] See also p. 126 below.

Bishop Cyprian's jurisdiction has published many capably written articles, books, and other materials against Ecumenism. However, of all the old calendar jurisdictions, Bishop Cyprian's certainly has some of the most unusual—and perhaps most self-contradictory—views on ecclesiology, and it may be worth our while to examine them at some length.

Bishop Cyprian justified his separation in 1984 by asserting that it was a matter of faith; that is, he taught that the new calendar State Church, though ailing, had not yet been condemned by a Church Council, and therefore still had full canonical status. He rested his argument on the 1937 private letter of Metropolitan Chrysostom[15] while ignoring both the Encyclical of 1935, which had been issued by the entire hierarchy of the True Orthodox Christians,[16] and Metropolitan Chrysostom's later Encyclical of 1950,[17] not to mention the Encyclical of 1974,[18] issued by Archbishop Auxentius's Holy Synod (to whose authority the then Archimandrite Cyprian was subject). Bishop Cyprian has maintained that Metropolitan Chrysostom's 1950 encyclical was not a true expression of his confession, but made under duress and with the hope that it would appease the Matthewite bishops. Here, however, it should be noted that the Encyclical of 1950 expressed not merely the view of Metropolitan Chrysostom, but of the entire Holy Synod of the traditional Orthodox Christians.

Furthermore, in making this claim concerning Metropolitan Chrysostom's Encyclical of 1950, Bishop Cyprian ignores certain other important elements. Metropolitan Chrysostom of Florina had spoken his convictions in clear conscience and maintained them with integrity. Nothing less could be expected from a man of his stature. Since he was a man of such stature, it is not entirely honest to dismiss so lightly the formal synodical and official Encyclical of 1950 in which Metropolitan Chrysostom repudiated and disavowed everything said and written by him previously. In this Encyclical, he affirmed that the new calendarists must be received by chrismation and that their mysteries are invalid. To say

[15] See pp. 59–62.
[16] See pp. 53–55.
[17] See pp. 67–69.
[18] See pp. 99–100.

that he did not believe in his last Encyclical cannot be supported by the historical facts. First, he suffered a two-year exile on account of this Encyclical, because it had especially infuriated the new calendar State Church. Secondly, he returned from exile in 1952 and lived three more years in freedom, but he did nothing to retract the Encyclical. Besides, in ecclesiastical matters, it is the official and public confession and statement which bears weight. Certainly, he was a man who did not fear to take a position because of its consequences. One may disagree with Metropolitan Chrysostom's stand; nevertheless, the facts are so clear that it is impermissible to ignore his position of 1950 or to discount it as mere hypocrisy.

Bishop Cyprian also ignores the earlier Encyclical of 1935. In addition, Metropolitan Kallistos, one of the bishops who illegally consecrated Archimandrite Cyprian as a bishop, had always expressed the same view taken by the Matthewite bishops (i.e., that sacramental grace had departed from the State Church the instant it had changed the calendar in 1924).

In connection with this, in his publication *Agios Kyprianos* (July 1983, p. 210), Bishop Cyprian complained that Metropolitan Kallistos, who consecrated him to the episcopate, "proceeded to publish and circulate a booklet entitled *Apologia* and an open letter entitled 'Epistle of Confession'.... *without previous consultation* [emphasis in original] with the other members of our Sacred Synod." Concerning these two publications of Metropolitan Kallistos, Bishop Cyprian wrote that the views expressed therein are "without witness, unprovable, anti-patristic, and hence un-Orthodox."

Yet Metropolitan Kallistos's confession of faith was known to all, both young and old, and it never changed throughout the years. Neither was it a "personal" matter, as Bishop Cyprian might have said, but rather was proclaimed publicly by Metropolitan Kallistos, both in writing and from the ambon: there was—he said openly and consistently—no sanctifying grace in the new calendar State Church.

For example, describing the events of 1924, he wrote the following:

Dismissing, disdaining, and trampling upon a multitude of sacred laws, this fellow, Chrysostom Papadopoulos, accepted the new calendar of renovation, innovation, and of modernism, and stripping himself naked of divine grace, clothed himself with the so-called new calendar of the astronomers of the most impious Pope, at the behest of Satan.[19]

Later, in the same book he records the following remarks made to an elderly new calendarist:

The priests of the new calendar do not have the grace of the All-holy Spirit, and whatever [prayers] they read are all invalid and bereft of divine grace. This is why they do not have the power to loose the sins of another. They themselves are under the anathema and curse of the Ecumenical Councils and of the Holy Fathers, and because of this they have no grace of the Holy Spirit whatsoever, nor any authority, because they are under the power of the devil, since they do his works.[20]

Whether one agrees with it or not, the fact remains that this theme is repeated again and again throughout this book, and in every other document that Metropolitan Kallistos composed or signed.

Simply, this was and still is the Matthewite confession of faith, and Metropolitan Kallistos espoused it to the end of his life.

If, therefore, Metropolitan Kallistos's credo was un-Orthodox, it was un-Orthodox from the very day he was consecrated in 1948 by Bishop Matthew of Bresthena. Why, then, did Bishop Cyprian accept in 1979 to be consecrated secretly and uncanonically by such an "un-Orthodox" bishop?

Also, given Bishop Cyprian's theological position, one wonders why he, while still an archimandrite, continued to remain in the Synod of Archbishop Auxentius after it published its 1974 Encyclical (which re-affirmed the Synodal Encyclical of 1935 and

---

[19] [Metropolitan] Kallistos Macris, *The History of the Sacred Monasteries of the Holy Supreme Commanders Michael and Gabriel, and of the Annunciation of the Theotokos,* Athikia, Corinth, 1972, p. 24 (in Greek).

[20] *Ibid.,* p. 163.

Metropolitan Chrysostom's Encyclical of 1950). Certainly, one cannot use the holy canons to justify the presence of two genuine Churches of Christ in one place, that is, both an old and a new calendar Synod of Greece. According to the canons, one cannot maintain that the Archbishop of the State Church is still the canonical Archbishop of Athens and All Greece, and yet not be in submission to him.

The publication *The Old Calendar Orthodox Church of Greece*, printed under the auspices of Bishops Chrysostom and Auxentius (both located in Etna, California and under the jurisdiction of Bishop Cyprian), deals with their particular views on ecclesiology. The section which addresses this question, "Addendum II: An Ecclesiological Position Paper," is marked by considerable ambiguity of definitions and terminology. Throughout the book, the authors state that the Church of Greece is "divided" over the calendar issue (some seventy years now). Nonetheless, the authors claim, this is not a schism.

But in Greek "schism" means a division or cleavage. Schism is defined by Saint Basil as a dispute over ecclesiastical rule and leadership, and insubordination to the legal bishop. (The Saint calls this the establishment of a parasynagogue, that is, an unlawful assembly.) The conditions in the Greek Church certainly conform to this definition of schism. The authors, however, state that the Church is divided yet there is no schism. In other words, the Church is divided yet there is no division. Since there exist separate hierarchies in the same region, and since there is no concelebration and no unity of administration manifesting the unity of Christ, a schism exists. Any other statement is a mere playing with words, and, as we mentioned above, lacks canonical support.

Another point that is unclear in the "Addendum" is the question: Who constitutes the Church? The Fifteenth Canon of the First-and-Second Council is quoted to justify Bishop Cyprian's actions in establishing a church structure separated from the State Church. Here we append the entire text of the canon:

CANON XV

The rules laid down with reference to Presbyters and Bishops and Metropolitans are still more applicable to Patriarchs. So that in case any Presbyter or Bishop or Metropolitan dares to secede from communion with his own Patriarch and does not mention his name as is ordered and appointed in the divine Mystagogy, but before a synodical arraignment and [the Patriarch's] full condemnation, he creates a schism, the holy Council has decreed that this person be alienated from every priestly function, if only he be proven to have transgressed in this. These rules, therefore, have been sealed and ordered concerning those who on the pretext of some accusations against their own presidents stand apart, creating a schism, and severing the unity of the Church. But as for those who on account of some heresy condemned by Holy Councils or Fathers, sever themselves from communion with their president, that is, because he publicly preaches heresy and with bared head teaches it in the Church, such persons as these not only are not subject to canonical penalty for walling themselves off from communion with the so-called Bishop before synodal clarification, but [on the contrary] they shall be deemed worthy of due honor among the Orthodox. For not Bishops, but false bishops and false teachers have they condemned, and they have not fragmented the Church's unity with schism, but from schisms and divisions have they earnestly sought to deliver the Church.

According to the canon, one is justified in separating from one's bishop or walling oneself off from communion with him if he openly preaches "some heresy condemned by Holy Councils or Fathers." Then one preserves the unity of the Church (the unity of true faith and teaching, i.e., unity in the Truth, Christ Himself) by separating from these "false bishops and false teachers." Obviously, a schism will then exist. However, the canon emphasizes that those who separate from an heretical bishop are not the ones who are creating a schism (even though they are apparently rending asunder the Church's external structure). Rather, they are separating themselves from a bishop who separated himself from the truth (a schism in the inner and true invisible unity of the Church), and by doing so, they are remaining in union with the truth, for the innovating bishops are false bishops, that is, outside the Church of Christ and bereft of spiritual authority.

The sentiments expressed by the authors of *The Old Calendar Orthodox Church of Greece* are certainly not in accord with this canon which they quote in order to justify their church policy. They separate from the new calendar bishops, yet they will not call them false bishops; the Church is divided, yet they say there is no schism; there is a "falling away from the faith" and teaching of heretical doctrines, yet there is no heresy; there are two bishops in one diocese, yet both are valid; we are the Church, yet they are also; etc. It appears to be a case of wanting to have your cake and eat it too.

Incredibly, in spite of the fact that his bishops in America cite Canon XV, mentioned above, to defend their separation from the new calendarists ("on account of some heresy condemned by holy Councils or Fathers," as the Canon states), Bishop Cyprian maintains that there *has been no conciliar decision* condemning the new calendar State Church for heresy![21]

Which of the two is it?

And what of the three Pan-Orthodox Synods (in 1583, 1587, and 1593) and the numerous local Councils and Holy Synods of local Churches which condemned and anathematized the new calendar?[22] Even Archbishop Chrysostom Papadopoulos—who adopted the new calendar—acknowledged, together with all the other local Churches, the legitimacy of these Pan-Orthodox Councils, and tried to avoid coming under their anathemas, using as an excuse the fact that he had not changed the Paschalion. In addition, the decrees of the Seven Ecumenical Councils and the *Synodicon of Orthodoxy* have most certainly synodically and officially condemned the teachings subsequently espoused by the "Orthodox" ecumenists of our days, as, for example, in their "Agreed Statement" with the Monophysites. The State Church of Greece—the nation in which Bishop Cyprian resides—is, like all

---

[21] See Appendix J, pp. 246-247. [22] See Appendix M, p. 265.

the other "official" Churches, in full communion with the Patriarchate of Antioch, which is presently under the condemnation of ✗ the last four Ecumenical Councils and of the *Synodicon of Orthodoxy*, since it is now in communion with the Monophysites.²³

Bishop Cyprian accuses the traditional Orthodox Christians of the greatest blasphemy against the Holy Spirit because of their denial of the validity of the mysteries of those involved in innovation and Ecumenism. Thus, he justifies his non-communion with them and hurls epithets against them.²⁴ But then, what of the undeniable fact that it was the new calendar bishops who first adopted this position *vis-à-vis* the traditional Orthodox Christians in 1926? Are, then, both the old and new calendar hierarchies of Greece guilty of blasphemy against the Holy Spirit, according to Bishop Cyprian? If they are, where does this leave Bishop Cyprian, who derives his priesthood from the one, and his episcopacy from the other?²⁵

It seems as though the Synod of Bishop Cyprian wants to believe that this is still 1937—a time, that is, when there was much uncertainty as to which direction the State Church of Greece and the other jurisdictions of "World Orthodoxy" would take.

This, however, is not 1937, but the final years of the twentieth century, when "World Orthodoxy's" official statements, acts, encyclicals, and ecumenistic resolutions have made it all too clear that this body finds itself clearly outside the official and canonical

---

²³ See Appendix F, pp. 216-219. See "On the Unity of the Eastern and Syrian Orthodox Churches" and "The Second Agreed Statement," *The Word*, April 1992. In addition, *The Synodicon of the Holy and Ecumenical Seventh Council for Orthodoxy* (see *The Triodion*, the Sunday of Orthodoxy) has the following clause: "To those who reject the definitions which were promulgated for the establishment of the true doctrines of the Church of God by the Holy Fathers Athanasius, Cyril, Ambrose, Amphilochius and the God-proclaiming Leo, the most holy Archbishop of Old Rome, and by all the others, and furthermore, who do not embrace the acts of the Ecumenical Councils, especially those of the fourth, I say, and of the sixth, *Anathema* (*thrice*)."

²⁴ See, for example, *Our Ecclesiological Position* in the periodical *Agios Kyprianos* (Nov., 1984), and *Orthodox Resistance and Witness* (Jan-Mar., 1987), both published by the Monastery of SS. Cyprian and Justina, Fili, Attica (in Greek).

²⁵ See pp. 39-41; 50; 53-55.

boundaries of the Orthodox Faith, as defined by the Holy Ecumenical and Local Councils.

Recently, Bishop Cyprian's jurisdiction has joined in communion with the Russian Church Abroad, in spite of some resistance from within this Russian jurisdiction,[26] which itself is in communion with the Patriarchates of Jerusalem and Serbia (both full and organic members of the World Council of Churches).

3) *The Synod of Chrysostom (Kiousis)*

In 1985, although Metropolitan Anthony and the bishops he had uncanonically consecrated (see pages 103-109) were, upon their repentance, forgiven and received by Archbishop Auxentius and his Holy Synod (Metropolitan Kallistos neither asked nor was ever received back into the Holy Synod), these bishops again rose up in rebellion against their Archbishop and tried to remove him on the charge that he had opened a diocesan office without the approval of the rest of the Holy Synod. The parish clergy and faithful were shocked at such a ludicrous accusation and rejected the claims of the bishops who wished to bring the Archbishop to trial for such a "transgression." The bishops again recanted, were forgiven, and were received back again.

Later in 1985, the same bishops again sought to bring Archbishop Auxentius to trial, this time for the alleged consecration of one Dorotheos Tsakos—a man of notoriously bad repute, who has since died—and then they sought out Chrysostom Kiousis to make him their Archbishop.

From the very beginning, there were many anomalies in this "trial" of the Archbishop. To begin with, Gerasimos of Boeotia, one of the bishops said to have consecrated Tsakos, kept giving completely contradictory testimonies as to where and when the consecration was to have taken place, or whether it took place at all. Metropolitan Maximos, the other bishop who allegedly took part in this consecration with the Archbishop's verbal approval, had numerous witnesses proving that he was not present during any of

---

[26] See Appendix J, p. 243.

the "times" the consecration took place.²⁷ There were also many other irregularities in the procedure, the certificate of consecration, and the presentation of evidence. In the meantime, several bishops belonging to the rebellious party invited Metropolitan Chrysostom Kiousis—a bishop who belonged to the Synod of Archbishop Auxentius, but had not actively taken part in Synodal proceedings for several years—to become their new Archbishop. This was a strange turn of events, for although Metropolitan Chrysostom Kiousis had stopped participating in the Synod meetings because of all the problems these very bishops had been causing before, he now accepted the invitation to become their Archbishop. Archbishop Auxentius and his Holy Synod declared in an official Synodal resolution on March 5, 1986 that, although the Archbishop was innocent of the charges brought against him, "if" any consecration of Tsakos had taken place, it was null and void because it took place without his knowledge and consent. Despite this, the bishops under Bishop Chrysostom Kiousis proceeded to form their own faction and to "depose" Archbishop Auxentius, who was left with three bishops, Metropolitans Athanasios of Larisa, Maximos of the Seven Islands, and Germanos of Aeolia. (Not long before his death in 1986, Metropolitan Gerasimos of Boeotia repented and asked forgiveness from Archbishop

---

²⁷ The committee that was delegated by the jurisdiction of Chrysostom Kiousis to examine the Tsakos case (Bishops Kalliopios and Kallinikos of Achaia) came to the conclusion that the consecration took place "probably during the period of Pascha, 1985." The "certificate of consecration" that Tsakos himself presents, however, is dated "3 December, 1983." (In its first edition, the same "certificate of consecration" was presented without a date, later added by hand.) It is astounding that the investigative committee could overlook such an important document, especially since it is a document that formed the very basis for all the accusations! Furthermore, one of the "consecrating" bishops, Gerasimos of Boeotia, twice confirmed that he performed the consecration and twice denied it. In his written deposition submitted to the court authorities in January 1986, he mentions vaguely that he performed the consecration ". . . at 12:30 p.m. one night in 1985." In his written statement of 6/19 July, 1985, he maintains that the consecration took place ". . . during the past year, 1984." What, indeed, is the validity of such depositions, made by witnesses who contradict and refute themselves?

Auxentius, and received the holy Mysteries from the Archbishop's own hands shortly before falling asleep in the Lord.)

In doctrinal matters, the Synod of Chrysostom Kiousis maintains a theological position that is, in theory at least, identical to the position of Archbishop Auxentius's Synod as regards the State Church of Greece and the other churches that are becoming more and more enmeshed in the heresy of Ecumenism. Nevertheless, there are bishops within the Kiousis Synod—namely Metropolitans Peter and Paisios and Bishop Vikentios, all of Astoria, New York—who officially, openly, and consistently give communion to adherents of ecumenistic jurisdictions. It is certainly inconsistent that the bishops of the Synod of Chrysostom Kiousis should presume to depose Bishop Cyprian of Fili for this same practice (although he was not under their jurisdiction), yet, for years, took no action at all against their own bishops in Astoria who were guilty of the same charges.[28]

An interview given by Archimandrite Paul Stratigeas, chancellor of Metropolitan Peter of Astoria, confirms these charges. In this interview published by a Greek-language newspaper in New York City (*The National Herald,* May 24, 1994), Father Paul Stratigeas said the following:

> ... I indeed belong to the Old Calendar Church. The bishop whom I am under is His Eminence Metropolitan Peter, who belongs to the synod of the T.O.C. [i.e., True Orthodox Church] of Archbishop Chrysostom [Kiousis]. A schism has entered into Orthodoxy. A difference has developed over the issue of the liturgical calendar. Many Orthodox Christians did not wish to follow the change of calendar and, unfortunately and unavoidably, a division took place which must not be perpetuated forever in the Church.... I wish and search for the termination of this schism because there are many contradictions within the problem of the schism and division.... I'll tell you about a problem that bothers and troubles my conscience. At Saint

---

[28] Bishop Cyprian had already been canonically deposed by the Synod to which he was subject—the Synod of Archbishop Auxentius—in February of 1979 (see pp. 103-109).

Markella's [i.e., Metropolitan Peter's church] thousands of our [Greek] people attend services. But I have a problem of conscience because they are the spiritual children of [the Ecumenical Patriarch] Bartholomew, all of them. They belong to the Church of Bartholomew. I belong to the Church of Chrysostom [Kiousis] ... Yet I provide the Mysteries to the followers of the new calendar.

Archimandrite Paul Stratigeas could be commended here, perhaps, for admitting that a schism does exist, and at least he candidly admits that he provides the Mysteries to those who follow the new calendar innovation. This policy continues to this day.

Also, there was ambiguity in the relations that these same bishops—especially Bishops Paisios and Vikentios—had with the hierarchy of the Jerusalem Patriarchate, with whom they have concelebrated, and to whom, for a time, they had been subject. Although the Church of Jerusalem still keeps the traditional ecclesiastical calendar, it is a full, organic member of the syncretistic World Council of Churches, the Middle East Council of Churches, and is in full communion with other local ecumenistic churches of "World Orthodoxy."

In its official publication *The Voice of Orthodoxy* (Φωνὴ τῆς Ὀρθοδοξίας), December 1989, the bishops of the Synod of Chrysostom Kiousis have also lauded the Moscow Patriarchate! Although this Patriarchate indeed observes the traditional calendar, it is a known fact (with the opening of the KGB archives) that its hierarchy and lower clergy are riddled with KGB operatives (including the Patriarch himself) and that it vies with Constantinople in its ecumenical activities. How, therefore, is one to evaluate this ambiguous attitude expressed in the pages of *The Voice of Orthodoxy*?

From all this, one may conclude that, at least for the present, the bishops of the Kiousis jurisdiction are not in agreement among themselves on their ecclesiology, and it remains to be seen what course they will ultimately follow.

Archbishop Auxentius of Athens.

4) *The Synod of Archbishop Auxentius*

The historical accounts that we have recorded here, with all the accompanying heroism and betrayals, self-sacrifice and self-aggrandizement, confession of the faith and human lapses, are, to a very large degree, the history of the Synod of Archbishop Auxentius also.

During his thirty-one years as chief hierarch, His Beatitude Archbishop Auxentius experienced the love and devotion of his flock and also many disappointments from fellow hierarchs and clergymen who sought to further their own interests. Sometimes, the bounds of common civility were sorely tested by these ambitious clergy. On one occasion, during a meeting with clergy and laity, His Beatitude was trying to reason with a clergyman who was upset over the fact that the Archbishop wanted to allow a certain layman to speak. The clergyman, completely forgetting his vocation, suddenly flared up and, in the presence of the others, attempted to slap the Archbishop in the face. He would have succeeded in doing so had not one nun, the Abbess Akakia of the Convent of the Dormition of the Theotokos in Peta Kouvara, intervened and forcibly stopped him. At this point, His Beatitude bowed his head meekly, took his walking stick, and with tears streaming down his face, quietly left the room.

Archbishop Auxentius was a gentle and kind man, and many took advantage of these attributes. Certainly, no man is perfect, and as a human being, Archbishop Auxentius also made errors, and he was the first to admit them. He once told His Grace, Bishop Ephraim of Boston, "There is a Greek proverb that says, 'To err twice in the same matter is not the mark of a wise man.' Well, Your Grace, I have erred not twice, but five times, ten times, twenty times, in the same matter."

Some of His Beatitude's mistakes were notable, while others were debatable. Some contend that he accepted—sometimes without investigation—clergy fleeing from the State Church not for reasons of faith, but for moral and canonical offences.[29] When

---

[29] Unpublished manuscript, Karamitsos-Gamvroulias, *The Ordinations of the True Orthodox Christians*.

such accusations were made, however, His Beatitude demanded signed affidavits from witnesses deemed trustworthy by the Church's canon laws.

One serious error was that, for a considerable time, he countenanced the presence of a certain abbess in his jurisdiction, though she had published a denial of the sanctity of Saint Nectarios of Pentapolis and had denounced him as a heretic.

The consecration of John Rosha as bishop of Portugal was another incident that caused considerable debate. This person had been a priest under Archbishop Anthony of Geneva of the Russian Church Abroad. Originally a Roman Catholic, he was received by Archbishop Anthony by chrismation and then ordained to the priesthood. Archbishop Auxentius received John Rosha without a canonical release, then had him baptized and re-ordained. This action caused a rupture between his jurisdiction and the Russian Church Abroad, primarily because of the insistent demands of Archbishop Anthony of Geneva, who had on many occasions demonstrated stronger sympathies for the new calendar jurisdictions than for the true Orthodox Christians of Greece. The fact is, however, that according to the practice of the Church in Greece (including even the new calendarists and the monasteries of the Holy Mountain, Athos, which commemorate the Ecumenical Patriarch), *all* non-Orthodox are baptized, regardless of their former religious affiliation. According to this perspective—completely justifiable from a canonical point of view—no one who has not been properly baptized can be ordained to the priesthood. Archbishop Auxentius would have caused a major scandal if he had *not* received John Rosha in this manner. Furthermore, before he undertook this action, he and the other hierarchs of his Holy Synod consulted canon law experts from the Theological School of the University of Athens, who concluded that, properly speaking, John Rosha had not been correctly received by Archbishop Anthony of Geneva, and that he should be baptized and ordained as prescribed by the strictness of the holy canons.[30]

---

[30] In the *Ecumenical News International Bulletin* (July 3, 1995), p. 13, there was an interesting article concerning a ruling by the Roman Catholic Church "to the effect that converts from other churches to Roman Catholicism have to

In this case, Archbishop Auxentius erred in not first consulting with the Russian Church Abroad before receiving John Rosha, but he cannot be faulted in his subsequent actions, since he consulted his fellow hierarchs and experts in canon law. Nevertheless, the administrative rupture that resulted between his Synod and the Russian Church Abroad was regrettable, although it might well not have occurred had it not been for the insistent demands of Archbishop Anthony of Geneva. Despite this unhappy event, which was of an administrative rather than a doctrinal nature, the faithful of both jurisdictions continued to receive the holy Mysteries in either jurisdiction.

In the fall of 1981, the Synod of Archbishop Auxentius entered into communion with the Free Serbian Church in the United States. This jurisdiction was founded by Bishop Dionisije, and headed at that time by Bishop Irinej. (Since then, this jurisdiction has re-entered into union with the Serbian Patriarchate.) The arrangements for this union with the Free Serbian Church were made by Metropolitan Paisios (Protocol Number 1529, September 11/24, 1980, Athens) and the decision was signed by Archbishop Auxentius, Metropolitan Paisios, and Metropolitan Euthymios of Thessalonica. This curious union with the Free Serbian Church broke down when it became known that both clergy and laymen of the Serbian jurisdiction were deeply involved in Freemasonry.

Another consecration that was most unfortunate for its relations with the Russian Church Abroad was the consecration of Akakios Douskos as Metropolitan of Montreal and All Canada, since there already was a hierarch—Archbishop Vitaly Ustinov—who bore that title.

As noted above, many of these actions were serious errors that were made because of a lack of administrative order and discretion. They were often hasty, *ad hoc* decisions made under the influence of

---

be rebaptized '*sub-conditione.*' Some found this ruling 'shocking' [says the *Ecumenical News International Bulletin*]. A Lutheran bishop complained about this and said, 'There is not much sign of visible unity when even baptism is not recognized. The Catholic partners say to us that we do not use enough water and that therefore they have to rebaptize.'" Of course, this too is another reason why the Orthodox baptize Roman Catholics: they do not use enough water!

The newly reposed Archbishop Auxentius.

that "persecution mentality" which had so greatly determined and influenced the earlier history of the traditional Orthodox Christians, and has persisted to this day even though they are not presently persecuted in Greece.

One should keep in mind that great saints of the Church also made mistakes in the matter of ordinations. Both Saint John Chrysostom and Saint Epiphanius of Cyprus ordained men who were not under their episcopal jurisdiction, without the approval of the appointed ecclesiastical authorities. In more recent times, Saint John Maximovitch of San Francisco also made serious errors in his *economias* for the Dutch Church by allowing them to observe the

"Forgive us, Father, for we have sinned against you. We embittered you, we slandered you . . ." Bishop Stephanos of Chios, of the Kiousis Synod which "deposed" Archbishop Auxentius, asking forgiveness at his funeral.

new calendar and the western Paschalion, as well as in consecrating dubious candidates to the episcopacy. No one is infallible, and even if the saints made mistakes at times, this in no way detracted from their sanctity. The same could be said of Archbishop Auxentius—his errors were often mistakes made in good faith, often on the advice of clergy who wittingly or unwittingly misled him.

Had His Beatitude not been so trusting, it is likely he would have been spared considerable grief. Despite the errors that occurred, the fact that he remained in his position with so many devoted faithful is a testimony to the love and devotion the faithful cherished for him, to the degree that even his greatest enemies and accusers came tearfully after his repose on November 4, 1994, to beg his forgiveness for having slandered and falsely accused him.[31]

One of the final accomplishments of his tenure was to bring a

---

[31] See the biography and the account of the repose of Archbishop Auxentius, *The True Vine*, issue no. 23.

great number of traditional Orthodox Christians from the United States, Canada, and Europe under his omophorion in the late 1980's.

The Synod of Archbishop Auxentius and the Traditional Orthodox Christians in North America and Europe

For twenty years, since the "lifting" of the Anathemas of 1054 by Patriarch Athenagoras in 1965, the Russian Church Abroad, under the leadership of Metropolitan Philaret of blessed memory, had accepted both clergy and laity from jurisdictions in the United States, Canada, and Europe that were sinking deeper into doctrinal innovations and their offspring, Ecumenism.

Although priests and monastics who had left the jurisdiction of the Greek Archdiocese were approached by bishops of the Matthewite and Florinite Synods, and although these Synods did have some parishes in the New World and Europe for decades, the facts of Church history demonstrate that there already was a local church in the western hemisphere that was fully canonical. It was unwise and unlawful to divide the traditional Orthodox Christians in the New World into different jurisdictions along ethnic lines, even as the new calendarists and "World Orthodoxy" jurisdictions are divided to this day. It could be well demonstrated that the Russian Church had uncontested jurisdiction in North America until the political upheavals in Russia, Eastern Europe, and Asia Minor made it possible for opportunists such as the former Archbishop of Athens, Meletios Metaxakis—who was later dethroned as Ecumenical Patriarch—to establish independent jurisdictions along national lines. Nonetheless, the Russian Church was the first to establish missions on this continent in the eighteenth century. Under its jurisdiction there were—for pastoral reasons—a number of exarchates for various ethnic groups. In contrast, the embarrassing overlapping of numerous new calendar jurisdictions seen today is indicative of a lack of canonical and doctrinal seriousness in other matters as well, as has become more evident with the passage of time. Also, since most of the Orthodox jurisdictions on this continent—with the exception of the Greek, Syrian, and

Metropolitan Philaret of blessed memory during a visit to the Holy Transfiguration Monastery in Boston in the early 1970's.

Romanian churches—observed the traditional festal calendar until fairly recently, the growing innovationism of these churches was not very obvious until the middle to late sixties and early seventies, when ecumenical meetings and dialogues gave way, with increasing frequency, to ecumenical and syncretistic joint prayers and intercommunion, on both an official and an unofficial basis.

After despairing of seeing any change of direction on the part of their innovating hierarchs, many Orthodox faithful were grateful to find a haven of Orthodoxy in the Russian Church Abroad. Over the years the Synod of Metropolitan Philaret accepted clergy without canonical releases from their former bishops who were obdurate in innovation and heresy.[32] Metropolitan Philaret made a heroic stand against the growing modernism, writing several "Sorrowful Epistles" to the bishops of "World Orthodoxy," warning them that they were on a dangerous path. This culminated in the Anathema against Ecumenism, which all the bishops of the Russian Church Abroad signed in 1983. The text of this historic document and the names of those who signed it are as follows:[33]

THE ANATHEMA AGAINST THE HERESY OF ECUMENISM AND ITS ADHERENTS

To those who attack the Church of Christ by teaching that Christ's Church is divided into so-called branches which differ in doctrine and way of life, or that the Church does not exist visibly, but will be formed in the future when all branches or sects or denominations, and even religions will be united into one body; and who do not distinguish the priesthood and mysteries of the Church from those of the heretics, but say that the baptism and eucharist of heretics is effectual for salvation; therefore, to those who knowingly have communion with these aforementioned heretics or who advocate, disseminate, or defend their new heresy of Ecumenism under the pretext of brotherly love or the supposed unification of separated Christians,

Anathema

✛ Metropolitan Philaret
  Chairman of the Synod of Bishops
 Members of the Council:
  ✛ Seraphim, Archbishop of Chicago and Detroit

---

[32] See Appendix E, p. 213.
[33] See *Orthodox Christian Witness,* Nov. 14/27, 1983, pp. 12–13.

✠ Afanasy, Archbishop of Buenos Aires and Argentina-Paraguay
✠ Vitaly, Archbishop of Montreal and Canada
✠ Anthony, Archbishop of Los Angeles and Texas
✠ Anthony, Archbishop of Geneva and Western Europe
✠ Anthony, Archbishop of Western America and San Francisco
✠ Seraphim, Archbishop of Caracas and Venezuela
✠ Paul, Archbishop of Sydney and Australia-New Zealand
✠ Laurus, Archbishop of Syracuse and Trinity
✠ Constantine, Bishop of Richmond and Britain
✠ Gregory, Bishop of Washington and Florida
✠ Mark, Bishop of Berlin and Germany
✠ Alipy, Bishop of Cleveland

In a letter to Father Anthony Gavalas of Astoria, New York, His Eminence, Metropolitan Philaret, personally explained the significance of this contemporary patristic statement:

14/27 October, 1983

Dear Father Anthony:

I pray that the blessings of our Savior be with you and your Parish.

Please be informed that the Bishops' Council during its meeting last August unanimously adopted the following resolution concerning the pan-heresy of Ecumenism, which in one word encompasses all forms of modernism and innovation:

> To those who attack the Church of Christ by teaching that Christ's Church is divided into so-called branches which differ in doctrine and way of life, or that the Church does not exist visibly, but will be formed in the future when all branches or sects or denominations, and even religions will be united into one body; and who do not distinguish the priesthood and mysteries of the Church from those of the heretics, but say that the baptism and eucharist of heretics is effectual for salvation; therefore, to those who knowingly have communion with these aforementioned heretics or who advocate, disseminate, or defend their new heresy of Ecumenism under

the pretext of brotherly love or the supposed unification of separated Christians:

Anathema.

The text of this Anathema is to be attached to the *Synodicon* of the Sunday of Orthodoxy, to be read with the rest of the text of the *Synodicon*.

Please extend my prayerful greetings to your family and the members of your Parish.

With much love in our Lord,

☦ Metropolitan Philaret
President of the Synod

After the blessed repose of Metropolitan Philaret on the feast of the Holy Archangels, November 8, 1985, many of the faithful began to note with alarm that, whereas for the past twenty years the Russian Church Abroad had been progressively cutting off ecclesiastical contact with the innovating local churches, these contacts now began to increase, especially at a hierarchical level. Those of non-Russian background especially protested, since they saw this turn of events as a repudiation of the reason they had left the ecumenistic jurisdictions they had belonged to before. Such tendencies had been observed for a time in some of the bishops of the Russian Church Abroad, but now, with the repose of Metropolitan Philaret, and the repose and retirement of other bishops, these tendencies became a full-fledged policy "by *economia*" and later by synodal decree.[34]

Despite the repeated protests of the clergy and the faithful over these violations, by November of 1986, the Anathema of 1983 had become a dead letter by all the observable facts. In the face of this turn of events, the clergy of the New England deanery addressed the following letter to Metropolitan Vitaly:

---

[34] On 4/17 February 1987, during its meeting in Montreal, the Synod of Bishops of the Russian Church Abroad officially commended Archpriest Alexander Lebedev's reply to Fr. Neketas Palassis of Seattle, Washington. In this letter, Fr. A. Lebedev states that it is permitted to give communion to members of the new calendar, ecumenist jurisdictions.

November 8/21, 1986
✠ Holy Bodiless Commanders,
Michael and Gabriel

His Eminence, Most Rev. Metropolitan Vitaly
Synod of Bishops
75 East 93 Street
New York City, New York 10028-1390

Your Eminence:
Bless!

On several occasions since the enthronement of Your Eminence as President of the Synod of Bishops, we have addressed you with our concerns regarding the life of our Church and Her struggle against the heresy of Ecumenism. We told you that we were encouraged by your reputation for being strongly opposed to Ecumenism, Sergianism, and dealings with the other jurisdictions that cooperate with the evil forces which are determined to undermine our Holy Orthodox Faith.

We cited many instances wherein even Synod clergy sullied the witness of our Church before the eyes of the whole world. We asked Your Eminence to publicly address the whole Church regarding these incidents. We stressed that a correction of the scandals and a clear public reaffirmation of our Church's longstanding posture would comfort and strengthen the faithful and preserve our Church as the defender of Orthodoxy. We assured you that, in your firm stand on behalf of our Church and Faith, you would have our unswerving support.

The response of Your Eminence was to reassure us of your continuing witness to our Faith in the same forthright spirit and manner of your holy predecessors of blessed memory, Metropolitans Anthony, Anastasy, and Philaret. You even noted that on your recent trip to Europe you heard the same concerns voiced by our brother clergy.

Sadly, Vladyka, there have been no public declarations specifically censuring these violations of our Church's Faith. The result is a continuing erosion of the integrity of our Church, a constant gnawing at the conscience of our faithful, and the fear that our Hierarchy is weakening in its defense of the Faith.

We are now imploring Your Eminence, therefore, to address

these matters at the forthcoming Sobor. We are expecting that you, in the name of the Synod of Bishops, will address each item publicly.

We call your attention to some courageous documents of Faith, which constitute the very foundation of our Church's existence, and on the basis of which we now so unhesitatingly address this letter to you. First, the Certificate of Incorporation of our Church, filed with the State of New York in 1952, states in article III:

> The corporation in its corporate function and operation, and all of its trustees and officers, shall maintain no relations whatever with the Russian ecclesiastical authorities and organizations within the boundaries of the Soviet Union and the satellites of the Soviet Union, so long as the said countries, or any of them, shall be subject to Communist rule.

Second, the spiritual last will and testament (1957) of Metropolitan Anastasy repeated this legally-codified position of our Church. He warned us never to have any "canonical, liturgical, or even simply external communion" with the clergy of the Moscow Patriarchate.

Third, in his letter (dated May 21 / June 3, 1968) addressed to Athenagoras I of Constantinople, Metropolitan Philaret stated that "the Patriarch of Moscow and his collaborators have . . . long ago fully surrendered themselves to the orders of the communists, fulfilling their every wish and instruction."

Fourth, continuing in the spirit of this policy, the decision of the Synod issued on March 18/31, 1970 repeats our Church's understanding "that the present Moscow Patriarchate is not the authentic representative of the Church of Russia, since it has an atheistic Government as the source of its authority." The Holy Synod states further:

> Entering thus into communion with the heterodox [Roman Catholics], the Moscow Patriarchate estranges itself from the unity of the holy Fathers and Doctors of the Church. By its action it does not sanctify the heretics to whom it offers the sacraments, but it itself becomes part of their heresy.

(Hence, by the Synod's own instruction to us, we are to have no dealings with the clergy of the Moscow Patriarchate not only because that church is uncanonical but also because it is heretical.)

Fifth, the two "Sorrowful Epistles" (1969 and 1972) of Metropolitan Philaret and several official pronouncements of the Synod over the years have consistently preached against the heresy of Ecumenism. We cite two additional documents in this area. One is authored by Your Eminence. In your 1969 Report to the Sobor of Bishops on the dangers of Ecumenism, you make this crucial point:

> Ecumenism is now at the very doors of our Church. All local Orthodox Churches have become members [of the WCC], the last being the Serbian Church which was accepted in 1968.

From the Western European diocese of Vladyka Anthony of Geneva emanates the other document, a declaration of the priests and laity in the May 1969 Ninth Diocesan Congress. In this paper, one of the essential pillars of the heresy of Ecumenism, the so-called "branch theory," is called a "perverse theory." Moreover, those who advocate this teaching are called "the false teachers of our own day," and a concelebration with the heterodox is termed "illusory."

Sixth, because the other so-called "Orthodox" jurisdictions have demonstrated an obstinate refusal to hearken to these warnings, and because the poisonous menace of Ecumenism has grown frighteningly worse, the Bishops of our Church pronounced the anathema of 1983, in which they very clearly condemn Ecumenism and "those who knowingly have communion with these aforementioned heretics or who advocate, disseminate, or defend their new heresy of Ecumenism." We note that both the teaching and its adherents are anathematized.

This confession of faith has brought down the blessings of God on us all. Many of our clergy and laity have come to our Church and remain with her precisely because She has not shied away from preaching and living this Truth.

Yet, witness now some of the gross violations that have

occurred within the bosom of our Church which totally undermine the legal and doctrinal basis for our Church's existence and the integrity of Her Orthodox witness:

1) In 1984, Father Victor Potapov of Washington, D.C. visited the Soviet Union, and came into contact with Soviet churchmen, although, as demonstrated above, such activity is expressly prohibited by our Church.

2) In 1985, the same Father Victor Potapov visited the Soviet Gorny Convent in Israel, and in his own letter to Bishop Gregory, Father Victor said he visited the same Soviet convent two years earlier. Again, the same ecclesiastical prohibition applies here.

3) Toward the end of 1985, Archimandrite Seraphim Bobich of the Prophet Elias Skete on Mount Athos complained that Father Theodore (the priest-monk who is now at our Church in Hebron in the Holy Land) was commemorating the ecumenist patriarch of Constantinople, Demetrios I, who, as shown above, falls under the excommunication of the 1983 anathema.

4) The same Father Seraphim also complained that Bishop Mark of Berlin served at the Serbian Hilandar Monastery on Mount Athos, even though our Synod, as evidenced by the documentation cited above, recognized that the Serbian Patriarchate is ecumenist (Patriarch German served as a president of the World Council of Churches for ten years), and, therefore, also falls under the excommunication of the 1983 anathema.

5) At the beginning of this year, Archbishop Paul of Sydney concelebrated a Vigil Service with the Serbian Protopriest, Father Chedomir Videkanich, and then concelebrated a Liturgy with the Serbian Bishop Vasily on January 11, though both Serbian clerics are excommunicated by the anathema of 1983 because they participate in Ecumenism.

6) In March of this year, Bishop Hilarion, on behalf of the Synod, officially reprimanded Father Neketas Palassis of Seattle for criticizing the blatantly uncanonical and ecumenistic actions of the Serbian Patriarchate, which, in

keeping with the Ecumenism it espouses, received the Anglican Archbishop of Canterbury as a Bishop of the Church, chanting to him "Many Years" and joining together with him in prayer. In effect, then, the Synod censures the correct confession of the Faith by Father Neketas and covers the heresy of the Serbian Church.

7) On the Sunday of Orthodoxy this year, Bishop Alipy of Cleveland was present at a "Pan-Orthodox" vespers celebrated by clergy from the other ecumenist jurisdictions which are excommunicated by the 1983 anathema.

8) Again this year, Archbishop Anthony of Geneva recirculated an earlier encyclical of his, the effective message of which is that clergy of our Church in his jurisdiction may, with his blessing, concelebrate with clergy of the other ecumenist jurisdictions, which, as noted, are excommunicated by the anathema of 1983.

9) On his pilgrimages to the Holy Land, Archbishop Laurus receives communion consecrated by clergy of the Jerusalem Patriarchate at the Holy Sepulchre and then administers this communion to members of our Church who are present there with him, even though the Jerusalem Patriarchate is both in communion with the Moscow Patriarchate and excommunicated by the 1983 anathema because it actively participates in the World Council of Churches and advocates Ecumenism.

At no time has the Synod publicly denounced these scandals. Indeed, it seems that, by its silence, the Synod is condoning these violations of our Church's Faith and order. Every sorrowful indication is that our Church, weakened by nostalgia for the Russian motherland and the urgent desire to see the godless authority overthrown, has been seduced into the heresies of Sergianism and Ecumenism by ever more frequent reports from the Soviet Union of a new religious freedom and a spiritual renaissance. While every Christian soul must continue to pray for the restoration of True Christianity and Holy Russia, nevertheless, these reports can be accepted only when they are accompanied by a categorical rejection of Sergianism and Ecumenism, both of which heresies the Soviet church continues to espouse.

Vladyka, as we have explained above, we belong to the Synod because of its Orthodox confession of faith and its renunciation of Sergianism and Ecumenism. Further, we believe that our concerns are justified by your own teachings and by the teachings of our Holy Hierarchs of blessed memory.

Finally, Vladyka, these blatant contradictions have caused a deep spiritual crisis of conscience within our souls. Therefore, we approach you with love and humility, and implore you, our Chief Hierarch, for counsel and guidance so that we and those who share our concerns may be delivered by your love and wisdom from the dangerous crisis of conscience that afflicts our souls.

Awaiting your archpastoral counsel, care, and love, we remain,
Your servants in the Lord,

Archpriest George Kochergin, Dean
Holy Nativity Convent, Brookline, MA

Archpriest John Fleser
St. Anna, Roslindale, MA

Father Christos Constantinou
St. Mark of Ephesus, Roslindale, MA

Father Spiridon Schneider
St. John the Russian, Ipswich, MA

Father Victor Melehov
Holy Resurrection, Worcester, MA

Father Theodore Stavru
Dormition of the Theotokos, Concord, NH

Father Deacon John Mihopoulos
St. Mark of Ephesus–Roslindale, MA

Father Deacon Peter Farnsworth
Holy Resurrection, Worcester, MA

Father Deacon John Routos
Dormition of the Theotokos, Concord, NH

Father Deacon John Bockman
St. John the Russian, Ipswich, MA

This letter, like the many other letters and clergy representations which had preceded it since February of 1986, went unanswered. In another sense, however, the letter was answered indeed. Shortly after this letter was sent, the clergy and the faithful in France communicated with members of the clergy in North America and confirmed that "point eight" of the foregoing letter—Archbishop Anthony of Geneva's encyclical allowing concelebrations with new calendar clergy of ecumenist jurisdictions—was now officially being implemented in France and elsewhere in Europe. For the clergy and faithful who had left these same modernist jurisdictions at great personal sacrifice, this was a total betrayal. Despairing, therefore, over this latest development and the consistent disregard with which their concerns had been treated, some thirty clergy, twenty-five parishes, one monastery, one convent, and many faithful in North America left the Russian Church Abroad in December 1986, and asked to be accepted by Metropolitans Akakios of Diavlia and Gabriel of the Cyclades.[35] Thus, these traditional Orthodox Christians, wishing to remain faithful to the legacy they had received from Metropolitan Philaret, were in accord with Church Tradition in their departure from the Russian Church Abroad. This departure was further justified within a few weeks by Metropolitan Vitaly's Nativity Epistle of 1986, in which he gave an entirely novel interpretation to the understanding the Church has always had of the terms "anathema" and "economy," thereby effectively negating the Anathema against Ecumenism.[36]

After half a year, it became evident that Metropolitans Akakios and Gabriel were not cooperating with each other as shepherds of the same flock. Upon further examination, it became evident that these bishops had no doctrinal reason to be separated from their lawful president, Archbishop Auxentius. Since Metropolitan Akakios had not left the Synod of Archbishop Auxentius but had only withdrawn from participating in it, the North American flock was entitled to appeal to the rightful Archbishop when it found that its own bishop could not or would not meet its pastoral needs. Further, at a meeting with the North American clergy in Boston in June of 1987, Metropolitan Akakios affirmed that he did not recognize the supposed "deposition" of Archbishop Auxentius by the Synod of Chrysostom Kiousis (which, he maintained, was itself

---

[35] The Russian Synod tried to claim that this departure was for personal reasons—to prevent an investigation of various accusations against the monastery in Boston. However, the charges against the monastery—which had been petitioning for a canonical investigation and trial for eleven months—were handled in complete violation of canonical order. Furthermore, the charges alleged against the monastery would hardly have precipitated such a mass exodus from the Russian Church Abroad if there were not valid doctrinal causes. This is clearly demonstrated by the subsequent departure of the French Mission, as well as additional clergy of the Russian Church Abroad, who departed for the same reasons of faith in the following year, 1987, after waiting in vain to see any change of direction in this Russian jurisdiction.

[36] See Appendix E, pp. 211-216.

uncanonical); he had even stated this in print only one year before in a publication entitled *An End to Silence*,[37] in which he declares:

> In view of the manner in which it was formed and established, we consider the formation and assembly of the new "Holy Synod of the Church of the True Orthodox Christians of Greece" [under Chrysostom Kiousis] as *lawless, anticanonical,* harmful to the lofty advancement and authority of our sacred struggle, and *therefore unacceptable* [emphasis in the original].

A good part of *An End to Silence* is devoted to quoting, word for word, many of Metropolitan Chrysostom Kiousis's letters, in which he relentlessly attacks on every possible canonical ground the very bishops who now formed the new synod under him!

At the meeting with the North American clergy in June of 1987, Metropolitan Akakios stated, in addition, that the clergy were free to find another hierarch who would be able to provide for their needs. In July of 1987, after meeting with Archbishop Auxentius and the clergy who accompanied him, the North American clergy, monastics, and laity petitioned to be received by them. The North American flock also appealed to Metropolitan Akakios of Diavlia to be reconciled with his archbishop, but he refused to do so. Thus, in September of 1987, Archbishop Auxentius received the American flock under his omophorion.

✻ ✻ ✻

In France, by late 1987, the traditional Orthodox faithful also had given up all hope that the Russian Church Abroad would ever correct the uncanonical activities that had been increasing at an alarming rate in that jurisdiction. Their own bishop, Archbishop Anthony of Geneva, was one of the Russian bishops who had been lax in his relations with ecumenistic Orthodox jurisdictions, even during Metropolitan Philaret's lifetime. In 1986, with the repose of Metropolitan Philaret, Archbishop Anthony issued an official

---

[37] *Λύσις Σιωπῆς* [*An End to Silence*], published jointly by Metropolitans Akakios of Diavlia and Gabriel of the Cyclades Islands, Athens, 1986, p. 4.

ukase which stated that his priests were free to concelebrate with clergy of the new calendar, ecumenistic jurisdictions. Finally, with Metropolitan Vitaly's Nativity Epistle of 1986, the French Orthodox Mission's worst fears were confirmed. The following letter to Metropolitan Vitaly directly addressed these fears:

Paris,
March 19/April 1, 1987

His Beatitude Metropolitan Vitaly
President of the Holy Synod
of the Russian Orthodox Church Abroad

War is better than a peace
that separates from God.
Saint Symeon the New Theologian

Master, Bless.

At the time of our meeting in the month of June 1986 at the Lesna convent, where you received us so paternally and where you listened to the statement of our problems, you asked us to have patience during the time you needed "to put on the shoes of a Metropolitan," according to your own phrase. We therefore were patient, keeping silent, and instead of seeing our questions resolved, it is with profound astonishment that we discovered in your Nativity Epistle that the ecclesiological theses of Vladyka Anthony of Geneva are now officially accepted by the Russian Church Abroad. We no longer find the rigor of your confession of faith, and that grieves us very much.

Concerning the anathema, you say, "We have proclaimed the anathema against Ecumenism for the children of our Church alone, but by this act we invite, so to speak, very modestly, but firmly, gently but decisively, the local Churches to consider."

We are dismayed by this definition of the anathema, which we find neither in the tradition of the Holy Fathers, nor in that of our canonists. An anathema is not an invitation to reflection, but a malediction on a false doctrine and on those who profess it—since there is no heresy without heretics. All the anathemas cast by the Fathers and the Councils took aim at the heretics and their heresies. Now, according to the theory of Vladyka Anthony of Geneva, which you have manifestly adopted, we may pray with those who belong to these heresies. But the "official" Churches, which you now recognize as constituting Orthodoxy, are all organic members of the World Council of Churches, which in its statutes acknowledges the principle that no particular Church can claim to possess by herself alone all the truth. By entering the World Council of Churches as an organic member, every Orthodox Church renounces being the unique Orthodox Church.

An anathema without a heretic, therefore, is abolished of itself, is annulled of itself, and puts to shame in turn those who cast it.

In his *Rudder*, Saint Nicodemos the Athonite distinguishes two meanings for the word "anathema." "An anathema is that which is 'set apart' by men and consecrated to God; and also we call anathema that which is separated from God by the Church of Christ and thus consigned to the devil.[38] Out of honor and respect for the Lord, no one may touch with his hands that which has been 'anathematized' or consecrated to God; and likewise he that has been separated by God or by the Church becomes 'consecrated,' consigned to the devil. No one should dare to keep company or to commune with him; rather, all the faithful separate themselves from him. In conclusion, the one anathema and the other—that which is set apart—differ between them in the sense that one is consecrated to God and the other consigned to the devil, and are therefore opposites."

You yourself, last summer, told us that the bishops knew very well what they were doing when they cast the anathema, and that every limitation of the sense of this anathema had been discarded. This is also what you affirmed in your explanation of the anathema published in 1984 where you said that "the spiritual destiny of all the local Churches within the universal Orthodox Church depends on their acceptance of this anathema."

Your new interpretation of this fearful anathema, in which we see a heresy and no heretics, reminds us of a humorous cartoon published some years ago in a Greek journal, in which a bishop cast forth anathemas and curses that issued from his mouth in the form of little black birds; but since they had no place to perch, they returned and perched on his own head.

---

[38] *Cf.* I Cor. 5:5.

In saying that the anathema is not directed at anyone—and therefore that there are no heretics—you justify on the one hand the concelebrations that Vladyka Anthony authorizes with his blessing—with the other local Churches—and which are in fact performed by himself and by the priests of Western Europe; but, on the other hand, do you not fear that the consequences of this anathema will come back down on us?

You also say, "If any of our clergy, by economy, has lent himself to such a concelebration . . ." But, as Saint Mark of Ephesus says, in matters of dogma, there is no economy, and here, economy cannot be applied, because the clergy who are allowed by Vladyka Anthony to concelebrate "by economy" [with ecumenistic clergy] do not in any way change the opinions and conduct [of the ecumenistic clergy]. As a consequence, certain of the faithful are deeply troubled, in particular those who know the writings of Metropolitan Philaret of blessed memory and of Archbishop Vitaly of Canada.

In short, by celebrating with the clergy of the Churches that you call "official," Vladyka Anthony is soliciting recognition from Churches, all of which consider us as a schism and which consider the Patriarchate of Moscow as the canonical Russian Church, and its Patriarch Pimen as legitimate. Thus we enfeeble our witness and we justify those who accuse us of being a "political schism."

"We remember days of old"—as the Psalmist says—when we would read with enthusiasm the writings of the Archbishop of Canada.

In your letter on the calendar you wrote that the Synod condemned, along with ecumenism, the cause thereof—the change of the calendar—"as having nothing in common with the dogmas of the universal Church."

In your Report of 1969, you invited the members of our Church "to free themselves from a certain scholastic ecumenism that has deeply penetrated our minds" and you foresaw that "the Antichrist will preside over the United Nations and the World Council of Churches, but in spirit he will draw nearer to the World Council of Churches."

In an article written two or three years ago, you write, "The Church says, 'I will not give Thee a kiss as did Judas.' Thus she warns us that in following an unorthodox mentality, a perverted

Christian teaching, a man immediately betrays Christ as did Judas, and joins himself to the camp of the enemies of God."

Finally in your beautiful article "The Apocalypse of our Times," read before the Synod of Bishops, you said that the times for spiritual diplomacy had ended. "We are already living at the beginning of that era of the great choice ... When the fateful question will be asked, every human soul will tremble, will be unsettled and shaken to its foundations and will be forced to make the inevitable choice. There will no longer be any place for spiritual neutrality, it will no longer be possible to stay on the sidelines, so to speak, it will no longer be possible to be spiritually evasive, to escape, to hide oneself: all will be hunted out, all will be driven out from the shadows, from the darkest corners, and that will be the end of spiritual diplomacy, of provisional neutrality. The choice is simple and clear: light or darkness, Christ or Belial."

You also added, "We are going to witness astonishing transformations in people." Today we no longer recognize, in Metropolitan Vitaly, the Archbishop Vitaly [we knew], as if you had "changed your spiritual face" according to your own words.

Wishing to remain faithful to the patristic interpretations of the concepts of anathema and of economy, as well as to your own [original] interpretation and to that of the Blessed Metropolitan Philaret, we ourselves and our faithful pose a question to you:

Do you condemn the circular of Vladyka Anthony which authorizes, with his blessing, concelebrations with new calendarists and ecumenists?

We hope, on behalf of the peace of our soul and conscience, for a clarification on your part. We continue to pray fervently for you and to love you as we have up to the present. We kiss your hand and ask your episcopal blessing.

Archimandrite Ambrose
Hieromonk Joseph
Patric, priest

A second letter, written five months later, this time to Archbishop Anthony of Geneva, demonstrates that the French Orthodox Mission had lost hope of seeing any correction in the course the Russian Church Abroad had taken:

RUSSIAN ORTHODOX CHURCH ABROAD
Deanery of the French Parishes

Paris,
August 21/September 3, 1987

His Eminence Vladyka Anthony
Archbishop of Geneva and of Western Europe
3, rue Toepffer 1206 Geneva
SWITZERLAND

Vladyka,

We read, with all the attention that they deserved, your recent circulars in which you expound your ecclesiology.

What astonished us is that you make no mention whatsoever of the fearful anathema of 1983—which you nevertheless signed. This act, so fearful, yet just, you have done everything to annul, whether by your restatement, the publication of which you imposed on us in our periodical *La Lumière du Thabor*, or again by the Nativity Epistle of Metropolitan Vitaly, which seems to have been inspired by you.

Troubled by these so unexpected interpretations, we consulted the *Rudder* of Saint Nicodemos of the Holy Mountain, where we found the true meaning of "anathema," in conformity with the decisions of the Ecumenical Councils and the *Synodicon of Orthodoxy*, in which Metropolitan Philaret—whom we greatly miss—stated that the anathema in question be included.

Saint Nicodemos, whose *Rudder* wields authority in the Church, says clearly that we call anathema that which is totally separated from the Church and consigned to the devil—and this has filled us with terror.

In your circulars, you assert also that, on the one hand, ecumenism is a great heresy and, on the other, that there are no heretics condemned by your anathema. By this subterfuge you annul *de facto* this anathema which, by necessity, falls back on you. This evokes the image of black birds representing the anathemas pronounced by a bishop and returning to perch on his head.

Not wishing to receive the repercussions of the anathema of '83 which would then come back down on our heads, we cannot in [good] conscience continue to commemorate your name in the diptychs as faithfully dispensing the word of truth.

Vladyka, you have always had the courage of your opinions and you have the sincerity not to hide your personal ecclesiology, going so far as publicly to oppose Metropolitan Philaret of blessed memory: you are saying, in fact, that for you, all the "official" Churches constitute Orthodoxy. Extending your reasoning to its conclusion, we conclude by necessity that the [Russian] Synodal Church, not being an "official" Church, is not Orthodox. And this is confirmed by the practice of all the "official" Churches which recognize as the "official" Russian Church the Moscow Patriarchate with which they all are in communion. Since all the Churches recognize the Patriarchate of Moscow and its Patriarch Pimen as canonical and legitimate, they all accuse you, openly or not, of schism.

We discover therefore with sadness, according to your own argumentation, that it is not for reasons of faith that you have separated yourself from the Patriarchate of Moscow, but for other reasons in which we have always refused to be implicated.

Therefore, after consultation with the lay presidents [of our communities], we have made the decision to leave your diocese. As a result we are no longer able to take into consideration any canonical measures that you might take against us.

With all the respect due to your rank,

Archimandrite Ambrose
Hieromonk Joseph
Patric, priest

After this, the French Orthodox Mission began to make contacts with the various Synods of the Traditional Orthodox Christians in Greece. In December of 1987, one full year after the parishes and clergy in North America had left the Russian Church Abroad for the same reasons of faith, the French Mission was also accepted into communion by the Holy Synod of Archbishop Auxentius.

With the passage of time two more priests of the Russian Church Abroad in the United States, with their parishes, also decided that the time to depart had come. They had been very disturbed by the events of 1986, but decided to proceed more slowly and see if the Russian Church Abroad would correct itself and change its course. Since this did not occur, they also petitioned the Holy Synod of Archbishop Auxentius to receive them into its North American Diocese. One of those priests, Father Seraphim Johnson, wrote the following to Metropolitan Vitaly:

Saint John of Kronstadt
October 19/November 1, 1987

Most Reverend Metropolitan Vitaly
Synod of Bishops
75 East 93 Street
New York, N.Y. 10128

Dear Metropolitan Vitaly:

    I am writing this letter to you with a heavy heart. Since 1970 I have been a member of the Russian Orthodox Church Outside Russia, being baptized in it when I converted to Orthodoxy. I have many friends in the Church and have been fortunate to have known several of our bishops well.

    It was difficult for me to leave my earlier affiliation with the Episcopal Church, to which I was tied by family and by sentiment; but the truth of Orthodoxy was more important to me than those ties, hard as they were to break. My wife and I joined the Russian Orthodox Church Outside Russia because it offered the purest expression of Orthodoxy, free of the compromises made by the other jurisdictions in this country. My parishioners have similarly chosen the Synod Church because of its uncompromising Orthodoxy: they have come from Judaism and the Protestant and Catholic Churches, and also from other Orthodox jurisdictions which no longer were teaching and practicing the Orthodox Faith. For all of us, the Faith has been more important than earthly ties or convenience. For many of us, also, the monastery in Boston and the parishes inspired by it have been important teachers and influences. We have learned from the fathers there and found they were teaching the same things we heard from such teachers as Metropolitans Anthony and Philaret, Archbishop Saint Hilarion, Archbishop Averky [of Jordanville], Bishop Gregory [Grabbe], and you, Vladyka Vitaly.

The events of the last year have been a great shock to us all. We have been puzzled by many things we saw in our bishops' dealing with accusations of sin, but we assumed that these were human failings, not something which truly affects the Faith. We were horrified when a number of parishes and the Holy Transfiguration Monastery withdrew from the Russian Orthodox Church Outside Russia last winter. At that time we were very confused, since our spiritual guides seemed to be going in different directions. We prayed that God would guide us, and for the time we felt that He wanted us to stay in the Russian Orthodox Church Outside Russia. We decided to wait and watch both sides, trusting that God would not abandon us, but would show us the way we should go. We decided as a parish to dedicate our Great Lent this year to asking for His guidance and enlightenment. We believed that He would make clear to us what we should do; we would see which Church He was blessing, which Church was sound, and then we would know what He wanted us to do.

The results of our patience have not been at all what we expected. You and many of your bishops and priests have written statements and clarifications to present the view of the Russian Orthodox Church Outside Russia on the questions which have been raised about Orthodoxy, the heresy of Ecumenism, and the role of economy in the life of the Church. And every time we have read an explanation, it has made things harder to understand; every clarification has muddied things more. Let me list a few of the things which we have been dismayed and amazed to learn:

A. *Concelebrations.* The Russian Orthodox Church Outside Russia is now said to be in full communion with the Serbian and the Jerusalem Patriarchates, even though both are very active in the ecumenical movement. In addition, we have learned of concelebrations with the Finnish Church (which not only uses the New Calendar, but even celebrates Pascha with the non-Orthodox), the Ecumenical Patriarchate (both with Greek parishes in this country and with its Russian priests in Europe), and others. We have heard of parishioners going back and forth to Moscow Patriarchate parishes in Europe with their bishop's blessing. Right here we have seen how, several years ago, the

Kursk icon—the Synod's greatest holy treasure—came to Washington and was taken by a local Synod priest to the OCA cathedral for a *moleben*, although we were given no opportunity to have it visit our own parish. Among my parishioners are several who left the Ecumenical Patriarchate; they made written promises, at Bishop Gregory [Grabbe's] direction, saying they would not receive the Mysteries in churches of the Patriarchate; they endured family conflicts and separation from friends by leaving their Patriarchate parishes. You can hardly imagine how they have been distressed by concelebrations with the church they left; now they ask why they had to leave, and what can I say? It seems they made a foolish choice and grieved themselves for nothing in the eyes of many of your bishops and priests. You have personally told me not to give Holy Communion to members of other jurisdictions; how can you then permit your clergy to concelebrate with their priests? How does it help bring someone to a correct understanding of the errors in his church, if he sees your clergy concelebrating with his own?

B. *Strange Teaching*. We thought we understood the Orthodox Faith and that the Russian Orthodox Church Outside Russia was a careful teacher of that Faith. But we have been unsettled by things which have been written in the last six months.

1) The teaching in your Nativity Epistle effectively denies the 1983 anathema and states that all the local Orthodox Churches are grace-bearing. It says that the anathema has no general meaning, but only applies to members of the Russian Orthodox Church Outside Russia who hold ecumenical views; for the rest it is only a warning; but that is not what an anathema is.[39] It is the Church's statement that anyone holding those views is cut off from the Church of Christ! When you cut someone off from the Church, you do not cut them off from just the Russian Orthodox Church Outside Russia, but from the whole

---

[39] *Editors' Note:* In an earlier, different interpretation of the Anathema Against Ecumenism, the then Archbishop Vitaly had written the following: "The spiritual fate of all the local churches within the universal Orthodox Church depends on their acceptance of this anathema" (*Orthodox Observer*, Montreal, April, 1984).

Church of our Lord Jesus Christ! And even if we were to grant that it applies only to our Church, how then can members of our Church serve with those condemned by it? At the very least, the members of our Church should follow the direction and "warning" of the anathema. When I read this Epistle to my congregation, the reaction was one of shock; it was only with difficulty that I was able to persuade some of my parishioners not to leave the Russian Orthodox Church Outside Russia at that moment; several initially doubted that they could continue to receive the Mysteries in our parish as long as it was a part of the Russian Orthodox Church Outside Russia. Those who had come to the Synod from other local Churches came to me in sorrow and asked why they had bothered to leave them, if there was still grace in them. My flock agreed that this was not the Orthodox Faith they had been taught in the past.

2) An amazing ecclesiology has been presented by Father Alexander Lebedev in his two Open Letters. I might have been able to dismiss this as his own personal misunderstanding of the Faith, except that you and the other bishops have adopted his letters as "official" answers to those leaving the Russian Orthodox Church Outside Russia. I received my copy of his first letter at the direction of Bishop Hilarion. You and Archbishop Laurus have printed and distributed copies extensively, the Synod of Bishops (as reported in the most recent issue of *Tserkovnaya Zhizn'*, the official Synod journal) has publicly gone on record as thanking Father Alexander for his letters, and now the second letter has been printed in *Orthodox Life*, thereby making these letters the public position of your Church. Father Alexander offers an ecclesiology which I had known well as an Anglican, but which I never expected to see in the Orthodox Church. He states that in the question of which Churches one is in communion with, each diocese can decide for itself. He says that one diocese can be strict, another lenient, but all can be in the same Church; therefore, the Los Angeles diocese is not in communion with any other local Ortho-

dox Churches; the Midwest diocese is in communion with the Serbs and the Constantinople Patriarchate; your diocese is in communion with some Serbian bishops, but not others (an impossible situation in itself); the Western European diocese is in communion with all local Orthodox Churches. This is not Orthodoxy! All I can think of when I read such things is the poor Episcopalians: for them, one diocese has women priests, another does not recognize such priests; in one parish the Holy Communion is the Body and Blood of Christ, while in another it is just a memorial, etc. And now I am told that the Russian Orthodox Church Outside Russia follows the same principle of ecclesiology.

3) In both your Nativity Epistle and Father Alexander's letters there is also a novel understanding of "economy." The theological textbooks which I have consulted define economy as a waiving of the strictness of the Church's rules to facilitate the admission of people to the Church and the Mysteries. As Father Alexander says, by economy you might admit someone to Holy Communion even though he had not kept the full fast beforehand for some weighty reason. But to turn around and use this as an excuse for concelebrating with those one has in fact anathematized, even if one pretends that the anathema is only a warning, is not acceptable. That does not help to bring anyone to the Church, but rather drives them away and confirms them in their error. Father Alexander disingenuously argues that by accepting clergymen from the other local Orthodox Churches, you have acknowledged that those Churches still have grace: but he fails to mention that those clergymen were received without observing the canonical rules, precisely because their churches were considered to be in heresy! It was an act of economy to receive them as priests; but if their churches were truly Orthodox, then you and your bishops have violated canonical procedure in accepting such clergymen without releases from their former bishops and have made yourselves schismatics. The concept of economy does not mean that a priest or bishop can do anything he

feels like [in this matter], although Archbishop Anthony of Geneva says this in a letter to his flock; economy is strictly limited in application and purpose, and the teaching we have seen from you and Father Alexander is a novelty with no place in the Orthodox Church.

Certainly it is possible that we have been misinformed on these points in the past. We have done much reading and study in the last nine months to see if this is so. I have even asked Father Alexander for enlightenment on "economy" and for sources for his teaching of it, but have received no reply from him. But whether we are right or wrong, we have concluded that we do not agree with the doctrines being taught now by the Russian Orthodox Church Outside Russia. Unless we can be shown by something other than invective and unsupported statements that we are in error in our understanding, we must continue to believe as we have in the past and as we have been taught by your predecessors.

c. *Admission to the Mysteries in Synod Parishes.* We have long been aware that in specific parishes of the Russian Orthodox Church Outside Russia, the stated policy of the Church in regard to admission to the Mysteries has not been followed. We have seen and heard of cases of non-Synod Orthodox being admitted to the Mysteries, for example, at Jordanville. This has been particularly distressing when it has involved members of the Moscow Patriarchate and the Orthodox Church in America, since in those cases there are explicit prohibitions by the Council of Bishops of such actions. I have found it awkward to have to turn away New Calendarists in my parish (at your direction, Vladyka), while I know they will be admitted to Holy Communion at the Russian parish of Saint John the Baptist in Washington, D.C. In fact, my parish would be much larger if I had been willing to admit New Calendarists to the Mysteries; it now seems that I have injured my parish in vain by turning them away when I need not have. But now the question of receiving the Mysteries has gone even beyond this. In western Massachusetts there is an open follower and propagandist for the teachings of Apostolos Makrakis, a Greek philosopher who was condemned as a heretic by the Churches of Greece, Russia, and Serbia; Bishop Gregory [Grabbe] would not admit this man to membership in the

Synod on the grounds that he was a heretic; but [this man's] own son testifies that [his father] has been admitted to Holy Communion in the monastery in Jordanville. Additionally, a case has come to light recently of the admission of a Monophysite Copt to Holy Communion in the Synod parish in Houston. This act occurred repeatedly, with the knowledge of the priest and also of Bishop Hilarion, who refused to stop it, saying that he could not, since it had been going on for a long time already.

D. *Canonical Disorder.* As if the above-mentioned items were not sufficient indication of canonical disorder in the Russian Orthodox Church Outside Russia, we have had several additional manifestations of this problem.

1) After the Synod parishes in both Mount Holly Springs and Atlanta joined the Greek Old Calendar Church,[40] Bishop Hilarion advised those who wished to remain in the Synod to attend parishes of the Orthodox Church in America; this was done despite the prohibition on any communion in prayer or mysteries with the OCA.

2) The Synod had generally maintained cordial relations with Metropolitan Cyprian of Oropos and Fili in Greece; his views on grace in the New Calendar jurisdictions generally agree with those now being proposed by the [Russian] Synod. But last spring the Russian Orthodox Church Outside Russia has directed its Greek parish in Thessalonica to join a different Old Calendar jurisdiction, that of Archbishop Chrysostom [Kiousis]. The Synod argues that geographical integrity requires the Greek parish to transfer its allegiance, but neglects to comment on the fact that one member of Archbishop Chrysostom's synod is Bishop Peter of Astoria, Long Island, New York. Is Bishop Peter to become a member of the Synod of Bishops of the Russian Orthodox Church Outside Russia on the same grounds of geographical integrity?

3) The Synod of Archbishop Chrysostom [Kiousis] has deposed Metropolitan Cyprian for Ecumenism because he teaches that the New Calendar churches have grace.

---

[40] *Editors' Note:* This is a reference to the True Orthodox Church of Greece.

How can the Russian Orthodox Church Outside Russia have entered into communion with this synod (by handing over a parish to it), when you maintain in your teachings and actions that there is certainly full grace in the New Calendar churches? This action has an appearance of opportunism, aimed at preventing the establishment of a hierarchy in North America for those parishes which have left the Russian Orthodox Church Outside Russia in recent months.

4) In the Second Open Letter of Father Alexander Lebedev, published in the March–April 1987 issue of *Orthodox Life* (Vol. 37, No. 2), he quotes with full approval a statement that the Synod of Metropolitan Cyprian is the only valid Old Calendar hierarchy in Greece and that "with two or three possible exceptions" all other Greek Old Calendar bishops are "an absolutely astonishing collection of erratic cranks, deposed renegades, self-important gurus, half-baked dabblers in theology, and other characters so bizarre, so fantastic, that, to discover parallels, one would be compelled to draw from the more exotic or comical specimens of fictional literature" [page 41]. If this is so, how can you hand over your Greek flock to these latter bishops, ignoring Metropolitan Cyprian and his "valid" synod? And if this is not the view of the Russian Orthodox Church Outside Russia on the Old Calendar bishops in Greece, why did Archbishop Laurus and Bishop Hilarion publish it in your at least semi-official English-language magazine? . . .

The end result of all the attempts to explain the issues raised by those who left the Russian Orthodox Church Outside Russia in recent months has been confusion and the revelation of heretical and disordered thinking in theology and the administration of the Mysteries of Christ in the Russian Orthodox Church Outside Russia.

We have contrasted this with what we have seen from those who left the Russian Orthodox Church Outside Russia and organized themselves under the omophorion of Archbishop Auxentius of Athens. Certainly there have been human weaknesses, with mistakes made and, sometimes, harsh words spoken; but on this earth we will find no perfection, and who among us could honestly say that he had never said or done anything which he later came to regret? But with these mistakes, we also see a firm commitment to the Orthodox Faith and a clear statement of the dangers of Ecumenism, the latest and most dangerous heresy yet. I am enclosing a copy of the oath[41] which all priests have to sign when they join with Archbishop Auxentius; if only the Russian Orthodox Church Outside Russia had such an oath and enforced it! Then there would be no question of its opposition to Ecumenism.

We have waited and watched with prayer for a correction of the Synod's course, but all that we have seen is further progress on the way of accommodation. And then we read Archbishop Auxentius's clergy oath, and we saw the Orthodox Faith being taught without compromise or equivocation. You cannot imagine how my heart was moved when I finally saw an Orthodox bishop speaking the truth of the Faith in opposition to what you have rightly called the "pan-heresy" of our time: Ecumenism. Now we must act as God has shown us. Therefore, with earthly sorrow, I must inform you that my parish of Saint Cosmas of Aitolia in Riverdale, Maryland and I have been received under the omophorion of Archbishop Auxentius. It gives me greater grief than you can believe to do this, Vladyka, but what else can I do, except follow the Orthodox Faith where it is taught most fully and clearly.

Please be assured that we bear you no personal ill-will and will continue to pray for you and your brother bishops as long as we all live. It is our greatest hope and prayer that you will be able to correct the problems which have arisen in the Russian Orthodox Church Outside Russia, and that someday soon we may once again be united in receiving the Body and Blood of our Lord and Saviour Jesus Christ.

With love in Christ,
Priest Seraphim Johnson

---

[41] *Editors' Note:* This is a reference to the Clergy Declaration required of the clergy of Archbishop Auxentius's Synod. The text follows Fr. Seraphim's letter.

DECLARATION OF THE CLERGY

The undersigned . . . . ,
having in mind that:

1) the introduction of the new calendar brought disastrous consequences into the liturgical order and harmony of the Church and created a schism in its midst;

2) the acceptance of the new or "corrected" calendar by the innovators and schismatic hierarchs stands in opposition to the law of God in that, according to Saint Theodore the Studite, "No authority has been given to the hierarchy to transgress in any matter whatsoever that which is the rule, but [it has power only] to continue in that which has been passed down and to follow in the steps of those who have gone before";

3) the faithful people of God acted in a manner pleasing to God when it rejected the innovation, because, according to Saint Cyprian of Carthage, "He that separates and divides the Church of Christ cannot possess the robe of Christ";

4) the Pan-Orthodox Councils (such as those of 1583, 1587, and 1593 under the Ecumenical Patriarch Jeremias the Illustrious, and the Council of 1848 under the Ecumenical Patriarch Anthimus) have forbidden and condemned the change or alteration of the calendar ("Whoever does not follow the customs of the Church . . . and wishes to follow the newly-devised Paschalion and new Menologion of the ungodly astronomers of the Pope, and sets himself in opposition in all these matters, and wishes to overturn and to destroy the doctrines handed down by our Fathers and the customs of the Church, let him be under anathema, and let him be outside the Church of Christ and the Assembly of the Faithful"—the Council of 1583);

5) the Encyclical of 1920 of the Patriarchate of Constantinople, "To the Churches of Christ Wheresoever They Might Be," proclaims that the union with the (heretical) churches of the West is not impeded "by the dogmatic differences which exist among them" and that this union is desirable and seemly, and that one of the first steps towards its accomplishment is "the adoption by all the Churches of one single calendar so that the great Christian feasts may be everywhere celebrated simultaneously . . .";

6) the ecumenistic innovation of the calendar change also cultivated the ground for the steps that followed, such as the meeting of Pope Paul VI and Patriarch Athenagoras in 1964 in Jerusalem, and all the subsequent acts and heretical pronouncements which were made "with bared head";

7) the "lifting" of the Anathema against the Papacy in 1965 is not a true lifting, in that the Papacy has not renounced its heresies, but, to the contrary, it places under its Anathema even the "Orthodox," according to the dictum of the Fathers: "If anyone does not anathematize all heretics, let his portion be with theirs";

8) the enrollment of a Church as a member of the World Council of Churches altogether constitutes an acceptance of the Branch Theory and a denial of Orthodox ecclesiology and faith, and the common prayers and pronouncements in themselves constitute a proclamation of heresy;

I therefore confess that I reject every ecclesiastical and liturgical relation or association with the ecumenistic churches and those who are in communion with them. I confess and proclaim with the Fathers of the Seventh Ecumenical Council: "We follow the ancient traditions of the Catholic Church. We keep the institutions of the Fathers. We anathematize those who add anything to or subtract anything from the Catholic Church."

I confess that I join and am united to the saving and true Church of the True Orthodox Christians of Greece under the jurisdiction of His Beatitude, the Archbishop, kyr Auxentius, under whose spiritual guidance and pastorship and obedience I shall be.[42]

The undersigned

On . . . .
     (date)   (name)

---

[42] Taking into consideration the recent "Balamand Statement" and the signed proposals and agreements with the Monophysites, this Declaration has been updated accordingly.

One of the principal concerns of the faithful when they met with Archbishop Auxentius in the summer of 1987 was that the Holy Synod under him would consecrate as bishops native-born Americans from the flock here. These hopes were fulfilled in August of 1988 when Hieromonk Ephraim of the Holy Transfiguration Monastery in Boston was consecrated suffragan bishop for the flock in North America.

The following year the Holy Synod of Archbishop Auxentius consecrated two more suffragan bishops, Photios of Lyons, France, and Theonas of Thessaly, Greece. The Holy Synod now had three ruling bishops and three suffragan bishops. Later, in January of 1991, Hieromonk Makarios of Holy Transfiguration Monastery in Boston was consecrated suffragan bishop of Toronto, Ontario. In a subsequent Synodal decision in 1993, all these hierarchs were made ruling bishops.

THE TRADITIONAL ORTHODOX CHRISTIANS OF RUSSIA

In November of 1990, members of the Catacomb Church of Russia established contact with Father George Kochergin, one of the Diocesan Deans of the Holy Orthodox Church in North America. Thus, the traditional Orthodox Christians in North America were made aware of the state of affairs of the Orthodox Church of Russia. While rejecting the KGB-infiltrated Moscow Patriarchate with its deep involvement in Ecumenism, the True Orthodox Church acknowledged the presence of the True Orthodox Church of Russia, from which scant pieces of information were received from time to time. This Orthodox Church had been struggling for existence under unbelievable persecutions for seventy years. With the disintegration of the Soviet Union, various catacomb Orthodox Christian groups began to emerge into the open.

Among those clergy who surfaced was Hieromonk Gury of Kazan, who was the leader of the commonly called "passportless" True Orthodox because they refused to take (internal) passports from the Soviet authorities which, in their estimation, did not represent a legitimate government. Hieromonk Gury's spiritual lineage was impeccable and his group was also known for its

Catacomb Bishop Gury of Kazan.

absolute integrity in its confession of faith. Father Gury first made contact with the Russian Church Abroad, but soon perceived that it had changed its theological course. It was then that some laymen in his group learned of the departure from the Russian Church Abroad of a substantial number of clergy, monastics, and faithful in 1986. On investigating this further, the traditional Christians of Russia were surprised to find out that those who had left the Russian Church Abroad were not all Russians, but that a majority were of other ethnic backgrounds, and that there were many converts. After learning more about the various divisions that existed among the True Orthodox of Greece, these faithful in Russia decided that the Synod of Archbishop Auxentius was the canonical Church of Greece, and that the other groups were in schism from it. In July of 1991, after nine months of communication, Archimandrite Gury was consecrated Bishop of Kazan for the True Orthodox Church of Russia by Metropolitan Maximos of Cephalonia, Bishop Ephraim of Boston, and Bishop Makarios of Toronto at the Russian Orthodox Church of the Holy Resurrection in Worcester, Massachusetts, with the vote and approval of Archbishop Auxentius.[43] Because at present there is an acute lack of clergy to serve the needs of the faithful in Russia, Russian-speaking clergy from the American diocese travel to Russia periodically to help Bishop Gury serve his widely dispersed flock, the members of this true Church of the New Martyrs. Presently, Father Victor Melehov of Worcester, Massachusetts, is serving as the Exarch of the parishes and missions in Russia.

THE CURRENT STATE OF AFFAIRS

Archbishop Auxentius was the leader of his Synod for thirty years, during a period of dramatic innovations within "World Orthodoxy." Indeed, in view of these developments, the calendar issue has become one of the least significant matters of concern for the traditional Orthodox Church of Christ. During this time, Archbishop Auxentius's confession of faith remained unchanged as he received it from his predecessors, Metropolitan Chrysostom of Florina and Archbishop Akakios. In the camp of World Orthodoxy, on the other hand, the pan-heresy of Ecumenism continues to grow with the "official" local Churches fully involved. Despite the personal piety of some of the priests and laity of the ecumenistic jurisdictions, their hierarchs consistently trample underfoot what the Holy Orthodox Church has taught about her very nature and boundaries for the past 2000 years.

Parthenios, Patriarch of Alexandria, affirms that, "The Prophet Mohammed is an apostle. He is a man of God" and "Those who

---

[43] See Biography of Bishop Gury, *The True Vine*, issue number 11, Vol. 3, no. 3, 1991.

are against Islam and Buddhism are not in agreement with God"[44]—and not one bishop of the new calendar Churches, or even of the presumably conservative Patriarchates of Serbia or Jerusalem, speaks out to demand a retraction. Ecumenical Patriarch Bartholomew expresses views tolerant of abortion,[45] and describes the "Roman Catholic Church and the Orthodox Church as the two lungs of the Body of Christ," and as "Sister Churches,"[46] and none of the bishops of "World Orthodoxy" objects, or, they object without following through with the required canonical sanctions. Both Ecumenical Patriarchs Demetrios and Bartholomew allow their Archdeacons to serve in papal masses in Rome in their presence, and Orthodox hierarchs participate in World Council of Churches assemblies interspersed with pagan ceremonies.[47] There are "Agreed Statements" with the Monophysites, who refuse to recognize the authority of the last four Ecumenical Councils.[48] The heads of all the local "World Orthodoxy" churches sign a document that condemns proselytizing the non-Orthodox so as "not to place obstacles in the path to unity." (In other words, it is wrong to try to convert a person in heresy, since, evidently, doctrinal error presents no danger to his salvation.)[49] Orthodox bishops sign "Church Leaders' Covenants," together with clergymen of various other denominations, including Unitarians (few of whom consider themselves Christians), seeking by means of such covenants "to manifest more clearly the oneness of the Body of Christ"—as if people who teach heretical doctrines, or who do not even think of themselves as Christians, could be members of the Body of Christ.[50] In the WCC's Barr Statement, the Orthodox representatives sign a document that confesses that "we find our-

---

[44] *Orthodoxos Typos*, #854, Athens, Greece (in Greek).
[45] *San Francisco Chronicle*, July 20, 1990.
[46] *The Orthodox Church*, Feb. 1993, p. 6.
[47] Videotapes of these events are available from both WCC and Orthodox Christian sources.
[48] See Appendix F, pp. 216-219, and footnote 23, p. 119.
[49] See Appendix G, p. 219.
[50] See Appendix G, pp. 223-224, and also *Hellenic Chronicle*, Jan. 2, 1986.

selves recognizing a need to move beyond a theology which confines salvation to the explicit personal commitment to Jesus Christ."[51]

In the "Balamand Agreed Statement"—signed by representatives of the Vatican and the Churches of Constantinople, Alexandria, Antioch, Russia, Romania, Cyprus, Poland, Albania, and Finland—it is acknowledged by both sides that both the Orthodox Catholic Church and the Roman Catholics are possessors of the true Apostolic Faith, and that both have sacramental grace and Apostolic Succession.[52]

Certainly, here one must ask: By which of the Church's acknowledged canonical and doctrinal criteria are these bishops and clergy Orthodox?

All of these developments—and there may well be more deviations in the future—justify the position of the Holy Synod of the True Orthodox Christians in their refusal to have any sort of liturgical communion with these churches, which are losing their continuity of traditional Orthodox belief and practice. All that remains is the empty title. The traditional Orthodox Christians scattered over the face of the earth take comfort in the Saviour's words "Fear not, little flock," and they proceed with reverence and caution lest they betray the deposit of the Faith committed to the holy Apostles of Christ, for they bring to mind the words of Saint Maximus the Confessor:

> Even if the whole world holds communion with the Ecumenical Patriarch, I will not communicate with him. For I know from the writings of the holy Apostle Paul: the Holy Spirit declares that even the angels would be anathema if they should begin to preach another Gospel, introducing some new teaching.[53]

In these days, it is not just the Ecumenical Patriarch, or only "certain church leaders," as some would maintain, but *all* the

---

[51] See Appendix B, p. 181.
[52] See Appendix H, p. 231.
[53] *The Life of Our Holy Father Maximus the Confessor,* trans. Fr. Christopher Birchall (Boston: Holy Transfiguration Monastery, 1982), pp. 38-9.

bishops of "World Orthodoxy" who are guilty of these crimes against the Holy Orthodox Faith, either directly or by their acquiescence and silence. It is no longer a matter of infractions of the canons, or lapses in the *Typicon,* but of consistent and profound violations of the Holy Faith. Simply, the hierarchs of "World Orthodoxy" are no longer speaking and acting as Orthodox bishops. This is all the more reason why the traditional Orthodox Christians are thankful to God that they have rightly-believing and rightly-teaching hierarchs.

If the traditional Orthodox Christians are divided today, they will once again, with the help of God's grace, be reunited, especially as the heresy of Ecumenism advances, and especially because their differences, with only few exceptions, are over secondary issues. If one finds these divisions distressing, one should consider the chaotic state in which the Church found herself in the fourth century, "the Golden Age." Certainly, the only ones who could be troubled over the current state of affairs are they who are quite unfamiliar with Church history. Indeed, Church history demonstrates that, despite all the turmoil and confusion during the tumultuous fourth century, the Church—the Body of Christ—emerged united and triumphant.

New calendarists and ecumenists who scoff at the divisions among the traditional Orthodox Christians should consider the disordered canonical state of the ecumenistic World Orthodox Churches in America, Europe, and Australia. The arguments, divisions, and confusion in the Russian Patriarchate over the Ukrainian jurisdictions, or in Greece over various dioceses, or in the Patriarchate of Bulgaria, or in the contention between the Ecumenical and Russian Patriarchates over Estonia, assuredly give them no grounds to condemn the True Orthodox Christians for "division and confusion."

The traditional Orthodox Christians have demonstrated both heroic traits and human flaws, and, as one writer said, "under the duress of persecution, or out of sheer desperation, or mistaken judgment, or just plain human weakness," they made mistakes. But they have kept the Orthodox Faith and fought the good fight against the heresy of Ecumenism without compromises or accommodations, whereas the new calendarist and ecumenistic jurisdictions have not. The traditional Orthodox Christians are willing to forgive the ecumenists the brutal sins of violence and sacrilege and the offenses they committed against helpless Orthodox clergymen and lay people. They are also willing to extend their love to the ecumenistic hierarchs and clergy who have maligned and persecuted them. But, until the time comes when the partition of the heresy of Ecumenism is removed, they will not be able to pray or be in communion with their erstwhile brothers in the Faith.

Archbishop Auxentius of Athens ✝ November 4, 1994.

Epilogue

IN 1582 POPE GREGORY XIII, without consulting either the Christian East or the Reformers in the West, unilaterally changed the calendar, ostensibly for reasons of astronomical accuracy. He then invited all the European nations to accept his modification. The Orthodox responded with the Pan-Orthodox Synod of 1583, under the presidency of Ecumenical Patriarch Jeremias the Illustrious of Constantinople. This Synod prohibited any of the faithful, under the pain of anathema, from accepting this papal invention.

What were the reasons for this prohibition?

Aside from the question of Uniatism, the calendar change which Pope Gregory implemented disrupted the entire cycle of the liturgical calendar which determines the celebration of all the moveable feasts (Triodion, Pascha, Pentecost, etc.) and the immovable feasts (Nativity, Epiphany, Annunciation, all the Saints' feasts, etc.). This liturgical unity in celebrating the feasts on the same day for all Orthodox Christians everywhere was a major concern of the First Ecumenical Council in Nicaea (325), and this is why the Council Fathers determined the reckoning of the Paschalion and the menologion once and for all. However, by changing the liturgical calendar, the Papacy disrupted this unity and, among other things, no longer abided by the decision of the First Ecumenical Council which prohibited the Christians from celebrating Pascha before the Jewish Passover. This change by the Pope contravened the theological considerations implicit in that historical sequence. The Christian calendar is solar; the Hebrew calendar is lunar (nor have the Jewish people introduced an innovation into their calendar in order to be more "scientifically correct"). Consequently, they celebrate their religious feasts according to the traditional manner of calculating when their Passover will fall each year. (Because they are based on a lunar calendar, all Jewish feasts are moveable.) By not accepting the papal innovation and continuing to follow the decisions of the First Ecumenical Council, the Orthodox Christians always celebrate Pascha after the Jewish Passover.

But one of the primary reasons Orthodoxy rejected the new calendar was because it believes no one bishop has the authority to make such changes and to legislate for the entire Church. This prerogative belongs exclusively to Ecumenical Councils. By making this calendar change in the name of "scientific correctness," and by inviting all the "separated brethren" to adopt it, the Papacy hoped that, should it be accepted both in the East and in the West, the Christians in these regions would have unsuspectingly accepted also the papal claims to universal jurisdiction, that is, that the Pope, as "the head of Christendom," has the prerogative to legislate for the whole Church. The calendar reform was, therefore, primarily a matter of papal prerogative. The Church, however, rejected this reform in many Pan-Orthodox and Local Synods up to this century, and continues to reject it categorically. The Protestant West also initially rejected this papal innovation for the same reasons, and continued to abide by the Julian Calendar. In the course of the subsequent centuries, the European nations capitulated one by one and accepted the calendar change, primarily because of the growing secularism of the government authorities. England was the last to accept this change, observing the Julian calendar throughout the eighteenth century and, in pockets, even until the beginning of the nineteenth century. Hence, in historical documents and other references in English publications, one may see "o.s." after the date, which signifies the Old Style date, that is, the date according to the Julian calendar.

The calendar innovation of the sixteenth century was not the first nor the only arbitrary change implemented by the Papacy. Some seven centuries before, during the pontificate of Pope Nicholas I, when Saint Photius the Great was Ecumenical Patriarch, the Papacy proclaimed the Filioque as a universal teaching of the Church. Disregarding the Third Ecumenical Council's prohibition against any additions to or omissions from the Creed, Pope Nicholas added the phrase "and from the Son," thus contradicting the Gospel teaching and that of the Church Fathers that the Holy Spirit proceeds eternally from the Father alone.

Archbishop Chrysostom Papadopoulos of Athens, who changed the Church calendar in 1924, himself attested to the true reason behind the calendar change in an article he wrote in 1918.

> The letter of Patriarch Jeremias II [1572-1584, 1586-1595] indicates in an excellent manner the position which the Orthodox Church immediately took against the Gregorian modification of the calendar. The Church considered it yet another of the many innovations of Old Rome, a universal scandal, and an arbitrary affront to the traditions of the Church. The reform of the calendar is not only a matter of astronomy but also pertains to the Church, because it is related to the celebration of the Feast of Pascha. *Hence, the Pope had no right to reform the calendar, [but by doing so, he] thus proved that he esteems himself superior to the Ecumenical Councils* [emphasis added].

In the Orthodox countries where the papal calendar was imposed upon the Church, the faithful, the guardians of the Faith, resisted it from the beginning—in some instances even unto blood—even as the faithful in the fifth century resisted the heretical teachings of Nestorius, the Archbishop of Constantinople; even as they later rejected the heresy of iconoclasm, the false unions of Lyons and Florence, and every other attempt to exchange the truth of Christ for the darkness of error.

Should the Ecumenists and modernists attempt to change the liturgical calendar in the remaining Churches that still follow the ecclesiastical calendar, the reaction will be the same.

A preview of what awaits those who seek to introduce innovations may be seen in the following incident:

> During his sermon in the Convent of Saint John of Kronstadt [on the Karpovka river in Saint Petersburg], Metropolitan Vladimir of Saint Petersburg spoke for adopting the new style calendar for the Moscow Patriarchate. This evoked such indignation in the Orthodox Christians, that the church resounded with exclamations of: "Heretic! Anathema!", and the abbess would not bless those in the *kliros* [choir] to chant *"Eis polla eti,*

Despota" for Metropolitan Vladimir. The church procession was cancelled, and Metropolitan Vladimir departed the church followed by the angry stares of the faithful.

(From the Saint Petersburg newspaper
Nashe Otechestvo, No. 64, 1997)

The forthright text that follows—addressed to the new calendar bishops of Greece in 1995—is a fitting end to this history and demonstrates that the voice of dissent within the innovating jurisdictions has not been quelled and forebodes many unpleasant developments for those bishops who refuse to turn back from their ruinous path of apostasy from the Orthodox Faith.

THE REASONS FOR THE CHANGE OF THE PATRISTIC CALENDAR[1]

Your Eminences, bless.

Keeping in mind from the start—in order to remove any misunderstanding—that I, as well as our holy monastery, follow the new calendar, we would like to note some essential points about the calendar problem so that we may contribute to its resolution, as far as possible.

As is known, the venerable, sacred and holy Synod of our Orthodox Church, under the leadership of His Beatitude, Archbishop Seraphim, heard the study on the old calendar issue prepared by His Eminence, Metropolitan Augustine of Florina, and decided that the issue should be considered by the upcoming Ecumenical [*sic*] Pan-Orthodox Council. We believe that what should be emphasized in this wonderful study by Metropolitan Augustine is that the issue is not about the calendar, that is, the thirteen days; nor is it an issue of salvation or an issue of faith, as Metropolitan Christodoulos of Demetrias stated truthfully. The issue is why we who follow the new calendar changed that which our Orthodox Church had for twenty centuries. It is a delusion to believe that the difference between us and the old calendarists is thirteen days. This is not the issue.

---

[1] By Archimandrite Nektarios Moulatsiotis, a clergyman of the new calendar Church of Greece.

The truth of the matter is, unfortunately, to be found in our Ecumenical Patriarchate's Encyclical of 1920.

Our venerable Ecumenical Patriarchate knows, as we do, why we accepted this change. It is therefore necessary to see what the Ecumenical Patriarchate says, and why the change of the calendar was introduced in the first place, followed by the rest of the changes that were proposed by the holy hierarchs of the Ecumenical Throne.

Let us therefore read the Patriarchal Encyclical of 1920, which introduces the calendar change, and its consequences will become apparent immediately and easily.

(*The text of the Patriarchal Encyclical of 1920, which was quoted in part in this letter, may be found in Appendix A, p. 177.*)

First, we can conclude the following from the above Encyclical: the holy hierarchs of the Ecumenical Throne call all the heresies "Churches of Christ" and emphasize that our dogmatic differences do not impede our approaching one another, and communion is not precluded. Having expressed their conclusions, what they end up saying is that in order for one church to approach the other and for union among the churches finally to occur, the eleven steps proposed by the Holy Synod of the Patriarchate must be taken.

The first step in the rapprochement and union of all the churches would be the calendar change, so that we might celebrate with those in heresy, as the above Encyclical states. Therefore, whoever wanted the union of the churches and their rapprochement, in spite of the existing dogmatic differences ("an unhealthy ecumenism," according to the Metropolitan of Demetrias), accepted the proposal of the Patriarchal Synod and changed the calendar. The "whoever" are all of us and whoever else followed or follows the new calendar. Our acceptance of the new calendar bears witness that we have an "unhealthy ecumenism." And the most frightening thing of all is that we attempt to persuade our people by telling them that we have a "healthy ecumenism"!

Unfortunately, we say one thing and do another. We are sometimes Orthodox in what we say, or sometimes unhealthy

Orthodox in what we say, but we are certainly unhealthy ecumenists in our deeds. How is it possible for us to say that "Orthodoxy considers dogmatic unity a presupposition to the common Cup; for this reason we do not concelebrate with the non-Orthodox" (as Metropolitan Christodoulos stated on February 21, 1995), while the Patriarchal Encyclical says the exact opposite?

Also, how can we say such falsehoods when our Ecumenical Patriarchs have gone to the Vatican in an official capacity and prayed jointly with the Latins, and the Latins come to Orthodox churches and pray with Orthodox hierarchs? How is it possible to fool ourselves and others when we knowingly say these falsehoods? There exist an abundance of videos and photographs of such concelebrations and common Mysteries (weddings); is it possible to say that these things do not go on in Orthodoxy? Why do we deny the truth? Further, the distinguished Professor Evangelos Theodorou wrote an extensive article in *Orthodoxos Typos* last year and testified that, unfortunately, most of our Orthodox hierarchs are possessed by "unhealthy Ecumenism." Let us, at least, admit our tragic mistakes.

Those, however, who did not desire these [ecumenistic] contacts with those in heresy, or these unions of the churches "without dogmatic union," did not adopt the proposals made in the Patriarchal Encyclical and they remained with the old calendar. Simply, that is how things are. Why do we try to complicate them?

Finally, our venerable Holy Synod must ask the clergy and the laity: "Do we, the Church of Greece, want the union of the churches despite the existing dogmatic differences, or do we not?" Because, if we do not want such a union, why then did we follow and continue to follow the proposals of the Patriarchal Encyclical of 1920?

Is it not ironic for us, on the one hand, to say "no" to such types of unions, and then, on the other hand, to enforce the proposals of the Encyclical of 1920?

This is the main point. This is the issue and the problem. We say one thing and do another. We as Orthodox say *no to such types of union*, therefore we must disavow the application of the 1920 Patriarchal Encyclical by abandoning the "unhealthy ecumenism" that we have today, and we must return to our former state. We believe that placing this issue on the agenda of the future Pan-Orthodox Council is not the correct solution to this matter, because the calendar change did not come about as the result of a Pan-Orthodox Council. Why, then, should we discuss its resolution today by means of a Pan-Orthodox Council? And, as the Metropolitan of Florina said, it is preferable for us (he means our entire official church) to return to the old calendar and be called anachronistic by some members of the press rather than to be condemned, or at some point to be characterized as *heretics*.

Your Eminence, there is, unfortunately, only one solution if we truly want to heal the open wound that was created by the change of the calendar. It is to eliminate the reasons which created it. Otherwise, we will be accountable before God and history, because we who accepted the new calendar created the problem, and not they who refused to change, thereby demonstrating that they refuse union with the Latins under the conditions outlined in the 1920 Patriarchal Encyclical.

Would not a new problem be created even today, should the representatives of the Ecumenical Throne and the other Orthodox churches undertake such unions, without dogmatic agreement, recognizing the errors of the western denominations as "local customs and usages"? The hasty handling of such serious issues, unfortunately, creates problems. Indeed, special care is required in endeavors that concern the union of the Orthodox with those in heresy.

The solution, therefore, is in our hands. We must eliminate the reasons that created this problem for us, because what is going on today is tragic: that is, we call those who follow the old calendar heretics and schismatics and urge our Christians to have no dealings with them, while we call those of the West—who are truly schismatics and heretics—"brothers" and "sister churches," and go into their churches and pray with them. Therefore, the only cure for this issue is to eliminate the causes that created it.

Let us decide, therefore, because the issue of the calendar is, in essence, the uncovering of our identity, that is, whether we are *pro-union* or *anti-union*.

We all know that His Beatitude, our Archbishop Seraphim, is anti-unionist, as he has stated many times. Therefore, let him make one more courageous pronouncement that will make his name go down in history: that he ceases, as an anti-unionist, to enforce the 1920 Encyclical, and that he is returning the Greek Church to its pre-1920 state—something which all the holy elders of the twentieth century, such as Father Philotheos Zervakos, sought, and which would immediately resolve the old calendar problem, if they [the new calendar bishops, such as those mentioned in the beginning of this letter] want to resolve it indeed, and are not just engaged in rhetorical discussions. May God help you proceed with boldness and courage to the solution of this problem that has already distressed our country for seventy years. It is certain that your names will go down in history and your Local Synod will be invested with the authority of an Ecumenical Orthodox Synod. AMEN.

Archimandrite Nektarios Moulatsiotis, Abbot.

Alas, three years after Abbot Nektarios's letter was published, the new calendar Church of Greece had yet to change back to the traditional calendar or terminate its involvement in Ecumenism. God grant that the hierarchs of this Church and of all other local Churches of "World Orthodoxy" resolve to reconsider and decisively reject this and every other innovation and heresy!

And may Christ God our Saviour preserve and keep our traditional Orthodox hierarchs, clergy, and laity in the One, Holy, Catholic, and Apostolic Faith, and restore to the bosom of the Church all those now found in innovation, heresy, and schism, so that all may be counted worthy to rejoice together with all the Saints and Confessors of the One Church, in the Heavenly Kingdom. Amen.

THE END

AND TO OUR GOD BE GLORY

THE STRUGGLE AGAINST ECUMENISM

PART TWO
Appendices

Though they might be very few who remain in Orthodoxy and piety, yet they are the Church, and the authority and protection of the Church's laws abides in them; and if it needs be that they suffer for the sake of piety, it is for them a perpetual boast and a cause of salvation for the soul.

Saint Nicephorus, Patriarch of Constantinople,
Confessor and Wonderworker
PG 100: 844-5

APPENDIX A

Encyclical of the Ecumenical Patriarchate, 1920[1]

"To the Churches of Christ Wheresoever They Might Be"

"Love one another earnestly from the heart." (I Peter 1:22)

Our own church believes that rapprochement among the various Christian churches and communion among them is not excluded by the doctrinal differences which exist among them, and that such a rapprochement is highly desirable, necessary, and useful in many ways for the edifying profit of each particular church and of the whole Christian body, and also for the preparation and facilitation of that full and blessed union that will be accomplished in the future with God's help. We therefore consider that the present time is most favourable for re-examining this important question and studying it together.

Even if in this case, owing to antiquated prejudices, practices or pretensions, the difficulties which have so often jeopardized attempts at reunion in the past may arise or be brought up, nevertheless, in our view, since we are concerned at this initial stage only with contacts and rapprochement, these difficulties are of less importance. If there is good will and intention, they cannot and should not create an invincible and insuperable obstacle.

Wherefore, considering such an endeavour to be both possible and timely, especially in view of the hopeful establishment of the League of Nations, we venture to express below in brief our thoughts and our opinion regarding the way in which we understand this rapprochement and contact and how we consider it to be realizable; we earnestly ask and invite the judgment and the opinion of the other sister churches in the East and of the venerable Christian churches in the West and everywhere in the world.

---

[1] Karmiris, pp. 958–959 (for reference, see footnote 2, p. 25 above). See also *The Orthodox Church in the Ecumenical Movement*, WCC, Geneva, 1978.

We believe that the two following measures would greatly contribute to the rapprochement which is so much to be desired and which would be so useful, and we believe that they would be both successful and fruitful:

First, we consider as necessary and indispensable the removal and abolition of all the mutual mistrust and bitterness between the different churches which arise from the tendency of some of them to entice and proselytize adherents of other confessions. For nobody is ignorant of what is unfortunately happening today in many places, disturbing the internal peace of the churches, especially in the East. So many troubles and sufferings are caused by other Christians and great hatred and enmity are aroused, with such insignificant results, by this tendency of some to proselytize and entice the followers of other Christian confessions.

After the essential re-establishment of sincerity and confidence among the churches, we think that, above all, love should be rekindled and strengthened among the churches, so that they should no more consider one another as strangers and foreigners, but as kinsmen, and as being a part of the household of Christ and "fellow heirs, and formed of the same body and partakers of the same promise of God in Christ" (Eph. 3:6).

For if the different churches are inspired by love, and place it before everything else in their deliberations and relations among themselves, instead of increasing and widening the existing dissensions, they should be enabled to reduce and diminish them. By stirring up a right brotherly interest in the condition, the well-being and stability of the other churches; by readiness to take an interest in what is happening in those churches and to obtain a better knowledge of them; and by willingness to offer mutual aid and help, many good things will be achieved for the glory and the benefit both of themselves and of the entire Christian body. In our opinion, such a friendship and kindly disposition towards each other can be shown and demonstrated particularly in the following ways:

1) through the adoption by all the churches of one single calendar so that the great Christian feasts may be everywhere celebrated simultaneously;

2) through the exchange of fraternal letters on the occasion of the great feasts of the ecclesiastical year, as is the custom, and on other special occasions;

3) through more fraternal relations among the representatives of the different churches;

4) through establishing relations between the theological schools and the representatives of theological science, and the exchange of theological and ecclesiastical periodicals and works published by each church;

5) through sending young men from one church to the schools of other churches for their studies;

6) through the convocation of pan-Christian assemblies for the examination of matters of common interest to all the churches;

7) through the dispassionate and more historical examination of the dogmatic differences from a scholarly point of view and by dissertations;

8) through mutual respect for the practices and customs of the various churches;

9) through reciprocal granting of houses of prayer and cemeteries for funerals and burials of the adherents of other confessions who have died in foreign lands;

10) through the implementation of common rules by the different confessions concerning the question of mixed marriages;

11) through a reciprocal and voluntary support of the churches in the realm of religious edification, philanthropy and other such activities.

Such a sincere and close contact between the churches will be all the more useful and profitable for the whole body of the Church, because manifold dangers threaten not only particular churches, but all of them. These dangers attack the very foundations of the Christian faith and the essence of Christian life and society. For the terrible world war which has just finished brought to light many unhealthy symptoms in the life of the Christian peoples, and often revealed great lack of respect even for the elementary principles of justice and charity. Thus it worsened already existing wounds and opened other new ones of a more material kind, which demand the attention and care of all the churches. Alcoholism, which is increasing daily; the increase of unnecessary luxury under the pretext of bettering life and enjoying it; the voluptuousness and lust hardly covered by the cloak of freedom and emancipation of the flesh; the prevailing unchecked licentiousness and indecency in literature, painting, the theatre, and in music, under the respectable name of the development of good taste and cultivation of fine art; the deification of wealth and the contempt of higher ideals; all these and the like, as they threaten the very essence of Christian societies, are also timely topics requiring and indeed necessitating common study and cooperation by the Christian churches.

Finally, it is the duty of the churches which bear the sacred name of Christ not to forget or neglect any longer His new and great commandment of love. Nor should they continue to fall piteously behind the political authorities, who, truly applying the spirit of the Gospel and of the teaching of Christ, have under happy auspices already set up the so-called League of Nations in order to defend justice and cultivate charity and agreement among the nations.

For all these reasons, being ourselves convinced of the necessity for establishing a contact and league (fellowship) among the churches and believing that the other churches share our conviction as stated above, at least as a beginning we request each one of them to send us in reply a statement of its own judgment and opinion on this matter so that common agreement or resolution having been reached, we may proceed together to its realization, and thus "speaking the truth in love, may grow up into Him in all things, Who is the head, even Christ; from Whom the whole body, being joined and knit together and compacted by that which every joint supplieth, according to the effectual working in the measure of each and every part, maketh increase of the body unto the edifying of itself in love" (Eph. 4:15-16).

> The Patriarchate of Constantinople, in the month of January, in the year of grace, 1920.
>
> The *Locum Tenens* of the Patriarchal Ecumenical Throne
> ✟ Dorotheos, Metropolitan of Prusa
>
> > The Members of the Holy Synod
> > ✟ Nicholas, Metropolitan of Caesarea

✠ Constantine, Metropolitan of Cyzicus
✠ Germanos, Metropolitan of Amasia
✠ Gerasimos, Metropolitan of Pisidia
✠ Gervasios, Metropolitan of Ancyra
✠ Anthimos, Metropolitan of Vizya
✠ Eugene, Metropolitan of Selyvria
✠ Agathangelos, Metropolitan of Saranta Ecclesiae
✠ Chrysostom, Metropolitan of Tyroloë and Serention
✠ Irenaios, Metropolitan of the Dardanelles and Lampsacus

APPENDIX B

The Barr Statement of the World Council of Churches[1]

At an official meeting of a WCC committee that met in Barr, Switzerland, from January 9–15, 1990, some twenty-one Orthodox, Protestant and Roman Catholic representatives drafted a 2,500-word statement on "Religious Plurality: Theological Perspectives and Affirmations." These twenty-one official representatives of their respective church groups cited the need for a "more adequate theology of religions" (it seems they feel that what the Church has taught for centuries about false belief and idolatry is not sufficient), and, in the section on Christology, the participants affirmed

> "that in Jesus Christ, the incarnate Word, the entire human family has been united to God in an irrevocable bond and covenant. The saving presence of God's activity in all creation and human history comes to its focal point in the event of Christ." But, they add, "because we have seen and experienced goodness, truth and holiness among followers of other paths and ways than that of Jesus Christ . . . , *we find ourselves recognizing a need to move beyond a theology which confines salvation to the explicit personal commitment to Jesus Christ*" (emphasis added).
>
> (*Ecumenical Press Service*, 16–31 Jan. 1990)

[1] "New Age Bishops," *Orthodox Christian Witness*, June 4/17, 1990.

APPENDIX C

A Letter from Metropolitan Philaret (Voznesensky) to Abbess Magdalena (Countess Grabbe), Superior of the Lesna Convent in France[1]

November 26/December 9, 1979

Your Reverence,[2]

I am writing this letter en route—on board the ocean liner *Orion,* which is sailing to Australia. The ship is a rather large one, 42,000 tons (that's roughly the size of the *Titanic*)[3] and comfortable enough. This morning my travelling companion, Protopriest Constantine,[4] served Liturgy in our cabin, and I took Communion. We did the same yesterday, it being the *apodosis* of the Feast of the Entry of the Most Holy Theotokos, since neither on the actual day of the feast, nor on the day following did we manage to serve—the ship was continually tossing. But since Thursday the ocean has grown calm, and now we are sailing peacefully.

For a long time now I have been wanting to share some thoughts of mine with you—on issues concerning which we proved to be of differing views. Of course, I write not in order to initiate a sharp polemic, but rather an exchange of opinions.

---

[1] Printed in *Tserkovnie Novosti* (*Church News*), No. 58, February 1997, by Matushka Anastasia Schatiloff (née Grabbe), niece of the recipient of this letter. As is evident from the photocopies of the original, this letter was typed on both sides of five sheets of Metropolitan Philaret's familiar letterhead bearing his stylized Cross. The photocopies also show that certain personal references have been deleted by having strips of paper taped over them, apparently by the person who first put the copies into circulation. These references have only been masked, not cut out, which would have resulted in loss of text on the reverse side of these sheets. For the sake of precision these deletions are noted below.

[2] Here the second half of the salutation, apparently "Mother Magdalena," has been masked in the photocopy.

[3] Quotation marks, parentheses, all emphasis, and ellipsis marks are those of Metropolitan Philaret. All bracketed insertions and footnotes are the translator's.

[4] Protopriest Constantine Fedorov.

You most likely recall that, not during my last visit to the Convent, but during the one previous to it, you and I had somewhat of an argument over the fact that the Convent[5] receives into its church those who, in essence, are followers, members of the former Exarchate,[6] and not of the Church Abroad. And conversely, many of our spiritual children regularly attend [the churches of] the Parisians, and there they go to confession and receive "Communion"...

You pointed out that the Convent acts thus for missionary purposes, in order to give the erring ones the opportunity to pray and be sanctified by the Mysteries in a true Orthodox church. But to this I will say: that may very well be so, just as the emissaries of Holy Prince Vladimir attended the Greek Orthodox Church. However... and it's a big "however"! The emissaries of the Prince reported to him concerning the beauty of the Orthodox Faith, and the result was that both they and the Prince himself did not remain in their error, but exchanged paganism for Christianity. And it seems clear to me that proper "missionary work" will exist in the Convent only then, when the Convent, while allowing "them" to visit the church, will, however, allow them to approach the Mysteries *only upon the condition* that, having received the Mysteries from us, they refuse the "Mysteries" performed at the "Rue Daru,"[7] and in general in the churches of the Exarchate.

---

[5] Here in the photocopy the name "Lesna" has apparently been masked before the word "Convent."

[6] The "Temporary Patriarchal Russian Orthodox Exarchate," based in Paris, had been formed in 1931 when Metropolitan Evlogy (Georgievsky), having already withdrawn from the Russian Orthodox Church Abroad, placed himself and his flock under the jurisdiction of the Patriarch of Constantinople. Although the Exarchate itself was abolished in 1965 under pressure from Moscow, the present successors of Metropolitan Evlogy and his adherents remain in submission to the Ecumenical Patriarchate as its Russian Orthodox Archdiocese of Western Europe.

For further information in English on this and other points of contemporary church history touched upon by Metropolitan Philaret in this letter, see *A History of the Russian Church Abroad: 1917–1971* (Seattle: Saint Nectarios Press, 1972).

[7] The street in Paris on which the Church of Saint Alexander Nevsky, the cathedral of the Evlogians, is located.

Otherwise what is the outcome? The outcome is that everything with them is in order, and there is no need for them to change or correct anything. And we, by admitting them to the Mysteries and not demanding any integrity or constancy in this regard, confirm them more strongly in the conviction that everything is fine with them and that their path is the true and correct path.

At the Third Pan-Diaspora Sobor[8] they started making speeches about how we should unite with the Parisians and with the American False-Autocephalites **"in a spirit of love."** Love, you see, should unite us, and there is no need to emphasize our differences. But such talk ceased when I cited the words of one of the Holy Fathers which read thus: if we, supposedly in the name of love, so as not to trouble our neighbors, are going to keep quiet about their error and not explain to them that they are on a false path, then this **is not love, but hatred!** Does he do well who, upon seeing a blind man approaching a precipice, does not tell him about it, so as not to "trouble" him? Is that then love?

At the latest Bishops' Sobor,[9] Vladyka Anthony of Geneva[10] began to deliver a speech in that vein ... He said: as regards Paris, there we have a common flock (that is, we and the Exarchate). We both alike service one and the same Orthodox people.

At that point I could not contain myself and I burst forth with a speech ...

First of all, I pointed out that we really do have a place where we have a flock in common with other ministers of the Orthodox Church. And that is Boston. We have our parishes there, and the monastery of Archimandrite Panteleimon[11] is located there too.

---

[8] The Third Pan-Diaspora Sobor of the Russian Orthodox Church Abroad took place at Holy Trinity Monastery, Jordanville, N.Y. from Aug. 26/Sept. 8 to Sept. 6/19, 1974.

[9] The previous Bishops' Sobor had been held in September 1978 at Synod headquarters in New York.

[10] Archbishop Anthony (Bartoshevich) of Geneva and Western Europe. Here in the photocopy "Anthony of Geneva" has been masked to simply read: "Vladyka A."

[11] Archimandrite Panteleimon (Metropoulos) of the Holy Transfiguration Monastery.

Metropolitan Philaret of blessed memory, during a visit to the Holy Transfiguration Monastery in Boston.

And it has Greek practices and *Typicon*. All the faithful there attend both one and the other equally, since that monastery is of our jurisdiction, is absolutely Orthodox, and has our Orthodox "spirit," despite the difference in *Typicon* and practices.

And to which I then added: but tell me, what sort of "common flock" could I have with the Parisians, when their head, Archbishop Georgy,[12] while passing by our Memorial Church in Brussels,[13] spits in its direction with the words—"Ugh, the

---

[12] Archbishop George Wagner.

[13] The Church of Saint Job the Much-suffering, consecrated in 1950 as a memorial to the martyred Imperial family and to all those who had lost their lives at the hands of the Communists in Russia.

Karlovci contagion!"[14] This was seen and heard by our people who were present there ... But the Exarchate spits not only upon our churches but upon the Church *Typicon* and the canons. They perform weddings there on Saturdays, and generally whenever you like—just so long as you pay the money. They served a funeral there for an *unbaptized* Jewish man—as was reported to us with indignation by our "Zarubezhniki."[15] What kind of "common flock" could there be here and what could we have in common with them? When I was serving in Brussels for the Day of Mourning,[16] a certain woman started to approach the Holy Cup. I said: Ask her whether she went to confession. The answer: "no." "Then you cannot receive Communion." She began to make a commotion—what is this, all that is needed is a clear conscience, and so forth ... But I, I didn't get into an altercation with her, but only thought to myself: "Ugh, the Exarchate contagion" ... For she was one of the "Parisians."

I am accused of excessive strictness and of "fanaticism." But I have sufficient basis for holding to my point of view, for behind me stand great authorities, both ancient and contemporary.

I shall begin with the ancient ones. First and foremost—was it, then, in the present spirit of "condescension" towards those who have broken away that these words were spoken: "But if he neglect to hear the church, let him be unto thee as an heathen man and a publican"?[17] We know **Who** said these words. Who then will dare to gainsay Him? ...

Let us turn to the great authorities. Here we have the hierarch Saint Gregory the Theologian, the incarnation of meekness and pure Christian love towards all, and in particular towards those

---

[14] "The Karlovci schism" was the disparaging term used for the Russian Orthodox Church Abroad by its detractors. The name is derived from the Serbian town of Sremski Karlovci where the Synod of the ROCA first convened in 1921, and where its headquarters were located until the end of World War II.

[15] Lit. our "Diasporites," a colloquialism for the members of the ROCA, formed from the Russian adjective *zarubezhnaya* (i.e., 'abroad, in diaspora'), as in *Zarubezhnaya Tserkov*, the Church Abroad.

[16] Apparently July 4/17, the anniversary of the execution of the Imperial family. [17] Matt. 18:17.

who have gone astray. However, he frankly states that not every peace is to be prized, nor is every war to be feared. "There is a shameful peace, and there is a good and praiseworthy division," says Saint Gregory.[18] And the context of these words clearly indicates that he had in view those who had broken away—who had gone off into schism.

Next is Saint Basil the Great—a man stricter than most. Yet we know that when it was a question of a schism that had only just begun to form, then the hierarch was in favor of showing the maximum condescension and, for the sake of facilitating for the fallen the matter of their return to the fold of the Church, strove in every way so that the least possible demands be made upon them as the condition for their return. But how drastically he shifts his position when he speaks of an obstinate and prolonged schism. "Such a schism," says Saint Basil, "is already in all things like unto heresy, and one must treat such schismatics *as one would heretics*, not permitting any communion with them."[19]

Severe and categorical. But even more severely and more categorically speaks the third of these great authorities, Saint John Chrysostom. It's a pity that I do not have here at hand with me on the ship his marvellous sermons, preached precisely concerning schismatics. But I remember them well and shall strive to convey them as accurately as possible. [20]

Saint John Chrysostom begins his talk on schism by citing the ancient testimony of that great saint, Hieromartyr Ignatius the God-bearer. Saint Ignatius says that there is no sin worse than that which brings division into the Church, and he warns that this sin is so great, that not even the blood of martyrdom can

---

[18] Saint Gregory the Theologian *Oration* VI:20. Of course, here and elsewhere in this letter the Metropolitan is citing the Holy Fathers from memory and not giving exact renderings from their works.

[19] In like manner, Canon VI of the Second Ecumenical Council reads in part: "We call those heretics . . . who, though pretending to confess the sound faith, have schismatically separated and have gathered congregations in opposition to our canonical bishops."

[20] For the full text of this and the subsequent quotations from Saint John Chrysostom, see his *Commentaries on the Epistle to the Ephesians*, Homily XI.

wash it away!²¹ Corroborating this, Saint John Chrysostom says: I say this for those who *indiscriminately go to all churches*—both to ours and to those of the schismatics. If they teach differently than we do—then for that very reason, of course, one ought not go to them. But if they teach the very same as we do—**then all the more cause why one ought not to go to them**, for here is the sin of lust for authority...

Was it not for this very cause that Evlogy, of sorry memory, broke away and became a schismatic leader, because he could not endure the seniority of Metropolitan Anthony?²² Alas, it is so! I recall how my late father, Bishop Dimitry, upon returning [to China] from the famous "conference of the four,"²³ for all his customary caution in making comments, said in grief: "I did not imagine that an Orthodox hierarch could be as insincere as this Evlogy, whom one simply has no desire to call 'Metropolitan'." And Bishop Nestor,²⁴ who, as a hierarch, received the minutes of the conference, showed them to Father Nathaniel.²⁵ They contained, incidentally, these words of Vladyka Dimitry: "Inasmuch as His Beatitude Evlogy is today saying the exact opposite of what he

---

²¹ Saint Nicodemus of the Holy Mountain, compiler of the *Rudder*, in turn cites this passage from Saint John Chrysostom in his own notes to Canon XXXI of the Apostolic Canons.

Saint Cyprian of Carthage, in his *Treatise I, On the Unity of the Church:* 13, writes: "If such men were even slain in confession of the Christian name, not even by their blood is this stain washed away... He cannot be a Martyr, who is not in the Church."

²² Metropolitan Anthony (Khrapovitsky) of Kiev, first Chief Hierarch of the Russian Orthodox Church Abroad.

²³ This conference had been arranged through the mediation of Patriarch Varnava of Serbia, with the approval of the other participants, in an attempt to reconcile these hierarchs and restore unity to the ROCA. It was convened in October 1935 in Sremski Karlovci with Patriarch Varnava presiding. The four Russian hierarchs participating were Metropolitan Anastasy (Gribanovsky, on behalf of the ailing Metropolitan Anthony), Metropolitan Evlogy of Western Europe, Metropolitan Theophil (Pashkovsky) of America, and Bishop Dimitry of Hailar (Far East). Vladyka Dimitry also acted as secretary for the conference, with Count George Grabbe (the future Bishop Gregory) as his assistant.

²⁴ Bishop Nestor (Anisimov) of Kamchatka.

²⁵ Archimandrite Nathaniel (Lvov), subsequently Archbishop of Vienna.

said yesterday, then I too am forced today to likewise say the opposite and I hereby declare my total disagreement with him"...

Saint John Chrysostom continues: Thou (he is addressing his interlocutor) sayest, "We are all the same—they serve, pray, and teach the same as we do." Very well—why then are they not with us? One Lord, one Faith, one Baptism![26] They have broken away—in that case, one of two things must be so: either all is well with us and they are in poor straits; or else all is well with them, and we are in trouble!

What do these clear and categorical words of this Holy Father signify? They indicate nothing other than that schism is **graceless.** Christ was not divided, and His grace is one. If one is to believe in the "state of grace" of schism, then one must either admit that we do not have grace—those who broke away having taken it with them; or else admit that there are *two* graces (and obviously two true Churches, for grace is given only in the true Church).

Continuing to expound his thoughts, Saint John Chrysostom finally draws his conclusion—inevitable and incontrovertible: "I do say and affirm that schism is just as terrible an evil as heresy."

And heresy separates the human soul from the Church, from God,—and from salvation.

Here are some more voices from antiquity. Saint Peter of Alexandria saw the Saviour in a torn robe—the Lord was clutching it in His hands. The hierarch made so bold as to inquire: Who has rent Thy garment, O Saviour? There followed the mournful and indignant reply of the Saviour: Arius the madman—he has separated My sheep from Me which I have purchased with My blood...[27]

In the lives of the saints it is related that the righteous Gregory once had a revelation. He beheld the future Dread Judgment of Christ. And at that judgment the Lord summoned Arius to Himself and threateningly asked him: Am I not the God-man Christ,

---

[26] Eph. 4:5.

[27] From the Life of Saint Peter, Pope of Alexandria, who is commemorated on November 24.

equal in Divinity to the Father and the Holy Spirit? How is it that you reduced My Divinity to the level of creation and have brought this assembly deceived by you (the followers of Arius) to eternal torment? ...

What do these terrible words tell us? That the heretic leads his followers to eternal torment! ... We have already seen that—not according to the present spineless reasoning, but according to the teachings of the Holy Fathers—schism is just as terrible an evil as heresy, and that obviously the end of it will be the same. I do not dare to pronounce judgment on our contemporary founder of schism, Metropolitan Evlogy; but I fear for his soul and I fear for all those who have been deceived by him and his successors and have been carried away into schism.

And I cannot understand the position taken on this issue by the late Vladyka John—a true minister of God and a man of God.[28] Why didn't he "dot the i" from the very beginning and explain to the Evlogians the total falsehood of their path and position? For it is precisely because of this, because it was not stated at once and clearly where the truth is and where falsehood (for two truths there cannot be), where is white and where black, where light and where darkness, which path is correct and which incorrect—there would not now exist this "inter-jurisdictional hodgepodge" and the position would be clear.[29]

That fact, that many from among the "Orthodox" indiscriminately attend whatever church, what does it tell us? Why, simply that people do not hold the truth dear. For this very reason they

---

[28] Archbishop John (Maximovitch) had been the ruling hierarch of the ROCA Western European Diocese from 1951 to 1962, with his residence first in Paris and then in Brussels. In 1964 Archbishop John had been one of two candidates for Metropolitan of the Church Abroad before the Sobor elected its youngest member, Bishop Philaret of Australia, to the office. Vladyka John was glorified as a saint in 1994.

[29] Although it is clear what the Metropolitan intends to say here, it appears that his thoughts were flowing more swiftly than he could write, and thus he seems to have gone on to the second clause without having completed the first. The translation reflects the original and nothing of the text has been inadvertently omitted here.

don't bother giving the matter much thought. "The services are identical, everything is the same—what need is there to philosophize?" Or, as our Father John Storozhev in Harbin (the last spiritual father of the murdered Imperial family), one of the best pastors of the Diaspora, used to say with poignant irony: "The bells ring; the popes[30] serve; the singing is good—what more do you want?" To which may be added the oh, so familiar: "After all, God is one!" . . .

If only people loved the truth and cherished it—would they really be content with such indifference? No, and a thousand times no! Their soul would ache, and it would not rest content until it had discovered where is the truth, which can only be one—for two truths cannot be. How correct Vladyka Nectary[31] is when he always affirms: there is no such thing as "different jurisdictions"; but there is only the Orthodox Church Abroad, and outside of her are schisms and heresies.

Now I should like to cite a contemporary authority, one not ancient, but an authority before whom we all must bow. This, of course, is that great "Abba of all abbas," His Beatitude, Metropolitan Anthony [Khrapovitsky].

Vladyka Anthony, when presenting the abbess' staff to Abbess Paula,[32] said to her: "Be condescending to all, know how to converse with those weak in faith and with scoffers. Behave wisely with heretics, but never agree with them that they supposedly have the grace of the Holy Spirit; know that the Roman Catholics, the Mohammedans and all other heretics are without grace." And we have already seen that the Holy Fathers equate obstinate and prolonged schism with heresy. Consequently? . . .

---

[30] *Pope:* colloquial Russian for the simple village priest.
[31] Bishop Nectary (Kontsevich) of Seattle.
[32] Mother Paula (Kliueva) had been appointed in September of 1929 as Abbess of the Convent of the Ascension on the Mount of Olives in Jerusalem. She was to replace the ailing Abbess Elizabeth. Metropolitan Anthony presented her with her staff of office while she was still in Serbia, and Archbishop Anastasy conducted her enthronement when she arrived in the Holy Land in October. (*Tserkovnie Vedomosty*, NN. 10 & 11, May 1930, p. 14.)

A quotation from a Paschal encyclical of Vladyka Anthony's (1934):

> The present age is rich not in ascetical feats of piety and confession of faith, but in cheating, lies, and deceits. It is noteworthy that several hierarchs and their flocks, for the most part Russians, have already fallen away from Ecumenical unity, and to the question: "What dost thou believe?"[33] reply with references to self-proclaimed heads of all sorts of schisms in Moscow, America, and Western Europe. It is clear that they have ceased to believe in the unity of the Church throughout the whole world and do not wish to admit it, attempting to bear calmly the refusal of the true Church to have relations with them, and imagining that one can supposedly save one's soul even without communion with her . . . Those who have cut themselves off from her deprive themselves of the hope of salvation, as the Fathers of the Sixth Ecumenical Council teach concerning this, *having recognized the renegades as being totally devoid of grace*, according to the word of Christ: But if he neglect to hear the church, let him be unto thee as an heathen man and a publican.
>
> Unfortunately, some Orthodox laymen, even, alas, many priests (and hierarchs) have subjected themselves to this state of gracelessness, although still retaining the outward appearance of the church services and *the apparent performance of the Mysteries*.

Ponder those last words of the great Abba: the apparent performance of the Mysteries . . . What horror! But these his words concur totally with my own conviction regarding the gracelessness and inefficacy of schismatic Mysteries.

When at the Sobor I cited these words of Vladyka Anthony in support of my conviction, the hierarchs received them in silence— Vladyka Anthony [of Geneva][34] likewise held his peace. While

---

[33] The question solemnly posed to a bishop at his consecration, to which he must reply publicly, declaring his confession of the Orthodox Faith and pledging to uphold the canons and teachings of the Church.

[34] Here again in the photocopy this has been masked to read simply: "Vladyka A."

Vladyka Philotheus[35] thanked me on behalf of the entire Sobor for such an exceptionally important explanation.[36]

Peace and God's blessing be with you. May the Lord and His Most Pure Mother preserve you and the Holy Convent in health and prosperity!

☩ Metropolitan Philaret

"ENCLOSURE"[37]

This letter has turned out to be rather long. But having re-read it, I see that I have not said all that I consider necessary to say, and so I add this enclosure.

You, Matushka, have no doubt caught the basic trend of my thoughts. I consider (I speak, of course, only for myself) that the schismatics—American and Parisian—do not have grace, for otherwise one would have to admit the absurd: the existence of several true Churches, which do not recognize each other, nor have any spiritual communion among themselves.[38] This is already manifestly absurd because the Divine Founder of the Church said: "I will build My Church,"[39] and not "My Churches." I was led to this conviction both by the words of the ancient Holy Fathers (cited by me above) and by the words of Abba Anthony concerning the *apparent* performance of the Mysteries among those who have

---

[35] Archbishop Philotheus (Narko) of Hamburg.

[36] At this point the bottom half of the front of this sheet of paper and three-fourths of the back side were taped over with blank white paper in order to mask the text when photocopied. The vertical strips of tape appear distinctly in the margins of the photocopy. In order to retain the Metropolitan's signature, which stands at the bottom of the reverse side, the sheet was not cut, but merely covered over.

[37] Metropolitan Philaret himself typed this title at the top of this separate sheet of paper.

[38] And as Bishop Gregory (Grabbe) pointed out in an article which he wrote not long before his repose: "Our previous Bishops' Sobors never raised the particular question concerning whether or not the New Calendarists have grace. But the fact that formerly concelebrations with them were never permitted already testifies with sufficient clarity that the Church Abroad considered them to be without grace." See *Tserkovnie Novosti* (*Church News*), No. 40, Sept.–Oct., 1994, pp. 2–4.

[39] Matt. 16:18.

broken away from the true Church. To such a degree do I not believe in the grace of the schismatics' "manipulations," that in the event that I were dying and it was necessary to give me Communion, I would receive it neither from the "Parisians" nor from the American False-Autocephalites, lest in place of the Holy Mysteries I should swallow a piece of bread and some wine.

But I have neglected still to emphasize that, the situation being such, it must be considered a most grievous thing that our "Zarubezhniki" also frequent the temples[40] of the schismatics—to "confess" and "commune" there. Of what are they communing? If the Holy Mysteries, then that means that we do not have the Holy Mysteries, as Saint John Chrysostom has elucidated so clearly. But if we **do have** the Holy Mysteries, then they do not, and these poor people go there in vain. "Apparent" Mysteries, according to the definition of Abba Anthony—that is what the ministers of the schism offer to these credulous people.

I quite understand what turmoil it would bring into the lives of those Russian people who believe in the exarchate and the false autocephaly, if that which I have written here were to be published. But will it really be better to remain silent concerning all this and take comfort in the "peace and quiet," as Vladyka Anthony [of Geneva][41] would have us do? Why, people are on a spiritually false path! This is terrifying! And will not the awesome judgment of God fall upon our heads, if we do not enlighten our erring brothers?

Some might raise an objection and say to me: Did not the Third Pan-Diaspora Sobor address both one and the other, the Parisians and the Americans, with a call for peace and unity? Yes, it did address them, but it addressed them not at all as was needed, and for that very cause this appeal produced no results, or rather, it produced a negative result. I had been *certain* that such would be the result. For we should have told them: You have gone astray, you

---

[40] The word employed here by the Metropolitan is not the usual *khram*, which can also be used (and is so used) for a Christian church, but rather *kapishche*, which designates a heathen temple only.

[41] Again masked in the photocopy to read: "Vladyka A."

have fallen away from the Church—strive to return to her! But the appeal as published speaks to them as though they were within the Church just as we are, with equal rights and position. Whereas what should have been told them then and there was: You are not some sort of "different jurisdictions"; you are simply schismatics, and have no rights whatsoever . . . Come to your senses and return in repentance!

Most likely **such** an appeal would have provoked only an outburst of rage from the leaders of the schism (God grant that I am mistaken; but then, we know their attitude). But among their "flock," many, very many may have pondered it over and come to understand that matters do not at all stand well with them, just as the late Sandrik Filatev and many others who have broken with the schism came to understand after hearing the serious and convincing explanations of Father Gerasim.[42]

The question might be posed to me: why I didn't mention at the Sobor that I felt the appeal to be inappropriate. I would reply: because I saw the attitude at the Sobor and I feared an explosion and a possible catastrophe. For I had been forewarned that the enemies of the Church wished to arrange such an explosion, in order to "blow up" the Sobor from within. Therefore I was compelled to avoid issues which might have provoked heated exchanges.

I wish to return to the issue of heresy and schism. His Beatitude, Metropolitan Anthony, asks: Is it permissible to be stern with heretics, who perhaps sincerely believe in the righteousness of their cause? One must never idealize heretics, he replies, since the basis for their departure is not virtue, but the passions and sins of pride, obstinacy, and malice. Sternness towards heretics, says Vladyka, is beneficial not only for the sake of protecting people from their influence, but also for the heretics themselves.

We have seen that the Holy Fathers equate obstinate schismatics with heretics. Consequently, is it proper to coddle them as, unfortunately, occurs among us? And all this for the sake of an evil and false "peace" . . .

---

[42] Father Gerasim Romanov.

If the Lord permits me to live until the next Bishops' Sobor, at it I shall pose this question "point blank."[43]

[*Written along the left-hand margin, in the Metropolitan's hand:*]

P.S. This letter was completed on board the ship, but is being sent only today, December 14/27, since I could not send it earlier—the mail system was overloaded before "Christmas" . . .[44]

APPENDIX D

A Letter from Metropolitan Philaret (Voznesensky) To a Priest of the Church Abroad Concerning Father Dimitry Dudko and the Moscow Patriarchate[1]

June 26/July 9, 1980

Dear Father ____,

For a long time now I have been intending to write a few words to you, but somehow I haven't managed to "get around to it."[2] But at last I have collected myself, and so I write.

When I, while still in Australia,[3] began to receive information

---

[43] Metropolitan Philaret was true to his word. The 1981 Bishops' Sobor was convened in New York chiefly to celebrate the official ecclesiastical glorification of the New Martyrs of Russia; therefore regular church business was kept to a minimum. However, the Bishops' Sobor met again in 1983 at the Holy Transfiguration Skete, near Mansonville, Quebec, to consider, among other things, the very issues raised by Metropolitan Philaret in this letter. The members of the Sobor resolved to solemnly condemn and anathematize the heresy of Ecumenism. (See pp. 132-134.)

[44] The Metropolitan wrote *Christmas* in English. His ship had docked in Sydney on Dec. 7/20.

---

[1] From *Tserkovnie Novosti* (*Church News*), No. 59, March–April, 1997.

[2] Quotation marks, parentheses, all emphasis, and ellipsis marks are those of Metropolitan Philaret. All bracketed insertions and footnotes are the translator's.

[3] Metropolitan Philaret had been in Australia on an extended pastoral visit from Dec. 7/20, 1979 until April 3/16, 1980. (See *Pravoslavnaya Rus*, No. 5, March 1/14, 1980, p. 8; and No. 8, April 15/28, 1980, p. 12.)

from America—already *post factum*,⁴—that here [in New York City] there had been protests, demonstrations, and even *molebens* in front of the Soviet consulate, I became quite alarmed and regretted that I was not here, since I would have decisively opposed much of what took place. In particular, holding a *moleben* in such a place.⁵ Did they not sing the Lord's song in a strange land?⁶ What cause was there to display the holy things of the Church's services before the gaze of the frenzied servants of Antichrist? Was it really not possible to pray in church?

I must say frankly that I am always seized by dismay when I hear of "protests," "demonstrations," and the like. In the USSR, life is governed by him (the one with horns) who fears only Christ and His Cross; and who fears nothing else in the world. And he merely chortles over protests and demonstrations. "Public opinion"? Why, the antichrist regime has nothing but the uttermost contempt for it! They wanted to seize Czechoslovakia—and they seized it, paying no heed to the commotion that was raised. They wanted to invade Afghanistan—and they invaded it, again paying no attention to the protests and threats of the various Carters & Co.⁷ All attempts to shape public opinion in the so-called Free World in favor of those suffering from Communism are powerless

---

⁴ Here Metropolitan Philaret had written the Latin phrase in by hand.

⁵ The first demonstration—held on Jan. 1/14, 1980, in front of the headquarters of the Soviet mission to the UN—had been organized by the Coalition for a Free Russia, as a protest against Soviet aggression in Afghanistan. Y. Mashkov, a participant reporting on the event, erroneously stated that it had been done "with the blessing of the First Hierarch of the Russian Orthodox Church Abroad, Metropolitan Philaret." (See *Pravoslavnaya Rus*, No. 3, Feb. 1/14, 1980, pp. 15–16.) A second demonstration, with a *moleben* followed by a procession, was organized by the Committee for the Defense of Persecuted Orthodox Christians, on Feb. 11/24, 1980, in support of the recently-arrested Father Dimitry Dudko, Father Gleb Yakunin and others. A similar demonstration was held in San Francisco on this day. (See *Pravoslavnaya Rus*, No. 7, April 1/14, 1980, p. 12.)

⁶ Cf. Psalm 136:5.

⁷ At the time of these demonstrations, the Synod had sent a telegram and then a letter to President Carter concerning the current persecutions in the USSR. (See *Pravoslavnaya Rus*, No. 8, April 15/28, 1980, p. 13.)

and fruitless, since the Free World stubbornly closes its eyes and imitates the ostrich, which hides its head under its wing and imagines that it cannot be seen...⁸

In bewilderment did I read in the newspaper how one journalist approvingly cites your words: "Father __ is correct when he writes: Russia is arising from the dead! We must believe in this; for we believe in Christ the Saviour Who arose from the dead."⁹

I cannot understand—what is the connection between the one and the other? Personally, I believe in the Resurrection of Christ—for me this is the most precious thing in the world. But I absolutely cannot see why **must** I believe that Russia is "resurrecting"? I hope that she truly will arise, when the all-powerful nod for it will be given by God. But at present, not only do I not share your enthusiasm, but I am greatly alarmed for the Russian people. The falsehood and emptiness of atheism is obvious to them. But alas, it is not true Orthodoxy that is being disseminated there. There, under the guise of Orthodoxy, the Russian people are being offered Bulgakovism, Berdyaevism, and similar rubbish of the Evlogian schism.¹⁰ The sects are flourishing there: the Baptists, etc. The official Church preaches cooperation with the God-hating regime,

---

⁸ For an Orthodox view on how to help our persecuted brethren, see the letter, "Compassion for the Suffering," in *Orthodox Christian Witness*, Vol. 14, No. 9, 1980, pp. 1-12.

⁹ Both "arise" and "resurrect" (and their various related forms) are derived from the same root in Russian.

¹⁰ In 1931 Metropolitan Evlogy (Georgievsky, 1868-1946), having already withdrawn from the Russian Orthodox Church Abroad, placed himself and his flock under the jurisdiction of the Patriarch of Constantinople, thus forming the "Temporary Patriarchal Russian Orthodox Exarchate," based in Paris. Although the Exarchate itself was abolished in 1965 under pressure from Moscow, the present successors of Metropolitan Evlogy and his adherents remain in submission to the Ecumenical Patriarchate as its Russian Orthodox Archdiocese of Western Europe. For further information in English, see *A History of the Russian Church Abroad: 1917-1971* (Seattle: Saint Nectarios Press, 1972).

Father Sergius Bulgakov (1871-1944) and Nicholas Berdyaev (1874-1948) were among a group of free-thinkers and intelligentsia who were expelled from Russia by the Soviet government in the 1920s. They were associated with Metropolitan Evlogy's Theological Institute of St. Sergius in Paris, of which Father Sergius was even dean. Their Gnostic, false teaching of "Sophiology" was condemned as heresy by the Second Pan-Diaspora Sobor of the ROCA in

lauding it in every possible way.¹¹ The true Orthodox Church has gone into the catacombs, hidden from the common masses ... Is that, then, the "rebirth of Orthodoxy"? ... And are you not perhaps taking a bit too much upon yourself, proclaiming to the whole world that Orthodoxy is being reborn in Russia? God grant that the Truth should overcome all errors and should triumph over them. But for the present it is still too soon to speak of it, since the influence of the anti-Orthodox elements is still so very strong there; not to mention the fact that the antichrist Soviet regime, as long as it rules Russia, will never permit the triumph of Orthodoxy. It is not without cause that the true Orthodox Church concealed herself in the catacombs and is fiercely persecuted.

Now a few words on the tragedy of poor Father Dimitry Dudko.¹²

From the very beginning of his activities, when his name was being mentioned more and more often as a pillar of Orthodoxy, and moreover, the members of the Synod, the hierarchs, were joining their voices to this; I, however, the author of these lines, immediately kept out of it and forewarned my fellow hierarchs that a disaster might happen here. How so? Because in the USSR, according to the precise definition of Archimandrite Constantine,¹³ there is now a **satan-ocracy**. There rules he whom the

---

1938. (For an English translation of the report submitted to the Sobor by Count Paul Grabbe [Bishop Gregory's father], see *Living Orthodoxy*, Vol. 16, No. 6, Nov.–Dec., 1994, pp. 15–28.) It should be noted that the Moscow Patriarchate also condemned Father Sergius Bulgakov as a heresiarch.

¹¹ Alas, they did not hearken to the wise admonition of Saint Theodosius of the Kiev Caves:

"Live in peace not only with your friends, but also with your enemies; but only with your personal enemies, and not with the enemies of God."

¹² Father Dimitry Dudko had been arrested on Jan. 2/15, 1980. After six months spent under arrest and in prison he publicly recanted on television and in the press.

¹³ Archimandrite Constantine (in the world, Cyril Zaitsev, 1887–1975), spiritual father of the brotherhood of Holy Trinity Monastery in Jordanville, N. Y., instructor at the seminary, and editor of *Pravoslavnaya Rus* and *Orthodox Life*. (For a short obituary see *Orthodox Life*, Vol. 25, No. 6, Nov.–Dec., 1975, p. 3; for a fuller biography, see *Orthodox Word*, Vol. 12, No. 1, Jan.–Feb. 1976, pp. 20–27.)

Saviour called a liar and the father of lies.[14] This lie reigns there. Therefore one cannot trust anything that occurs there. Any seemingly spiritually encouraging fact may turn out to be a falsification, a forgery, a deception, or a provocation . . .

Why did this calamity befall Father Dimitry Dudko? Let's assume the best, not suspecting him of conscious collaboration with the KGB and betrayal of his convictions, but simply noting the sad fact that he did not endure, but was "broken"; he capitulated before the enemies of the Church. Why? It would seem that he did display courage and daring; and then suddenly, such an inglorious end. Why?!

Because his activity took place **outside of the true Church** . . .[15]

What then is the "Soviet church"? Archimandrite Constantine has often and insistently stated that the most horrible thing that the God-hating regime has done in Russia is the creation of the "Soviet church," which the Bolsheviks presented to the people as the true Church, having driven the genuine Orthodox Church into the catacombs or into the concentration camps.

This pseudo-church has been twice anathematized. His Holiness Patriarch Tikhon and the All-Russian Church Sobor anathematized the Communists and *all their collaborators*. This dread anathema has not been lifted till this day and remains in force,

---

[14] John 8:44.

[15] At this time the then Archbishop Vitaly (Ustinov) of Montreal concurred totally with Metropolitan Philaret's evaluation. In a sympathetic yet uncompromising article which he published in the August 1980 *Parish Newsletter* of his St. Nicholas Cathedral in Montreal (and which was subsequently printed in English, at his request, in the *Orthodox Christian Witness*, Vol. 14, No. 51, 1981, pp. 7–9), he wrote: " . . . And in this good, urgent impulse of ours we somehow completely forgot a very important fact which no power can erase from life . . . Father Dimitry forgot, as we all did, this fact which cannot be wiped away by time or by life. And this fact is the Soviet Moscow Patriarchate. We are in no way mistaken when we call the Patriarchate Soviet . . . Such a corrupt, anti-canonical organism was not able, of course, to inspire Father Dimitry to follow the way of confession, much less of martyrdom, to the end. Father Dimitry's whole mistake is found in the fact that, although he often condemned and exposed his Soviet hierarchs, still he never separated himself from the Patriarchate as an organism, but even defended it as his own legal authority."

since it can be lifted only by a similar All-Russian Church Sobor, as the canonical supreme ecclesiastical authority.[16] And a terrifying thing happened in 1927, when the head of the Church, Metropolitan Sergius, by his infamous and apostate Declaration, subjected the Russian Church to the Bolsheviks and proclaimed collaboration with them.[17] And thus in a most exact sense was fulfilled the expression in the prayer at the beginning of Confession:[18] "having fallen under their own anathema"![19] For in 1918 the Church anathematized all the confederates of Communism, while in 1927 she herself joined the camp of these collaborators

---

[16] Some have asserted that Patriarch Tikhon (Bellavin, 1865–1925) himself subsequently retreated from this bold position and cooperated with the Soviets, and that Metropolitan Sergius's Declaration of 1927 was the logical and organic development of Patriarch Tikhon's policy. Such was not the case:

"In fact, the text of Tikhon's Epistle had been doctored. The opening of Russian archives makes it possible to ascertain that Tikhon had significantly qualified his call for obedience to the regime by adding that it was due only to the extent that its orders did not 'contradict the faith and piety (*vere i blagochestiu*).' Since in the eyes of the Church virtually all of the Communists' actions violated the tenets of Christianity, the injunction—as actually written, not as made public—had a rather hollow ring." (Richard Pipes, *Russia Under the Bolshevik Regime* [New York: Vintage Books, 1995], pp. 345–46.)

[17] Metropolitan Sergius Stragorodsky (1867–1944), one of the deputies of the *Locum tenens* of the Patriarchal Throne. On July 16/29, 1927, he issued his infamous Declaration. At a historic meeting with Stalin on Aug. 22 / Sept. 4, 1943, permission was received to convoke a Bishops' Sobor in order to elect a new "Patriarch" of Russia. Four days later, on Aug. 26/Sept. 8, the duly assembled Sobor of nineteen hastily summoned bishops chose Metropolitan Sergius to be the first Soviet Patriarch.

[18] In the Russian order for this rite, the prayer in which this phrase occurs precedes the penitent's recitation of his sins.

[19] In like manner, as Bishop Gregory [Grabbe] noted in sorrow: "Indeed, by not investigating the matter seriously and by forgetting about this previously confirmed anathematizing of the New Calendarists/Ecumenists (or perhaps not venturing to abrogate this resolution), our Sobor, as frightful as it may be to admit it, has fallen under its own anathema. Had it probed the net spread before it more carefully, it would never have issued such a contradictory Decision." (See *Tserkovnie Novosti* [*Church News*], No. 40, Sept.–Oct., 1994, pp. 2–4, and Appendix J, pp. 243-250 of the present book.)

and began to laud the red, God-hating regime—to laud the red beast spoken of in the Apocalypse.[20]

As if that is not enough. When Metropolitan Sergius promulgated his criminal Declaration, then the faithful children of the Church immediately separated themselves from the Soviet church, and thus the Catacomb Church was formed. And she, in her turn, has anathematized the official church for its betrayal of Christ.[21]

And it was within this very church of the evil-doers that the activities of Father Dimitry Dudko occurred, who has frankly declared in the press that he is not going to break with the Soviet church but will remain in her.[22] Had his spiritual eyes been open, and had he seen the true nature of the official church, he might have found within himself the courage to say: "'I have hated the congregation of evil-doers, and with the ungodly will I not sit'[23] —I am breaking off with the company of the enemies of God, and I am withdrawing from the Soviet church." Why, then for us he

---

[20] Rev. 12:3. The Moscow Patriarchate's collaboration with the godless regime was not a passive, but a very active betrayal—especially abroad, through the Peace Programs, the Ecumenical Movement, and the World Council of Churches. By denying before the whole world that the Church in Russia was undergoing persecution, by assisting in the closure and destruction of churches, by surrendering the persecuted faithful over to the Soviet authorities for supposedly "political" offenses, and by making common cause with the murderers of the true Orthodox Christians, the Moscow Patriarchate is guilty likewise of the blood of all the New Martyrs.

See the sobering account of an incident from the life of Saint Martin of Tours (as related by his biographer, Sulpitius Severus), and the commentary on it, in the article "An Evil Communion," *Orthodox Christian Witness*, Vol. 14, No. 1, 1980, pp. 1-11.

[21] See the testimony of the first Catacomb hierarch, the New Martyr, Bishop Maxim (Zhizhilenko) of Serpukhov. Vladyka Maxim also testifies to Patriarch Tikhon's true feelings about the Russian Orthodox Church Abroad. (Ivan Andreyev, *Russia's Catacomb Saints* [Platina: St. Herman of Alaska Press, 1982], pp. 52-68.)

[22] For a penetrating analysis of the case of Father Dimitry Dudko and his relation to the Soviet hierarchy, see the article "Shadows in the Midst of Light and Darkness," in *Orthodox Christian Witness*, Vol. 13, No. 38, 1980, pp. 1-18.

[23] Psalm 25:5. The word here rendered as "congregation" is, in the original Greek and Slavonic texts, *ecclesia / tserkov*, i.e., "church."

would have become one of our own—his courage would have destroyed the barrier which irrevocably stands between us by virtue of the fact that the Sobor adopted as its guiding principle the Testament of Metropolitan Anastasy.[24] For in this Testament it is ordered that we must not have any communion **whatsoever** with the Soviets, not only no communion in prayer, but not even ordinary contact in daily life.[25] But as long as Father Dimitry would have refused to remain in the Soviet pseudo-church, and would have withdrawn from membership in her—the barrier would no longer have applied to him.[26]

I recall a marvellous case of the direct and miraculous aid of God to those who remained faithful to the end. They banished a

---

[24] Metropolitan Anastasy (Gribanovsky, 1873–1965), Metropolitan Philaret's predecessor as First Hierarch of the Russian Orthodox Church Abroad.

[25] The pertinent concluding passage of the Testament reads thus:

"As regards the Moscow Patriarchate and its hierarchs, for so long as they are found in close, active, and benevolent cooperation with the Soviet regime, which openly confesses its total godlessness and strives to implant atheism in the entire Russian nation, then the Church Abroad, maintaining her purity, must not have any canonical, prayerful, or even ordinary communion with them whatsoever, at the same time leaving each one of them to the final judgment of the Sobor of the future free Russian Church."

For the full English text of Metropolitan Anastasy's Testament, see *Orthodox Life*, Vol. 15, No. 3, May-June, 1965, pp. 10–12. The Russian is found in *Pravoslavnaya Rus*, No. 10, May 15/28, 1965, pp. 1–2.

In 1980 Archbishop Vitaly was still of the same opinion, and—as though echoing Metropolitan Philaret on this point—stated in his article on Father Dimitry Dudko cited above (p. 200, note 15, of this present letter):

"Then the True Church went into the catacombs, into a position of illegal existence. From that time to this day the Soviet Moscow Patriarchate is liable to judgment, and until that future true council there can be no kind of contact, not even in everyday matters, as Metropolitan Anastasy, reposed in God, commanded us in his last will and testament."

[26] As it turned out, Father Dimitry Dudko's decision to loyally "remain with the hierarchy that has been given us" (to quote his own words), did him little good. The Moscow Patriarchate refused to lift a finger to help him. The then Metropolitan Alexis of Tallinn and Estonia (Ridiger, the present Patriarch), while on a visit to Austria, in reply to questions about the numerous recent arrests of Orthodox believers, stated: "In the Soviet Union citizens are never arrested for their religious or ideological convictions." (*Keston News Service*, Keston College, England, Issue No. 94, March 21, 1980, p. 1.)

group of nuns belonging to the Catacomb Church to Solovki.²⁷ The Chekists told them: "Get settled now, and tomorrow you will go to some sort of work." But they received an unexpected answer: "We will not go and work."

"What, have you gone out of your minds? Do you know what we will do with you?" screamed the Chekists. There followed the calm reply of people who in their faithfulness feared nothing: "What shall be, shall be—but what is pleasing unto God shall be, and not what suits you executioners and criminals. You may do with us what you please: starve us, torture us, hang, shoot, or burn us with fire. But we give you notice once and for all: we do not recognize you, you servants of Antichrist, as the lawful authority, and we will not fulfill your orders in any way! . . ."

In the morning the infuriated Chekists drove the nuns up onto the "hill of death." Thus was called a high hill where in winter an icy wind always blew. In that wind a man would freeze to death within a quarter of an hour. The nuns, clad in their shabby *rassas*, are led up the hill by Red Army men in their sheepskin coats. The nuns go happily, joyously along, chanting psalms and prayers. The soldiers left them at the top of the hill and then descended. They hear how they continue their chanting. Half hour, an hour, two, yet more—all the while the sound of chanting carries from above. Night fell. The guards approach the nuns—they are alive, unharmed, and continue chanting their prayers. The amazed soldiers led them home to the camp. News of this spread immediately throughout the entire camp. And when on the following day the guards were changed and yet the same thing happened, the camp authorities were bewildered and they left the nuns in peace . . .²⁸

Is this not a victory? Behold what it means to be faithful unto death—as the marvellous words of the Apocalypse say: "Be thou faithful unto death, and I will give thee a crown of life."²⁹ In this

---

[27] The infamous concentration camp for clergy and monastics, located in the former Solovets Monastery on islands in the White Sea.

[28] For the full account in English, see Ivan Andreyev, *Russia's Catacomb Saints* (Platina: St. Herman of Alaska Press, 1982), pp. 78–84. For the Russian, see *Pravoslavnaya Rus*, No. 3, Feb. 1/14, 1977, pp. 12–13.   [29] Rev. 2:10.

instance, it's an obvious miracle, as it was with the three youths in the Babylonian furnace, only there the death-bearing element was fire, but here a death-dealing and killing cold. Behold how God rewards faithfulness!

And hear my heartfelt conviction: if the entire mass of the many millions of Russians would evidence a like faithfulness as did those nuns, and would refuse to obey the bandits who have been oppressing the Russian nation, then Communism would collapse in a second. For the succor of God, which had saved in a miraculous manner the nuns while on their way to certain death, would come likewise to the Russian people. But as long as the nation recognizes the regime and obeys it, even if all the while cursing it in their hearts, that regime will remain in place.

Of course, the nuns were strengthened by the power of God, just as the ancient martyrs; without this aid they would not have endured. But their *podvig* [martyric exploit] was accomplished within the true Church, filled with grace and Truth. For the true Church, according to the apostolic teaching, is the **Body of Christ**—the Lord abides in her and leads her as her Divine Head.

Will anyone dare to assert that the Lord and His grace abide in the church of the evil-doers,[30] which lauds His demonized enemies and collaborates with them, which because of this is found under a twofold anathema, as indicated above? Can a church which has united with the God-haters possess grace?! The answer is obvious!

The hierarch Theophan the Recluse[31] in his own day warned that a terrible time was approaching when people would behold before their eyes all the appearance of church grandeur—solemn services, church order, and such—while on the inside there would be total betrayal of the Spirit of Christ. Is this not what we see in the Soviet church? Patriarchs, Metropolitans, all the priestly and

---

[30] This harks back to Psalm 25:5, "the congregation of evil-doers" cited earlier.

[31] Bishop Theophan (Gorov, 1815–1891), glorified as a saint by the Moscow Patriarchate in 1988.

monastic orders—and at the very same time, an alliance with the God-haters, that is, a manifest betrayal of Christ.[32]

To this company belongs also Father Dimitry Dudko. Of course, his sincere religious feelings compelled him to preach concerning God and not to condone many of the disgraceful happenings in the lives of Russian people. But for him, Pimen was, and likely still is, his spiritual head, the head of the Soviet hierarchy; while for us it is not at all so. For our Sobor in 1971 passed a resolution: on the basis of such and such canons to consider the election of Pimen as unlawful and invalid, and to consider all his acts and decrees as having no force or significance.[33]

How difficult is poor Father Dimitry Dudko's position now! What is he to do? Continue his pastoral work? And what can he say to the faithful? Say the same thing that he said before his

---

[32] Even pious and astute laymen within the Moscow Patriarchate came to realize that her hierarchs were "betraying the Church not out of fear, but for conscience' sake," to quote Boris Talantov, one of the authors of the famous "Open Letter of the Kirov Believers to Patriarch Alexis" which so enraged Metropolitan Nikodim (Rotov, 1929–1978) of sorry memory. In June of 1969 Boris Talantov was arrested and later sentenced to two years in prison for "anti-Soviet activities." He died in prison in January 1971. See his exposé, "The Leaven of Herod," by B. Talantov, *Orthodox Word*, Vol. 7, No. 6, Nov.–Dec. 1971, pp. 273–293. Concerning Metropolitan Nikodim, see "On the Death of a Soviet Bishop," *Orthodox Christian Witness*, Vol. 12, No. 10, 1978, pp. 1–8.

[33] This Bishops' Sobor met in September of 1971 in Montreal. One of the issues which it discussed was the election, in June of 1971, of Metropolitan Pimen (Izvekov, 1910–1990) as "Patriarch" of Russia. The pertinent passage of this resolution, signed by all the hierarchs present, reads thus:

"Therefore, elections of patriarchs performed in another manner [i.e., than the Sobor of 1917] which is not free, do not express the voice of the Russian Orthodox Church and are not lawful. Not only the election of the present Pimen, calling himself patriarch, but likewise the elections of his two predecessors must also be considered unlawful.... All the elections of the Patriarchs of Moscow, beginning in 1943, are invalid on the basis of the Thirtieth Canon of the Holy Apostles, and the Third Canon of the Seventh Ecumenical Council..."

If Sergius, Alexis, and Pimen were unlawful "hierarchs," then what can be said of the "ordinations" and the other "mysteries" performed by them? If both his predecessors were invalid, what of Pimen's own "ordination" to the priesthood and episcopacy? Manifestly, neither they, nor those ordained by them, have any grace to impart to anyone.

"repentance"? But then, he has already renounced this! Say the opposite? Why, they believed him before when he preached that which won for him the trust and respect of the faithful—and now, how will he look them in the face? One girl correctly said that there is one way out for him: make a genuine repentance in atonement for the one he just now made. But in order to do that he must depart from the church of the evil-doers for the true Church, and there make his repentance. However, in return, the red church will undoubtedly deal with him with particular malice and cruelty. Of course, by crossing over to the true Church, he will pass over into the realm of Divine grace and strength, which can fortify him just as it fortified those catacomb nuns. God grant that he find the true and saving path.

I should also like to note the following. The Catacomb Church in Russia relates to the Church Abroad with love and total confidence. However, one thing is incomprehensible to the Catacomb Christians: they can't understand why our Church, which realizes beyond a doubt that the Soviet hierarchy has betrayed Christ and is no longer a bearer of grace, nevertheless receives clergy of the Soviet church in their existing orders, not re-ordaining them, as ones already having grace. For the clergy and flock receive grace from the hierarchy, and if it [the hierarchy] has betrayed the Truth and deprived itself of grace, from where then does the clergy have grace? It is along these lines that the Catacomb Christians pose the question.

The answer to this is simple. The Church has the authority in certain cases to employ the principle of *economia*—condescension. The hierarch Saint Basil the Great said that, in order not to drive many away from the Church, it is necessary sometimes to permit condescension and not apply the church canons in all their severity. When our Church accepted Roman Catholic clergy "in their orders," without ordaining them, she acted according to this principle.[34] And Metropolitan Anthony [Khrapovitsky],

---

[34] Note that here Metropolitan Philaret put the words *in their orders* within quotation marks, as if to emphasize their invalidity.

elucidating this issue, pointed out that the outward form—successive ordination from Apostolic times—*that* the Roman Catholics do have; whereas the grace, which the Roman Catholic church has lost, is received by those uniting [themselves to the Church] from the plenitude of grace present in the Orthodox Church, at the very moment of their joining. "The form is filled with content," said Vladyka Anthony.[35]

In precisely the same manner, in receiving the Soviet clergy, we apply the principle of *economia*. And we receive the clergymen from Moscow not as ones possessing grace, but as ones receiving it by the very act of union. But to recognize the church of the evil-doers as the bearer and repository of grace, that we cannot do, of course. For outside of Orthodoxy there is **no grace**; and the Soviet church has deprived itself of grace.[36]

In concluding my lengthy letter, I should like to point several things out to you, Father. The Bishops' Sobor resolved to be guided by and to fulfill the Testament of Metropolitan Anastasy, in which the late First Hierarch bade us not to have any communion with the Soviet church whatsoever, not only no prayerful commu-

---

[35] In an earlier letter written to Mother Magdalena, Abbess of Lesna Convent, Metropolitan Philaret had quoted Metropolitan Anthony as having specifically referred to the Roman Catholics as heretics (*Tserkovnie Novosti* [*Church News*], No. 58, Feb. 1997). See Appendix C above.

At the same Bishops' Sobor of 1971, mentioned above by Metropolitan Philaret, it was resolved, in view of the growing confusion caused by Ecumenism concerning the true boundaries of the Church, to follow henceforth the stricter practice and baptize all heretics who come to the Church. For the full text of this resolution and an excellent exposition by the then Father George Grabbe on the application of strictness and *economia*, see *Orthodox Life*, Vol. 29, No. 2, March–April, 1979, pp. 35–43. The text of this resolution had also appeared earlier in *Orthodox Word*, Vol. 7, No. 6, Nov.–Dec. 1971, pp. 294–301.

[36] That this is not merely the personal opinion of Metropolitan Philaret can be ascertained from a perusal of the writings of many of the hierarchs of the Catacomb Church and of the ROCA. For an excellent survey and analysis of this material, see the two-part series in *Orthodox Christian Witness*, "Worse Than Any Heresy," *OCW*, Vol. 15, No. 28, 1982, pp. 1-16; and "A Sequel," *OCW*, Vol. 15, No. 34, 1982, pp. 1–10.

nion, but not even ordinary contact.[37] On what basis then have you and other clergymen had direct relations with Father Dudko? And have written him letters, etc.? No matter how sincere a man you[38] may have considered him to be, nevertheless, can your private opinion annul a ruling adopted by the Church? Now, had Father Dudko said: I am breaking with the official church and leaving her—then you could have entered into lively contact with him. But in the absence of that, your actions constitute a violation of ecclesiastical discipline. Dudko wrote to me personally, but I did not answer him—although I could have said

---

[37] The Third Pan-Diaspora Sobor of 1974 paraphrased this passage from Metropolitan Anastasy's Testament in its Resolution No. V (*Pravoslavnaya Rus*, No. 21, Nov. 1/14, 1974, pp. 12–13).

In its *Epistle to the Flock,* signed by all eighteen hierarchs present, the Bishops' Sobor of 1976 again makes mention of this passage:

"Our Church Abroad, as is well known, constitutes a part of the Russian Mother-Church, her free part. Although we, following the Testament of His Beatitude, Metropolitan Anastasy, of blessed memory, have no communion whatsoever with the Moscow Patriarchate; yet we have never broken with the Russian Church, our Mother-Church." (*Pravoslavnaya Rus,* No. 21, Nov. 1/14, 1976, pp. 1–4.)

In an earlier epistle written by Metropolitan Philaret on behalf of the hierarchy, and in response to Alexander Solzhenitsyn's letter to the Third Pan-Diaspora Sobor, the First Hierarch speculated on what might be the future role of the ROCA in Russia:

"Your fear that we are counting on returning to Russia as some sort of judges or commanders can only be attributed to a misunderstanding or to disinformation which someone has foisted upon you. We know of no one amongst us with such thoughts. But if the liberation of Russia should take place and we could be reunited with a restored Orthodox and canonical authority, then we would assume that we are a part of the Russian hierarchy. We simply have not considered how much weight we would carry in such an event. Numerically the flock abroad is a drop in the sea when compared with the ocean of the Russian nation" (*Pravoslavnaya Rus*, No. 19, Oct. 1/14, 1974, pp. 5–6).

[38] Here, and in the two following sentences, the Metropolitan has switched from the singular *thou* to the plural *you* in order to indicate that these passages refer to both the recipient of this letter and his like-minded fellow clergymen.

much.[39] By the way, on what basis did you,[40] even before this, take it into your head to commemorate an archbishop of the Soviet church during the Great Entrance? Who gave you the right to do that, which hierarch—who, how, where, when? . . . Be more careful, my dear, zealous, but, ah, too impetuous fellow minister!

Peace to you and the mercy of the Lord. To Matushka and the children too.

With love,
✟ Metropolitan Philaret

---

[39] For the full English translation of Father Dimitry Dudko's letter to Metropolitan Philaret, see *Orthodox Life*, Vol. 29, No. 6, 1979, pp. 28–30. This is followed by a lengthy, related article by Bishop Gregory [Grabbe] entitled: "The Russian Church in the Wilderness and in this World," pp. 31–44.

It should be noted here that the editorial introduction to Father Dimitry Dudko's letter makes the following statement:

> "In an exchange of correspondence which took place between the Synod's Archbishop Anthony [Bartoshevich] of Geneva and Father Dudko, the archbishop allayed Father Dimitry's fears somewhat by informing him that the Synod does not in fact deny that there is grace in the mysteries of the Soviet [*sic*] Patriarchate, accepts baptisms performed by its clerics, and has even received certain priests into its own fold. Father Dudko replied that he himself had evidently fallen victim to misinformation concerning the true state of affairs, supplied him by 'friends,' and expressed his continued and abiding respect for the Synod's official stance . . . ."

As can be seen from all that Metropolitan Philaret has written above, this statement is simply not true. It would appear that it is the editors themselves, and *not* Father Dimitry Dudko, who have "evidently fallen victim to misinformation concerning the true state of affairs."

[40] Here the Metropolitan reverts to the singular *thou*.

APPENDIX E

Reflections on Metropolitan Vitaly's Nativity Epistle[1]

At the present time the majority of local Churches have been shaken throughout by a dreadful twofold blow: the new calendar and the heresy of Ecumenism. Despite this lamentable situation, however, we dare not assert (and may God preserve us from this; for such is the duty only of an Ecumenical Council!) that they are devoid of the grace of God. We have pronounced an anathema upon the heresy of Ecumenism for the benefit of the faithful of our Church alone, yet we thereby also call upon the local Churches (in a modest but firm, gentle but decisive manner) to give serious thought to the implication of our action. This is the role of our small, modest, somewhat persecuted, but always vigilant, true Church. *De facto*, we can celebrate neither with new calendarists, nor with the Ecumenists; but if any one of our clergy, indulging in ecclesiastical leniency [*"economia"* is the term used in the original Russian text], has ventured to take part in such a celebration, this isolated fact in no way affects our stand for the truth.

(From the "Nativity Epistle" of Metropolitan Vitaly, 1986)

It was with deep sadness that we read Metropolitan Vitaly's Nativity Epistle for 1986. It was a more substantive document than is normal for such epistles, and was evidently a sincere statement of His Eminence's understanding of our Orthodox Faith and its opposition to Ecumenism. And that is the source of our sorrow, for the Epistle showed that his theology and understanding of terms is not the same as that which we have learned from our Fathers in the Faith, including the late Metropolitan Philaret.

In this Epistle, His Eminence introduces a different meaning into the term "anathema": he speaks of an anathema as an invitation to the other local Orthodox Churches to "give serious thought" in regard to the heresy of Ecumenism; but was this

---

[1] *Orthodox Christian Witness*, Feb. 16 / March 1, 1987.

not the function of our late Metropolitan Philaret's sequence of Sorrowful Epistles? According to Saint Nicodemos of the Holy Mountain in his commentary on the canons, an "anathema" is precisely a statement that those who follow or promulgate this teaching are cut off from God, that is, outside the Church. In his Epistle to the Galatians (1:8-9), the Apostle Paul uses the word "anathema" in this same meaning. An anathema is not an admonition or a warning at all; it is the final act after all admonitions and warnings have been ignored. One might argue that the Russian Orthodox Church Outside Russia should not have pronounced such an anathema, saying that this is a prerogative of an Ecumenical Council (even though such an assertion does not stand historically); but one cannot deny that it did pronounce an anathema against Ecumenism, and that this anathema implies that the Church has clearly exhausted all other means of recourse and has marked its boundaries from the heresy it condemns. Once an anathema has been pronounced, then by implication all ties in prayer and Mysteries with those who profess the condemned heresy must stop. Otherwise, the anathema is simply empty of meaning. If communion in sacred things is not stopped, then the anathema is not even an admonition or a warning, since those issuing it are seen not to be serious about it. His Eminence wishes to view the anathema only as a warning, an interpretation not supported by the clear meaning of the term; but even as a warning, it has value only if his church takes it seriously and ceases all contacts in prayer and Mysteries with those who are guilty of what is condemned in the anathema.

His Eminence further states that the Russian Orthodox Church Outside Russia does not now and never will declare that there is no grace in the other local Orthodox Churches. We can agree that such a judgment is a fearful one and is best left to God; but safety and common sense require that when we see the local churches departing from the Orthodox Faith, we should cut off all ties with them to protect our flock. If a parent even thinks a food might be poisoned, will he give it to his children? No, he will take no chances with the health of his little ones when the food seems doubtful, considering it better to err on the side of prudence. How much more, then, should this apply to the spiritual food of the Holy Mysteries! And, in fact, the practice of the Russian Orthodox Church Outside Russia in recent years can only be understood logically if we assume that it does not deny that at least some of the local churches have separated from the Church of Christ, and, at the least it has assumed that their possession of grace is questionable. Over the last fifteen or more years the Russian Orthodox Church Outside Russia has repeatedly accepted clergymen from other local churches, even though those clergymen had no releases from those churches. In fact, many of these clergymen were suspended and eventually deposed by the local churches from which they came, but the Russian Orthodox Church Outside Russia ignored these suspensions and depositions, since the clergymen left their previous jurisdictions because of heresy in those churches. Priests and deacons have been received into the Russian Orthodox Church Outside Russia from the Greek Archdiocese, the Syrian Antiochian Church, and the Orthodox Church in America. In one case, a Uniate Roman Catholic priest, Father John (George) Lewis, was received into the OCA as a priest; when he joined the Russian Orthodox Church Outside Russia several years later, he was baptized and then ordained to the diaconate and priesthood in that church. There could hardly be a clearer statement that the Russian Orthodox Church Outside Russia considers the OCA to be in heresy. Unless the Russian Orthodox Church Outside Russia has considered the other local churches to be at least to some degree in heresy and cut off from the true Church, it should never have received clergymen from those churches who were protesting the heresy found in those bodies. Since it nevertheless did accept them with a disregard for normal canonical procedures, the Russian Orthodox Church Outside Russia at least implied that they were cut off from the Church of Christ. This implication was then made plain in the statement of the "anathema" applied to the teachings and actions which these protesting clergymen rejected when they left other local Orthodox churches and joined the Russian Orthodox Church Outside Russia.

His Eminence states that the Russian Orthodox Church Outside Russia *de facto* does not concelebrate with the other local churches, but here he is unfortunately in error. *In principle* the clergy of the Russian Orthodox Church Outside Russia should not concelebrate with those of other local churches, but *in fact* (the meaning of *de facto*) they do concelebrate. The Russian Orthodox Church Outside Russia has explicitly forbidden communion in prayer or Mysteries with the OCA and the Moscow Patriarchate, even stating that the latter had left the Orthodox Church by admitting Roman Catholics to Communion. By the anathema, it has also implicitly forbidden concelebration with all local Orthodox churches involved in the Ecumenical Movement, which should logically include at least all members of the World Council of Churches. But in fact, such concelebration not only occurs, it is reported in semi-official Synod publications, for example, *Pravoslavnaya Rus* for 1/14 January 1986. His Eminence argues that such concelebration does not affect the Synod's standing for the truth, but in actuality it does. When public acts of error occur, they must be rebuked publicly to avoid confusing the faithful and teaching them error by example. When even bishops serve with or in other local churches (as many as five Synod bishops do so), and there is no public rebuke or disavowal of their actions, the implication is that there is no difference between the Russian Orthodox Church Outside Russia and the churches with which they are serving. Serving together implies the same faith; but if the faith is the same, then what has happened to the anathema? Is it not made a dead letter, devoid of all meaning when even the bishops of the Russian Orthodox Church Outside Russia violate it without censure? One of the firmest rules of the Church states that the "law of prayer determines the law of belief;" if this is so, then sharing in prayer certainly speaks more strongly of a church's beliefs than do high-sounding words which are ignored in practice. His Eminence would be right in saying that isolated acts would not affect the Russian Orthodox Church Outside Russia's standing in the truth if those acts were promptly and publicly repudiated by the Church, but when they are ignored or tacitly condoned, they become the *de facto* position of that church.

Metropolitan Vitaly's understanding of the concept of economy in his Nativity Epistle is, unfortunately, also different from ours. As normally understood, economy means that the Church permits its priests and bishops to use condescension in admitting people to membership in the Church or in reconciling them to the Church when they have fallen away through sin or heresy. But the critical point is that it can only be applied when the person is *returning* or *entering into union* with the Church of Christ; it is used then to ease his return or admission to Communion in the Body of Christ. Economy cannot be used to confirm a heretic in his errors by acting as if he were already in the Church when he is not. The acts His Eminence is referring to involve cases where clergymen of the Russian Orthodox Church Outside Russia have served, or serve, in churches belonging to other jurisdictions or allow members of other jurisdictions to serve or receive the Mysteries in Synod parishes when they have no intention of leaving their jurisdictions and joining the Russian Orthodox Church Outside Russia. If this is economy, then the Russian Orthodox Church Outside Russia might just as logically start admitting Anglicans and Roman Catholics to the Mysteries in its parishes. Experience has shown beyond doubt that people are brought to awareness of the errors in their own churches only when they are denied participation in the Mysteries by those who wish to preserve Orthodoxy. When they are admitted to the Mysteries while remaining in their own jurisdictions and, even more, when they see Synod clergymen serving in their churches or with their clergymen, they are taught that there is no real difference between their jurisdictions and the Russian Orthodox Church Outside Russia. This same message is given to the faithful of the Russian Orthodox Church Outside Russia by such concelebrations.

We have always loved and respected Metropolitan Vitaly, and we will not cease loving him and praying for him now. But we also now see that he and those with him in the Russian Orthodox Church Outside Russia at this time simply do not have the same theology that we do. We believe that an anathema has a certain, definite, historical meaning; they do not. We believe that accepting clergymen from the other local Orthodox churches for reasons of conscience implies that those churches are in heresy; they do not. We believe that repeated, unrebuked, public concelebrations with heretics confuses the faithful and destroys a church's witness to the truth, since the "law of prayer" is more significant than fine words; they do not. We believe that economy can only be used to help people into the Ark of Salvation, not to discourage them from coming because there is no need for it if they wish to receive the Church's Mysteries; they do not. We believe that our understanding agrees with what we have been taught by such instructors as Saint Nicodemos of the Holy Mountain, Archbishops Hilarion (Troitsky) and Averky (Taushev), and Metropolitan Philaret in his "Sorrowful Epistles." We intend to remain faithful to this teaching which we have received, refusing to change it "even if an angel from Heaven should preach a different Gospel."

APPENDIX F

Monophysitism and the Orthodox Church "Let Them Resist"[1]

There came into my hands two old calendarist booklets that spoke about the "betrayal of Orthodoxy" on the part of us, the [new calendar] Orthodox Churches. These booklets refer to the "Agreed Statement" of the "Joint Commission of the Theological Dialogue" between the Orthodox Church and the Oriental Orthodox Churches (Chambesy, Geneva; 23–28 September, 1990).

My curiosity was aroused and I looked up the Minutes of this Agreed Statement of the "Joint Committee." Well, I really got scared. Those who present themselves as representatives of the Orthodox Catholic Church seemed to me to have dared to do that which is not permissible. They propose that the local Orthodox Churches countersign what they themselves signed with those who are evident heterodox and Monophysites. I say "evident

---

[1] Translated from the new calendar Greek periodical, *I Drasis Mas*, November 1991, and published in *Orthodox Christian Witness,* July 6/19, 1992.

heterodox" because, in paragraph eight of their Agreed Statement, I read the following:

> Both families accept the first three Ecumenical Councils, which form our common heritage. In relation to the four later Councils of the Orthodox Church, the Orthodox state that *for them* the above points 1-7 [of the "Second Agreed Statement"] are the teachings also of the four later Councils of the Orthodox Church, while the Oriental Orthodox consider this statement of the Orthodox as *their* interpretation. With this understanding, the Oriental Orthodox respond to it positively.[2]

What is this twisted and obscure Agreed Statement saying? Let us try to decode it so that it may become clearly evident that perhaps the old calendarists are not exaggerating when they speak about a betrayal of Orthodoxy, regardless of whether this betrayal is conscious or not.[3]

Well then, this text does not accept the 4th, 5th, 6th and 7th Ecumenical Councils—because, what do we read in it? "Both families accept the first three Ecumenical Councils." They do not deign to call "the other four" by their name "Ecumenical," but they merely refer to them condescendingly as "the four later Councils of the Orthodox Church."

Then, even without the term "Ecumenical," do they accept those Councils or not? Do the Monophysites accept their decisions? Things are crystal clear: they do not accept them. Even the representatives of the Orthodox accept them only because, in their estimation and opinion, the "four later Councils" are in agreement with paragraphs 1-7 of the Second Agreed Statement, which the "Joint Commission of the Theological Dialogue" formulated, giving itself super-Ecumenical authority.

What do the Monophysites—or Monothelites—reply [to the Orthodox statement that the first part of the Agreed Statement is

---

[2] All italics in this and the following article have been added by the editors.

[3] *Editors' Note:* This statement is perplexing. Is the author saying that the new calendar theologians do not really understand this Agreed Statement that they themselves have prepared; or does it mean that they signed it while being unconscious?

the teaching of the "four later Councils" also]? They reply: "What you are saying is your *own* interpretation. Keep it. We allow you." Very well, we keep it, but do *you* accept it? No reply. Or rather, there is a reply couched in convoluted terms: "With this understanding, the Oriental Orthodox respond to it positively." In other words, absolutely nothing.

And now we come to the conclusion: What do the World Council of Churches (the inspirer of this dialogue), or international Freemasonry, or worldly "diplomacy" (which—though profane—presumes to enter into our holy of holies), or the naive Orthodox who walk without fear in this minefield—what do all these institutions and individuals imagine? Do they imagine that there will not appear another Mark Eugenicus,[4] who with heroic faith will overturn this unacceptable and defeatist concoction of Chambesy? Are there no young Orthodox warriors who will defend the Orthodoxy of the Seven, Holy, God-inspired and immutable Ecumenical Councils of eternal authority?

I believe that there are. Let them stand up and resist—quickly!

S. Aspirtis

✳ ✳ ✳

Editors' Note: Despite the concerns expressed by the new calendar writer above, the "Holy Synod of Antioch" under Patriarch Ignatius IV of Antioch has already issued directives regarding its relations with the Monophysite "Syriac Patriarchate" (*The Word*, April 1992). Here are some highlights:

> The Holy Synod of Antioch has decided the following matters:
>
> 1) The complete and mutual respect between the two churches for their rituals, spirituality, heritage *and holy fathers.*
>
> 3) The refraining from accepting members of one church in the membership of the other, whatever the reasons might be.
>
> 6) If two bishops of the two different churches meet for a spiritual service, the one with the majority of the people will generally preside. But if the service is the sacrament of holy

---

[4] I.e., Saint Mark of Ephesus.

matrimony, the bishop of the church of the bridegroom will preside.

9) If one priest of either church happens to be in a certain area, he will serve the divine mysteries for the members of both churches, *including the divine liturgy . . .*

The Patriarchate of Antioch has made it clear that these directives are in force only with the "Syriac Patriarchate" in the Near East. This is equivalent to saying that we are in communion with the Roman Catholic Church only in the Province of Quebec!

APPENDIX G

An Encyclical on the "Summit Message"

TO THE BELOVED AND PIOUS PRIESTS, DEACONS, MONASTICS, AND FAITHFUL FLOCK OF OUR TRUE ORTHODOX CHRISTIAN CHURCH.

In the Name of the Father, the Son, and the Holy Spirit. Amen.

My beloved brethren and children in the Lord,

It was with great sorrow that we read the *Summit Message* of the "Primates of the Orthodox Churches" who gathered in the Phanar in Constantinople, on the Sunday of Orthodoxy, the fifteenth of March, 1992 (according to the new calendar).

This *Message* was signed and issued at an unprecedented meeting, in which virtually all of the heads of the autocephalous churches were gathered.

Since it is an official document, it would be of profit to examine some important aspects of this *Summit Message,* so that we may discover its full implications.

The Question of Proselytism

One significant paragraph of the *Summit Message* reads as follows:

> We remind all that every form of proselytism—to be distinguished clearly from evangelization and mission—is absolutely

condemned by the Orthodox. Proselytism, practiced in nations already Christian, and in many cases even Orthodox, sometimes through material enticement and sometimes by various forms of violence, poisons the relations among Christians and destroys the road toward their unity. Mission, in contrast, carried out in non-Christian countries and among non-Christian peoples, constitutes a sacred duty of the Church, worthy of every assistance. Such Orthodox missionary work is carried out today in Asia and Africa, and is worthy of every Pan-Orthodox and Pan-Christian support.

The *Summit Message* distinguishes between proselytism and mission. Mission, it says, is "carried out among non-Christian peoples . . . in Asia and Africa." This type of missionary work "is worthy of every Pan-Orthodox and Pan-Christian support." Proselytism, on the other hand, which is practiced "in nations already Christian, and in many cases even Orthodox," is "absolutely condemned."

Both proselytism and mission involve converting people of one faith to another faith. Why is one "worthy of every support" and the other "absolutely condemned"? The *Summit Message* itself answers this question: Mission involves converting "non-Christian peoples" to Christianity. This type of work, which is carried out in Asia and Africa, is a "sacred duty of the Church." Proselytism, on the other hand, practiced "in nations already Christian, and in many cases even Orthodox," involves converting Christians of one denomination to another. Why is this wrong? Because it "poisons the relations among Christians and destroys the road toward their unity."

We read this *Summit Message* with grief because we saw that a great opportunity to witness to the unadulterated and Holy Orthodox Faith was lost. In these days, despite the fact that our society holds truth and morality to be relative, many are searching to find an absolute criterion of what is true and false, and what is right and wrong. But the message that most hear today is that truth, if it exists at all, is a matter of personal opinion. One will hear such sentiments as, "It does not make any difference what one believes, just as long as one is a good person." Yet, it is here, exactly, that we find a very great fallacy: one's beliefs are what determine for each person what is good and what is evil, what is right and what is wrong.

One will act according to what one believes is right or wrong, truth or falsehood. If one believes that there is no right or wrong, truth or falsehood, one will act accordingly. Our society reflects this "private interpretation" of morality (or amorality): "abortion rights," "pro-choice," "gay rights," "euthanasia rights." If truth is relative, then morality—which is the reflection of the truths we uphold—is also relative. As Dostoyevsky writes in *The Brothers Karamazov*, "If there is no God, then all things are permissible." If it does not make any difference what one believes, then belief—or unbelief—is irrelevant. As a consequence, so is morality.

Yet, beyond all expectation, we see that the *Summit Message* promotes this very mentality, this notion of a multiplicity of "truths." How so? If we examine this matter further, it will become apparent that we are here dealing with a new theology.

A New Theology that Leads to an Erosion of Witness to Orthodoxy

Although this new theology we speak of has never received such an official episcopal endorsement as in the *Summit Message*, it has already been articulated elsewhere. For example, the well-known academic theologian, John Karmiris, of the School of Theology of the University of Athens, wrote the following in his book, *Ecclesiology*:

> Even as there is one God the Father, and one Christ, and one Holy Spirit, in like manner, by the power of this unity, the Church also is one, and unique, and united in the presence of the Triune God, in Whose name all her members are baptized, thereby gaining justification for themselves, regardless of what confession [of Faith] they belong to, united with Christ and with one another in one body, which cannot be divided into many bodies.
>
> (*Ecclesiology*, Athens, 1973, p. 241)

Two years later, in 1975, at the World Council of Churches General Assembly in Nairobi, the Orthodox delegates, reflecting this new mentality, were already hinting at their disapproval of proselytism:

The Orthodox do not expect that other Christians be converted to Orthodoxy in its historic and cultural reality of the past and the present and to become members of the Orthodox Church.[1]

Recently, the practice of converting those of other Christian denominations has been disparaged more explicitly. In the Athenian newspaper *Bema* (March 1, 1992), Metropolitan Nektarios, the new calendar Bishop of Kalymnos, wrote the following:

> Even when hundreds of Roman Catholic priests abandoned the priesthood and their Church during the past three decades, the Orthodox Eastern Church systematically avoided receiving them into her bosom in order to avoid poisoning her relations with the elder Church of Rome. And when whole parishes in Europe, in Italy, for example, wished to embrace Orthodoxy, once again, we discreetly shut the door to them. Since Orthodoxy is persuaded that she does not need proselytism, she preferred to leave these thousands of former Roman Catholics by themselves and without guidance . . .

Here we have a more blatant application of the new theology now officially articulated in the *Summit Message*. Thousands of Roman Catholics who were pleading to be accepted into the Church had the door "discreetly shut to them"! Plainly and simply they were told, "You are not wanted. We prefer to leave you by yourselves, abandoned and without any pastoral or theological guidance (since it does not make any difference 'what confession of faith one belongs to'). If you join us, it will only poison our relations with Rome and upset the ecumenical dialogue."

From these developments, one can easily see that, for these men of the cloth, interdenominational relations and the ecumenical dialogue are more important than doctrinal truth. It makes no difference that the Pope affirms repeatedly that the papacy is a gift

---

[1] Quoted by Rev. Robert C. Stephanopoulos, "The Inter-Church Relations of the Orthodox Church," *A Companion to the Greek Orthodox Church* (New York: Department of Communication, Greek Orthodox Archdiocese of North and South America, 1984), p. 213.

from God and that the doctrine of papal infallibility is irrevocable. What is paramount are interchurch relations and the ecumenical dialogue.

This lack of concern for doctrinal truth is demonstrating itself in other quarters as well.

Further Developments

In January of 1986, Greek Orthodox, Roman Catholic, and Protestant leaders met in Boston, Massachusetts, and jointly signed "The Greater Boston Church Leaders' Covenant," an agreement among thirteen local church bodies "to manifest more clearly the oneness of the Body of Christ." Among the clergymen who signed this "Covenant" were Bishop Methodios of the new calendar Greek Archdiocese of North and South America; the local Roman Catholic cardinal; the Lutheran, Methodist, and Episcopalian bishops; ministers of the United Church of Christ, the Baptist Church, the Presbyterian Church, and the Salvation Army; an executive from the Massachusetts "Council of Churches;" and a Unitarian minister.

We know that the above-mentioned denominations espouse many divergent teachings. Some even reject Christian doctrines, such as the Divine nature, Virgin Birth, bodily Resurrection, and Ascension of Christ, to mention only a few. Yet, no matter what they believe—or do not believe—they are all esteemed "Christian" members of the Body of Christ, and, as such, we are not to proselytize them, that is, strive to convert them to the Orthodox Faith, according to the principles laid down by the *Summit Message*.[2] What is especially noteworthy is that the Unitarians were included

---

[2] At this point, it would be profitable to know what the Saints of the Church teach concerning the use of the name "Christian." In his work, *On the Holy Spirit* (chapter 17, paragraphs 130-1), Saint Ambrose of Milan writes the following: "'Not everyone,' He says, 'that saith to me Lord, Lord, shall enter into the Kingdom of Heaven.' Although many call themselves Christians, they usurp the name and do not have the reward.... Let not the Arians flatter themselves by the name which they have usurped, because they say that they are Christians. The Lord will reply to them: 'You put forth My name, and you deny My substance; but ... I do not recognize My name where I do not recognize My doctrine.'"

in this Boston Covenant, in spite of the fact that a recent survey prepared for the Unitarian Universalist Association in America found that only 15% of the Unitarian membership considered themselves Christians. According to one newspaper report, another Unitarian minister stated that his work as a clergyman is not impeded by the fact that he is an atheist! This, indeed, is something new and unheard-of: non-Christians and even ministers who do not believe in God can now be considered members of the Body of Christ!

The inclusion of the Unitarians in the "Body of Christ" reveals the true nature of the new theology that is now emanating from those Orthodox who are so deeply involved and committed to the heresy of Ecumenism. This new theology also explains the "absolute condemnation" of proselytism expressed in the *Summit Message*.

Nor Does Such a Policy of Weakness Stop at a Condemnation of Proselytism

What is, indeed, even more grievous is that this new theology is beginning to evolve into a New Age Theology. The *Summit Message* affirms that "mission, carried out in non-Christian countries and among non-Christian peoples, constitutes a sacred duty of the Church. . . . Such missionary work is carried out today in Asia and Africa."

But only a short time ago, one of the leading Patriarchs of "World Orthodoxy," Parthenios of Alexandria, publicly affirmed that:

> The prophet Mohammed is an apostle. He is a man of God, who worked for the Kingdom of God and created Islam, a religion to which belong one billion people. . . . Our God is the Father of all men, even of the Moslems and Buddhists. I believe that God loves the Moslems and the Buddhists. . . . When I speak against Islam or Buddhism, then I am not found in agreement with God.

If we are "not in agreement with God" when we speak against Islam or Buddhism, then . . . ?

*Earlier Orthodox Statements were Ones of Strength,
Following the Church's Traditional Exposition*

All these recent doctrinal aberrations and developments in the realm of Ecumenism stand in sharp contrast to the Church's traditional teaching concerning the conversion of the heterodox. As Orthodox Catholic Christians, we have always been taught that the Church *is* already one, and that the Holy Orthodox Church *is* the One, Holy, Catholic, and Apostolic Church. She is the undivided Body of Christ. Unity has always been understood as meaning that people of other religions and denominations would unite themselves to the Orthodox Church of Christ. This, in fact, is precisely what the Orthodox delegates pointed out at the World Council of Churches "Faith and Order Conference" in Oberlin, Ohio, in September of 1957:

> It is not due to our personal merit, but to divine condescension that we represent the Orthodox Church and are able to give expression to her claims. We are bound in conscience to state explicitly what is logically inferred: that all other bodies have been directly or indirectly separated from the Orthodox Church. Unity from the Orthodox standpoint means a return of the separated bodies to the historical Orthodox and Catholic and Apostolic Church.

Elsewhere in this statement the delegates affirmed that:

> The Orthodox Church teaches that the unity of the Church has not been lost, because she is the Body of Christ, and, as such, can never be divided.

This statement is clear and unambiguous: The Orthodox Church—i.e., the One, Holy, Catholic, and Apostolic Church—is the Body of Christ, and therefore cannot be divided. "Unity" means the return (i.e., conversion) of the separated bodies to this one, undivided Church.

The *Summit Message,* on the other hand, teaches us that proselytism—that is, the conversion of Christians belonging to "separated bodies"—is "absolutely condemned."

What has happened?

It is obvious that the *Summit Message*—signed by the Patriarchs of Serbia and of Jerusalem, as well as virtually all of the heads of the autocephalous Churches—proclaims an official change in doctrine.

The Orthodox delegates at Oberlin—and more pertinently, all the Saints and Confessors of the Church of Christ in ages past—identified the Holy Orthodox Church with the Body of Christ: both are one and the same. The hierarchs that gathered recently in Constantinople, in contrast, believe that members of other denominations should not be proselytized because they are already Christians, and hence, members of the Body of Christ.

The Branch Theory

The only reason we try to convert another person to our faith is because we believe that our faith is true and his is erroneous. Since the *Summit Message* "absolutely condemns" proselytism, this can only mean that the beliefs of the heterodox—no matter how divergent, or contradictory, or erroneous they may be—are somehow pleasing to God, or, at least, they are not so serious as to warrant our concern; therefore, we *must not* try to convert these people to Orthodoxy. In fact, it is *wrong* for us to do so.

But this is a renunciation of what Saint Paul the Apostle proclaimed to the Ephesians: "One Lord, *One Faith*, One Baptism."

Further, it is an adoption of the "Branch Theory."

The Branch Theory, which teaches that all churches and denominations are "branches" of the one great Church of Christ, was devised in the nineteenth century by Englishmen who wished to claim their place in the historic One, Holy, Catholic, and Apostolic Church while yet remaining Anglicans. Since all the "branches" differ from one another in faith, doctrinal truth plays an inconsequential role in this theory.

It is the same with the multiconfessional "Body of Christ." Since doctrines and beliefs are not taken into account, all denominations can be members of this Body. A proof of this is the fact that even Orthodox and Unitarians can belong.

But this is in direct contradiction to what the Saints of the

Church teach us regarding the Church and right belief. Here, for example, is what Saint Maximus the Confessor says concerning this matter:

> Christ the Lord called that Church the Catholic Church which maintains the true and saving confession of the Faith.[3]

And Saint Gregory Palamas affirms that:

> They that are of the Church of Christ are they that are of the truth; and they that are not of the truth are not of the Church of Christ ... for we are reminded that we are to distinguish Christianity not by persons [who have ecclesiastical titles], but by the truth and by the exactness of the Faith.[4]

In complete concord with the above, Saint John Chrysostom instructs us that:

> The universal Church is a great paradise ... and should anyone be found in the Church ailing with heretical error from the teaching of the serpent ... then he is cast out of this paradise, even as Adam was cast out from the paradise [of old].[5]

In contrast to these patristic teachings, both the Branch Theory and the ecumenistic "Body of Christ" teach that there are many divergent "Christian" truths and traditions—all of them of value, no matter how contradictory they may be. Therefore, the next conclusion is inevitable: there is no one, absolute Christian truth; truth is relative. It is all a matter of personal preference, if it is "meaningful" to one. Yet, my beloved, as we observed earlier, if truth—including Christian "truths" and "traditions"—is a matter of personal preference and opinion, to the degree that we must not try to convert the non-Orthodox, then this immediately spills over into the matter of morality, into the question of what is true and false, right and wrong, good and evil. This, too, becomes a matter of one's personal preference and opinion, for one acts according to what one believes. There is no longer a single criteri-

---

[3] *Life of Our Holy Father Maximus the Confessor*, p. 14.
[4] *Collected Works*, II, 627, pp. 10-16.   [5] *PG* 59: 545CD.

on of truth; therefore, there is no longer a single criterion of what is right or wrong.

This is the type of mentality that has brought our society to the lamentable state in which it finds itself today, and this, too, is the type of thinking that is cultivated and promoted—unwittingly perhaps—by the *Summit Message*.

An Errant Search for Unity

In addition, the authors of the *Summit Message* affirm that they are working for Christian unity, and this is why they are against proselytism. But what sort of unity are they seeking? Archbishop Iakovos, the primate of the Greek Archdiocese of North and South America, provides the answer. "The unity we seek," said the Archbishop, "cannot be Orthodox, Roman Catholic, or Protestant. It has a wider dimension, that of Catholicity."[6]

But if this future unity will be neither Orthodox, Roman Catholic, nor Protestant, then what will this as yet unformed religion believe? This new denomination, affirms Archbishop Iakovos, will have a wider dimension, "that of Catholicity." Yet in the Divine Liturgy of Saint John Chrysostom, used by all the Orthodox Churches throughout the world, the sacred text states clearly in the Litany of the Catechumens:

> Ye faithful, let us pray for the catechumens....
> That the Lord may have mercy on them....
> That He may unite them to His Holy, *Catholic*, and Apostolic Church.

Is it possible that for all these centuries the faithful have been praying that the Lord may unite the catechumens to a Church that does not yet exist? Again, we ask: what sort of unity is this?

The Only Source of Unity

My beloved, as Orthodox Christians, we believe that truth is from God alone, that love and justice and goodness are from God alone. And God alone is the Way to the acquiring of these heavenly virtues. Nothing is more ennobling than God. Therefore,

---

[6] *The Orthodox Observer*, March 15, 1988.

the truth and the virtues that ennoble mankind cannot exist independently of God.

There is no worldly or human substitute for these heavenly gifts, no worldly alternative or worldly redefinition possible. As Christians, we know, for example, that the love of fallen man is not really love at all, for the love of God is selfless, whereas the "love" of man is self-seeking. When God loves us, it is for the purpose of uniting us to Himself in an eternal bond, transcending this mortal existence and the aspirations of earth-bound ties of human kinship. Since we are mortal, when we love each other it is for the sake of uniting ourselves with some other mortal human being for "immediate purposes"—happiness, self-satisfaction, or worldly joys and pleasures. When we love God, it can only be done by beginning with a change of heart, a putting down of our fallen selves in humility, a setting at nought of our pride, and then, a genuine outpouring of selfless love for Him Who loved us in extreme humility, taking on our nature and our mortality in order to give us the opportunity to love Him eternally in an attitude of extreme humility. Human love and truth, then, cannot be compared with the divine love and truth of our Saviour, because He alone is the source of this love and truth. If we long for this truth, for this love for both Him and all mankind, and for the light that will guide us to true justice and goodness in our world, we must look to Him alone in order to receive it. This is why He said, "I am the Way, the Truth, and the Life."

This Way, this Truth of God, this Life which is the guide and source of our own life, is the rock upon which we must build the house of virtue during our lifetime. The multiple, constantly shifting sands of personal opinions cannot support this house, nor will it be able to withstand the many waves of temptations and afflictions that will inevitably assault it. If we lose this Way, this Truth, this guide for our life which brings us to Him Who alone is Life, then every standard becomes arbitrary, then "all things are permissible," as Divine truth and love fade from our hearts, and a mortal, selfish "love" and fickle and arbitrary "truths" replace them. Then, rather than unity, we will find only further fragmentation such as we already see all around us, where no one can agree any longer on what is right or wrong, good or evil, true or false, where even the concept of love itself is warped.

In the Orthodox Christian soul, it is not possible to separate truth and love. "But speaking the truth in love" (Ephesians 4:15), as the holy Apostle Paul says, we are called upon to fulfill both commands: to love both God and man, and to know and cleave to the truth that He has given us. In his *Twentieth Hymn on Faith*, Saint Ephraim the Syrian writes:

> Truth and Love are wings that cannot be separated,
> for Truth cannot fly without Love,
> nor can Love soar aloft without Truth;
> their yoke is one of amity.
>
> The eyes' two pupils see and move together;
> although the nose separates them,
> they are not divided;
> for not even the slightest blink of one eye can escape the other's attention.
>
> Nor were the feet ever divided
> so as to travel in two different directions ...
> A man's feet and eyes reprove him for being thus divided.

My beloved faithful, let us ever cleave to this concord of truth and love, for both have been bestowed on us as precious gifts from our Triune God: Father, Son, and Holy Spirit. If we stand firm in the One Holy Orthodox Faith of Christ, and in the love of God and in repentance, humility, and unceasing prayer, partaking of the Holy Mysteries with faith, fear, and longing, then, even though we may be surrounded by waves of conflicting beliefs and inconstant standards, they will not be able to hurt us or deprive us of our rightful inheritance in the Kingdom of Heaven, through the never-failing love and truth of God, revealed in His Church, which is already, and always has been, One, Holy, Catholic, and Apostolic.

This is the only true source of unity, my beloved; this is the only source of our, and every man's, union with God, in His truth, in His love, in His One Faith. This is the Message that the world needs to hear today.

If we cherish and fulfill in our lives the sacred precepts of love and truth that are ours in the Body of Christ, the Holy Orthodox and Catholic Church, and if we remain steadfast in this love and truth, and strive to bring others also to this knowledge, then, together with the Saints of all ages past, we the unworthy ones will be counted worthy to hear our Saviour's blessed voice, saying to us, "Come, ye blessed of my Father, inherit the Kingdom prepared for you from the foundation of the world" (Matt. 25:34).

My beloved children, may this be our portion in the age to come. Amen.

Your fervent supplicant before God,
✠ Ephraim, Bishop of Boston

Feast of the Holy Apostles Peter and Paul
29 June, 1992

APPENDIX H

An Encyclical on the Balamand Statement
A Warning to the Faithful

Let these offences, introduced into the Church by Ecumenical Patriarchs Sergius, Pyrrhus, and Paul, be removed; let those who have introduced them be deposed; and then the path to salvation will be cleared of all barriers, and you will walk on the smooth path of the Gospel, cleansed of all heresy! When I see the Church of Constantinople as she was formerly, then I will enter into communion with her without any exhortation on the part of men. But while there are heretical temptations in her, and while heretics are her bishops, no word or deed will convince me ever to enter into communion with her.

Saint Maximus the Confessor's reply to Theodosius,
Bishop of Caesarea in Bithynia

In the Name of the Father, and of the Son,
and of the Holy Spirit. Amen.

It was with deep sorrow, my beloved Orthodox Christians, that we read the "Balamand Agreed Statement," issued by the "Joint International Commission for the Theological Dialogue between the Roman Catholic Church and the Orthodox Church" in its Seventh Plenary Session at the Balamand School of Theology in Lebanon. This Commission met from the seventeenth to the twenty-fourth of June, 1993; the Statement was endorsed by the papal representatives, and the Churches of Constantinople, Alexandria, Antioch, Russia, Romania, Cyprus, Poland, Albania, and Finland.

We waited over one year to see what "World Orthodoxy's" reaction would be to this Statement, this latest step away from the One, Holy, Catholic, and Apostolic Faith.

Clergy of our own Archdiocese, both in Greece and abroad, have written articles against the Balamand Statement. Responses have also appeared on the part of jurisdictions that call themselves "traditionalist," although they officially maintain full communion with ecumenistic "World Orthodoxy," which has for some time officially espoused synodically condemned heresies.

New calendar periodicals and newspapers have also published sharp protests. For example, the new calendar newspaper *Orthodoxos Typos* (March 18, 1994) presented a very detailed letter to Ecumenical Patriarch Bartholomew, signed by all the representatives of the monasteries of the Holy Mountain, Athos, refuting and denouncing the Balamand Statement. According to *Orthodoxos Typos*, Ecumenical Patriarch Bartholomew—ostensibly out of administrative concerns, but actually because of the letter—was "provoked to wrath" and demanded that the monks repent of their action and ask his forgiveness. After a series of "depositions" and other unveiled threats on his part, the Athonite monks capitulated.

One new calendar priest, Father John Romanides—whom I and several clergy of our diocese had as professor of dogmatic theology at Holy Cross Theological School in Brookline, Massachusetts—also wrote a statement critical of the document adopted at Balamand.

Other new calendar clergy and theologians have written protests. But—as is always the case—none of their bishops, the hierarchs of "World Orthodoxy," have sided with them.

Finally, after almost a year, a bishop under the Ecumenical

Patriarchate wrote an article concerning the Balamand Statement. In *The Illuminator* (March–April, 1994), Bishop Maximos of Pittsburgh of the new calendar Greek Archdiocese of North and South America came to the wholehearted defense of the aforementioned Statement, as might be expected of a bishop belonging to an ecumenistic jurisdiction. In his "Introductory Note," Bishop Maximos explains that his defense of the Balamand Statement was necessary especially for those who "cannot understand some of the theological terms and the fine connotations that only trained theologians can understand." He then offers to guide his readers "through some of the 'rough spots' of the Balamand Statement, which are often misunderstood and misinterpreted by untrained theologians and lay people."

By assuming this patronizing approach, Bishop Maximos evidently feels that he can sweep away the protests of traditional Orthodox Christians, monastics, and even his own new calendar colleagues ("untrained theologians and lay people").

Such being the case, perhaps the best response to Bishop Maximos would be one written by a "trained theologian" (even though this term, somehow, has an un-Orthodox ring to it). We have already mentioned the critique of Father John Romanides, who is Professor of Theology at Balamand Theological School in Lebanon, Professor Emeritus of the School of Theology at the University of Thessalonica, and former Professor of Dogmatic Theology at Holy Cross Orthodox Theological School in Brookline, Massachusetts. Aside from Father John Romanides's short article, there is a very extensive, detailed, and excellent refutation and condemnation of the Balamand Statement written by the Reverend Protopresbyter Theodore Zeses, Professor of the Theological School of the University of Thessalonica, whose theological credentials, together with those of Father John Romanides, appear to be considerably superior to those of Bishop Maximos.

What follows is a summary of Father Theodore's argumentation:

As this professor of theology demonstrates in the March 16, 1994 issue of *Ekklesiastike Aletheia* (an official publication of the new calendar Church of Greece), ever since the Orthodox-Roman Catholic dialogue officially began in 1980, the Orthodox representatives have consistently demanded that the "Eastern-rite" Uniate churches be repudiated by the Papacy. This repudiation and condemnation was officially espoused, in fact, by both the Orthodox and the Roman Catholic representatives at the meetings held between them at Vienna (January 1990), and especially at Freising near Munich (June 1990). Nonetheless, Rome was not pleased with these decisions. Indeed, even at Freising, Cardinal Willebrands would not endorse the repudiation of Uniatism. Furthermore, the Vatican's official publication, *Osservatore Romano,* which normally gives full reports of all these proceedings, suppressed any news concerning the decisions taken at Freising, and the Polish papal theologian and representative Wl. Hrynievicz, who sided with the Orthodox in condemning the Unia, was dismissed from his post by Rome (*Ekklesiastike Aletheia,* April 16, 1994).

In contrast, the recent Balamand Statement, signed by the papal delegation and all the Orthodox representatives present, overturns all the former decisions and for the first time fully accepts and legitimizes the Unia, and even accepts the Uniate hierarchy as participants "in the dialogue of love."

In matters of doctrine also, as Father Theodore Zeses points out, there were serious compromises of the Orthodox Faith. Previous theological dialogues between Orthodox and the Roman Catholics dealt only with "those things that unite" rather than "those that divide." Nonetheless, when the document "Faith, Sacraments, and the Unity of the Church" was discussed at Crete (1984) and Bari (1986), the papal representatives sought to raise the matter of the Orthodox Church's practice of baptizing the non-Orthodox. However, the Orthodox at that time maintained that the subject of baptism should be discussed at some future date. Now, however, in the Balamand Statement, without any previous discussion of the subject, says Father Theodore, *all* the sacraments "of each Church" are mutually and fully recognized, and, in addition, "a new ecclesiology" is proposed.

"This creates a very serious problem," as Father Theodore Zeses correctly observes, "because it makes the Roman Catholics and the Orthodox Church equal, insofar as [the Balamand Statement] considers both possessors of the true Apostolic Faith, of sacramental grace, and Apostolic succession . . . Orthodox theologians are denying that the Orthodox Church is the One, Holy, Catholic, and Apostolic Church—because the statements made in the [Balamand] text signify that the Orthodox Church, together with the Roman Catholic Church, constitute the One Church, and that both in common are responsible to this One Church for the maintenance of the Church of God. The teaching of the great Saints and Fathers of the Orthodox Church concerning the fact that the Latins are schismatics and heretics is now forsaken and set at nought." And he continues, "Are, then, the *filioque*, the primacy and the infallibility of the Pope, purgatory, unleavened bread, created divine grace . . . and the multitude of other innovations, all elements of the Apostolic Faith? Have we returned again to the false council of Ferrara and Florence? Is this how the Roman Catholics and the Orthodox have become 'Sister Churches'?" he asks. Indeed, he says, "confessional syncretism and ecumenistic ecclesiological confusion have begun to bear fruit."

If the Papacy is a "Sister Church," as the Balamand Statement maintains, "then what are the local autocephalous [Orthodox] Churches which are of one doctrine, which are united in the same faith, worship, and administration, and partake of the one cup?" writes Father Theodore.

"And what is this 'theology of communion,' which the text [of the Balamand Statement] frequently mentions?" asks Father Theodore Zeses. "There do not exist 'degrees' of ecclesiastical communion, so that one could speak [as the Balamand Statement does] of seeking for 'full communion,' as though there could be a partial or incomplete communion. One either partakes or does not partake of the Body of Christ. Of course, it is well known that Roman Catholic ecclesiology is quite elastic, and can accept degrees of a community's 'ecclesial nature' according to one's recognition of and relationship with the bishop of Rome as the successor of Peter and head of the entire Church. According to this [papal concept], a community's 'ecclesial nature' can exist even in heresy and schism, and can achieve wholeness and full communion when various Christian groups become members of the 'Catholic Communion' and recognize the primacy of the Pope. This is the 'full communion' that Roman Catholics signify and seek as regards us Orthodox also—and not the unity in faith and doctrine [that we Orthodox espouse], so that being united in concord and peace, with one heart and one mind, we might in oneness partake of the Body and Blood of Christ. This is obvious from the fact that even 'heretics' can be received into the 'Catholic Communion' through the Unia; all that is necessary is that they recognize the Pope's primacy."

These are a few of the observations expressed by Protopresbyter Theodore Zeses in *Ekklesiastike Aletheia*, in a series of articles which began on March 3, 1994.

The perennial question remains, however: will there once again only be words and no action? Will these "trained theologians" follow through with their protests over this latest betrayal of the Orthodox Faith? Will they finally separate themselves from their bishops, who have ceased being Orthodox? Or will this continue to be yet another "paper war" of written protests and then capitulation and silence, as in the case of the monks of the Holy Mountain?

Some laymen, indeed, have expressed concern over the "seduction of Orthodoxy" by ecumenism. From every official indication, however, "World Orthodoxy's" hierarchy has acquiesced to not only the seduction, but the complete and shameless ravishment of Orthodoxy.

Many have concluded that there is no longer any point in appealing to the conscience of such bishops. Nevertheless, my beloved, we must appeal to the conscience of individuals who are found in innovationist jurisdictions, because many of them are sincere and good people who are being betrayed by their own bishops.

How can we appeal to their conscience? By patiently endeavoring to educate the unsuspecting Orthodox, through preaching, through writing, through our publications, and especially through our own practice of the Holy Orthodox Faith. But of course—and above all—only the grace of our Saviour can touch their hearts and their conscience and lead them to the path of salvation.

Simply by their silence, the bishops of "World Orthodoxy" have betrayed Orthodoxy—another betrayal in a chain of former betrayals, in which either the hierarchs keep silence before flagrant violations of the canons and the spirit of the Faith, or in which they will not apply the measures ordained by the Holy Ecumenical Councils, that is, breaking off communion with their erring colleagues.

The Ecumenists have succeeded in silencing and quelling any active resistance from within. Whenever they cannot suppress a protest, as Patriarch Bartholomew did with the monks of Mount Athos, they hurriedly say that these statements are mere proposals, or that these actions are mere courtesy with no theological import. The Balamand Statement contains merely "strong recommendations," they say. Yet, how could any faithful Orthodox even propose that the Scriptures, the holy Fathers, the canons, the whole life and history of the Church be abrogated in this fashion? Their "strong recommendations" demonstrate that in their hearts they have already renounced the Faith. Do not their proposals express their own beliefs? Furthermore, these proposals are never retracted—or even discussed; but history has proved that as soon as the rumblings have quieted or been stilled, the Ecumenists proceed to further enormities, as if what they called proposals were already approved and confirmed decisions. These tactics of the Ecumenists appear to have succeeded in breaking all opposition from within.

This is the very reason, then, why we have felt it imperative to issue this warning: a warning for us to stand fast in every way, a warning against this most recent betrayal, a warning against feeling any sort of discouragement. Rather, we must prepare ourselves for even greater struggles, and cultivate within ourselves even greater devotion to the "Faith which was once delivered unto the Saints" (Jude 3).

After completing his paralogical "Introductory Note" to the Balamand Statement, in which he attempts to deny what the document actually says, Bishop Maximos writes with elation, "The Balamand Statement . . . is a feather on the hat of those Orthodox theologians who are on the international Orthodox-Roman Catholic team! They are to be commended for a fine piece of work." Such an assessment might indeed be expected from a bishop who, after all, received his theological training and formation at the hands of Roman Catholic professors.

Protopresbyter Theodore Zeses, on the other hand, writes that the Balamand Statement brought "despondency and bitterness to the Church's faithful."

Obviously, this is a matter that the clergy of "World Orthodoxy" will have to settle among themselves. For our part, my beloved Orthodox Christians, following the example of Saint Maximus the Confessor, we are grateful to God that we have no portion, or part, or communion with those who are betraying our most holy Orthodox Faith, and we pray that our Saviour and God may ever preserve us from such a betrayal, by the intercessions of the three great Pillars of Orthodoxy, Photius the Great, Gregory Palamas, and Mark of Ephesus, and of all the Saints. Amen.

Your fervent suppliant unto God,
✝ Ephraim, Bishop of Boston

Dormition of the Holy Theotokos
August 15/28, 1994
Protocol Number 617

APPENDIX I

Saint Joseph of Arimathea English-Speaking Orthodox Parish, Toronto, Canada
The Tenth Anniversary[1]

Father David writes:

As Anglicans we had often visited Holy Trinity Monastery, Jordanville, New York, and had always been warmly received. I

---

[1] *The Arimathean,* October–November, 1995.

subscribed to and avidly read *Orthodox Life* from cover to cover. Consequently, we had a very positive feeling about the Russian Church Abroad. When we finally became Orthodox, however, we were received into the OCA (Orthodox Church in America) parish in our town, simply because it was the only Orthodox church in the area, and because services were conducted entirely in English. I went off to Saint Vladimir's Seminary in New York, was ordained to the priesthood in 1979, and subsequently was assigned to the OCA cathedral parish in Toronto. However, we always felt a certain affinity for the Russian Church Abroad. The more antagonistic my colleagues in the OCA were toward that jurisdiction, the more curious I became about their reasons.

In 1984 I attended the dedication of the new Serbian Orthodox Centre in Mississauga, Ontario. After the liturgy, talking with a young priest from the Serbian parish in Niagara Falls, Ontario, I asked him if there were a parish of the Russian Church Abroad in that town. To my astonishment, he replied that he was a priest of the Russian Church Abroad on loan to the Serbian parish there. I was surprised, because, according to the OCA, we were not in communion with the Russian Church Abroad, and we did not serve together with them, nor they with us.

Subsequently I learned that this arrangement was not an isolated case. It certainly made nonsense of the claim that the Russian Church Abroad was in communion with no one else!

(It was evident to me that by virtue of the Serbian connection, the Russian Church Abroad was in communion with everyone with whom the Serbians were in communion, including the Greek Archdiocese, the Antiochians, the OCA, and even the Moscow Patriarchate.)

This young priest with whom I was speaking went on to say that the Russian Church Abroad (his own church) was "out on a limb" and "the sooner the Church gets back into the 'mainstream' the better it will be." With amazement I asked him where we would all be today if saints like Athanasius, Maximus the Confessor, and Mark of Ephesus had thought along those lines. They were certainly not in the "mainstream" of their day.

Saint Athanasius, for example, had been *contra mundum*, one man against the world, while Saint Maximus the Confessor had said: "When the Patriarch (of Constantinople) returns to Orthodoxy, I shall return to the Patriarch." Saint Mark of Ephesus was the *only* Orthodox bishop who refused to sign the concordat with the pope at the council of Florence, thus saving Orthodoxy.

From this time on, then, though I pursued my interest in the Russian Church Abroad, I knew there were "two minds" in that church, even before we were received therein.

Archbishop Vitaly was most gracious to us and in 1985 received me as a priest from the OCA, along with my flock from Hart House, University of Toronto, by Holy Chrismation. This marked the founding of Saint Joseph's.

With the repose of Metropolitan Philaret, author of the Anathema Against Ecumenism which I had used even as a priest in the OCA, things began to deteriorate rapidly in the Russian Church Abroad. The other of the "two minds" seemed to me to be gaining the upper hand. With the election of Metropolitan Vitaly, a new and different interpretation was given to the anathema, one contrary to the meaning and intent of Metropolitan Philaret. The Nativity Epistle of Metropolitan Vitaly in 1986 claimed: "We have pronounced an Anathema upon the heresy of ecumenism for the benefit of our Church alone."

This had not been my understanding of the anathema at the time I had used it in the OCA. If it had been devised solely for the benefit of the Russian Church Abroad, as a priest of another jurisdiction I would not have used it. I did use it only because it seemed to me to be a clarion call to all of Orthodoxy from that late great confessor of the faith, Metropolitan Philaret.

The *Orthodox Christian Witness* said in response to Metropolitan Vitaly's 1986 Nativity epistle:

> His Eminence introduces a different meaning into the term "anathema": he speaks of an anathema as an invitation to "give serious thought" in regard to the heresy of Ecumenism. But was this not the purpose of our late Metropolitan Philaret's sequence of "Sorrowful Epistles"? According to Saint Nicodemos of the

Holy Mountain in his commentary on the canons, an "anathema" is precisely a statement that those who follow or promulgate this teaching are cut off from God, that is, are outside the Church. In his epistle to the Galatians (1:8–9), the Apostle Paul uses the word "anathema" in this same meaning. An anathema is not an admonition or a warning at all; it is the final act after all admonitions and warnings have been ignored. . . .

We have always loved and respected Metropolitan Vitaly, and we will not cease loving him and praying for him now. But we also now see that he and those with him in the Russian Orthodox Church Abroad at this time simply do not have the same theology as we do.

A manifesto, signed by thirty priests formerly of the Russian Church Abroad states:

> Having realized that the Russian Orthodox Church Abroad has now taken irrevocable steps towards ecumenism and accommodation with the Serbian Church which is deeply committed to ecumenism, as well as the ecumenist jurisdictions, and has not shown a desire to correct these breaches of its own policy, we have established ties with the True Orthodox Church of Greece.

I was therefore not surprised, when, having been in the Russian Church Abroad for only a year, we found ourselves "opting out" after Metropolitan Vitaly's new interpretation of the anathema against ecumenism. Before we committed ourselves to this action, however, Father Panagiotes Carras, Rector of Saint Nektarios Greek Orthodox Church, who had graciously extended hospitality to our congregation during the preceding year, said to me: "Father David, you and your people have only been with us for a year. Perhaps you are not ready for this move from the Church Abroad. If you are not, you are perfectly welcome to remain here; we will just commemorate different bishops." I told Father Panagiotes that not only was I substantially in agreement with his and the other clergy's reasons for leaving the Church Abroad, but that we had received no invitation from any of the three parishes of the Church Abroad in Toronto to relocate with them.

Bishop Gregory (Grabbe), the oldest and most respected member of the Synod of the Bishops of the Church Abroad, served as Secretary of the Synod under Metropolitans Anthony, Anastasy, Philaret, and Vitaly for a total of almost sixty years. Now in his nineties, he wrote the following to Metropolitan Vitaly of the Church Abroad on March 24, 1994:

> For a very long time now, actually from the first days of your being at the head of our Church Abroad, I have, with great distress and anxiety of heart, observed how quickly she has begun to slide into the abyss of administrative disintegration and canonical chaos...
>
> Thanks to the ignoring of the Canons, our Church has lost more than twenty parishes, two monasteries, and a whole series of clergymen. This brought our Synod to another great loss of prestige. I make no mention of the thousands of lay people scandalized by us—Greeks and Americans. Among the priests who left us, we lost several of the more outstanding ones: Father Panagiotes Carras and others. The Greek priests, having given up their very wealthy parishes in order to join us, suddenly found themselves hounded out of the Russian Church...
>
> For all the years of the Church Abroad's existence, we were held in respect and repute for nothing else save our uncompromising fidelity to the Canons. They may have hated us, but they did not dare not respect us. Whereas now we have shown the whole Orthodox world that for us the Canons are mere empty words, and we have become a laughingstock in the eyes of all who have anything at all to do with ecclesiastical matters.
>
> I am writing this letter solely in order vividly to demonstrate to you, how we, having left the canonical rails in 1985, have begun to depart all the further from the fundamental ecclesiastical canons and statutes of our Local Church....
>
> I was a witness and a participant in the glorious period in the life of the Church Abroad, and now with pain of heart, I behold what I consider to be her inglorious end.
>
> ✟ Bishop Gregory (Grabbe)

APPENDIX J

The Dubious Orthodoxy of Metropolitan Cyprian's Group

(Translated from *Church News* [in Russian], No. 5, Sept.–Oct. 1994, pp. 2–4.)

The newspaper *Pravoslavnaya Rus*, in its issue number seventeen of the present year, published the Decision of the Russian Orthodox Church Abroad concerning the establishment of prayerful eucharistic communion with the group of Old Calendarists headed by Metropolitan Cyprian of Oropos and Fili.[1]

In its concluding section the Decision elucidates the causes that prompted the Sobor to take this step. However, in not one of its six points does it mention that the Sobor of 1975 resolved not to have communion with the Greek groups until they themselves had become united, and the Synod, already presided over by Metropolitan Vitaly, reaffirmed this wise decision in the spring of 1993, that is, a mere year and a half ago. Everyone is aware that the Greek groups can in no wise boast of having already achieved unity, yet the present Conciliar Decision offers no explanation whatsoever for this abrogation by the Sobor of its previous resolutions.

Thus, in the Decision it is stated,

> After deliberation and analysis of all aspects of these questions [concerning the history and ideology of this group][2] the Council of Bishops maintains that at the present time, when apostasy is spreading and the so-called official representatives of Orthodoxy, such as the Patriarchate of Constantinople and other patriarchates, are succumbing to and embracing the position of the modernists and ecumenists, it is very important for the True Orthodox to unite, make a stand together, and oppose the betrayers of the Orthodoxy of the Holy Fathers. In this regard, the Council of Bishops has decided:

---

[1] For the complete English text of this Decision, see *Orthodox Life*, no. 4, 1994, pp. 49–50.
[2] Addition in brackets made by Bishop Gregory.

Metropolitan Kallistos of Corinth and Father George (later Bishop Gregory) Grabbe at the Russian Synod headquarters in New York, in 1973.

1) To establish communion in prayer and the Eucharist with the Greek Old Calendarist synod of Metropolitan Cyprian, as well as with His Grace, Bishop Photios of Triaditsa, who heads the Bulgarian Old Calendar diocese.

Bishop Photios was consecrated for the Bulgarians by the selfsame Metropolitan Cyprian, and thus his legitimacy is dependent upon the legitimacy of Metropolitan Cyprian.

It is of interest that our Sobor, while seeking union with the "True Orthodox" Greek groups, made no effort whatsoever toward unity with the far more numerous and decent group of Archbishop Chrysostom [Kiousis] of Athens, who has a sobor consisting of nineteen bishops.

The second point [of the Decision] deals with informing the flock abroad of this event.

In point number three it is stated, "During the deliberations, the statements of those opposed to the union were also taken into account, in which the question was raised concerning the canonicity of Metropolitan Cyprian's group and their allegedly un-Orthodox teaching on grace."

Aside from his personal teaching on grace (more on this below), Metropolitan Cyprian has likewise been accused of preaching the heresy of chiliasm.

Concerning the "canonicity" of this group, quite enough has already been said and written. But what then is their "allegedly un-Orthodox teaching on grace"?

Preparing the ground for possible union with the Church Abroad well in advance, Metropolitan Cyprian issued a pamphlet entitled "An Ecclesiological Thesis, or Exposition on the Doctrine of the Church, for the Orthodox Opposed to the Heresy of Ecumenism."[3] It would seem that, judging from the title of the pamphlet, nothing could be said against such a program. The pamphlet is quite handsomely printed, even to the point of using the old orthography [i.e., pre-Revolutionary]. It was very widely distributed, and each member of the Bishops' Sobor undoubtedly received a copy.

However, with great consternation and dismay one is forced to point out that apparently the very members of the Bishops' Committee investigating the Greek question themselves,[4] and all the members of the Bishops' Sobor together, failed to pursue sufficiently what is called "reading between the lines" of this pamphlet, which abounds in ancient texts and is deftly put together, but which bears little relation to the contemporary ecclesiastical situation.

Moreover, it is obvious that they took scant notice of the canonicity (very doubtful) of Metropolitan Cyprian's group, for the subject is not at all reflected in the text of the Sobor's Decision. Likewise evident is the fact that the committee took no account whatsoever of the motives behind our own previous resolutions.

Let us now attempt to determine precisely what sort of Orthodoxy Metropolitan Cyprian does confess and whether or not one

---

[3] For the English text of this thesis see *The Old Calendar Orthodox Church of Greece*, by Bishop Chrysostom Gonzalez (Etna, California: Center for Traditionalist Orthodox Studies, 1991), pp. 83–92.

[4] The committee was comprised of Archbishop Laurus, Bishop Daniel, and Bishop Mitrophan.

can actually say with a clear conscience that both he and his synod "adhere wholly to the exact same ecclesiological and dogmatic principles as our Russian Church Outside Russia" (point five of the Sobor's Decision).

In the chapter [of the pamphlet] entitled "The Church and Heresy," page two, it says:

> Sinners and those who err in correctly understanding the Faith, yet who have not been sentenced by ecclesiastical action, are simply considered ailing members of the Church. The Mysteries of these unsentenced members are valid as such, according to the Seventh Ecumenical Council, as, for example, the President of the Council, Saint Tarasios, remarks: "[their] Ordination" "is from God."[5]

Later, in the third chapter, the author turns to the matter, "The Division in the Church Over Ecumenism"—as he calls it.

It seems strange to hear from a bishop who proclaims his Orthodoxy the idea that the Church can be "divided." The holy Fathers have taught that she always was, is, and shall be the indivisible Bride of Christ. One can only fall away from her or be reunited to her through repentance. Metropolitan Anthony [Khrapovitsky] especially emphasized to his priests the necessity, after confession, of reading the ancient prayer of absolution which contains the words, "reconcile and unite him to Thy holy Church," thereby indicating that he who sins falls away from the Church. Although private confession can heal personal moral falls, it in no wise cures a public and obdurate inclination to heresy.

Metropolitan Cyprian correctly points out that the beginning of the malady was the introduction of the Western calendar into the life of the Church in 1924. But then later he advances an opinion which in no wise corresponds to the present ecclesiastical situation. "The followers of the festal calendar innovation," says he,

> have not yet been specifically judged in a pan-Orthodox fashion, as provided for by the Orthodox Church. As Saint Nicodemos

---

[5] See Editors' Note on pp. 250-254 for more on this question.

of the Holy Mountain writes, the violator of established precepts is considered sentenced, insofar as he is judged by "the second entity (which is the Council or Synod)." Since 1924, the innovators have been awaiting judgment and shall be judged on the basis of the decisions of the holy Councils, both Ecumenical and local, and, to be sure, on the basis of the ecclesiastical pronouncements of the sixteenth century against what were then Papal proposals for changes in the festal calendar. *In this respect those who have walled themselves off from the innovators have actually broken communion "before conciliar or synodal verdict," as is allowed in the Fifteenth Canon of the First-and-Second Council. That is to say, the innovators are still unsentenced. Consequently,* [according to the teaching of Metropolitan Cyprian],[6] *their Mysteries are valid.* [Emphasis mine.][7]

Metropolitan Cyprian chooses a convenient quotation from this canon to suit his purpose, but intentionally does not cite the subsequent text of the canon concerning those who separate themselves from their presidents before a synodical judgment in cases where the open preaching of heresy is taking place:

> Such persons as these not only are not subject to canonical penalty for walling themselves off from communion with the so-called bishop before synodical clarification, but [on the contrary] they shall be deemed worthy of due honor among the Orthodox. For not bishops, but false bishops and false teachers have they condemned, and they have not fragmented the Church's unity with schism, but from schisms and divisions have they earnestly sought to deliver the Church. (Canon Fifteen of the so-called First-Second Council)

The adherents of Roman Catholicism in Russia have from of old cited the fact that not one Ecumenical Council has ever condemned Roman Catholicism and therefore it, they say, is not a heresy. Such an opinion was quite widespread among our intelligentsia, and especially in military circles.

---

[6] Addition in brackets made by Bishop Gregory.
[7] Bishop Gregory's note.

Chapter Four is entitled "Repentance and Return." That which is expounded therein concerning the principle of repentance is entirely correct and in accord with the canons. Yet while offering us numerous examples of repentance which took place at one or another Ecumenical Council, Metropolitan Cyprian never so much as mentions the fact that the New Calendarists/Ecumenists not only have no intention whatsoever of repenting, but on the contrary, they persecute the True Orthodox in a most cruel manner. We have before our very eyes the example of how quite recently they "strangled," one could say, Patriarch Diodoros of Jerusalem, who was attempting to defend the Orthodoxy of the holy Fathers. Only a few months have now passed since they—by means of threats of expulsion from their monasteries, and canonical sanctions—have forced to repent before them that last bastion of Orthodoxy, the Holy Mountain, which was defending the Church from the inroads of the heresy of Ecumenism.

Metropolitan Cyprian sees no grounds for severing communion with the New Calendarists/Ecumenists until such time as it will be possible for a future Ecumenical Council to judge them. But who could not be aware (including the Metropolitan himself) that for almost twenty years now the ecumenists have been preparing the program for the future—and not in the least Orthodox—"Eighth Ecumenical Council"? The Preconciliar Committee has already on more than one occasion published its drafts for the reports to be delivered at this future "Council." The issues to be discussed at it include the unification of all Christians, the total abolition of the fasts, married bishops, and second marriages for the clergy.

Who, then, will be the president of this dishonorable assembly, which, according to Metropolitan Cyprian's daydreams, is supposed to condemn the Ecumenists/New Calendarists? Obviously that crypto-Roman Catholic, the Ecumenical Patriarch Bartholomew. And those like unto him will prove to be its members: the Patriarch of Alexandria, Parthenios (who has officially declared Mohammed to be a great prophet and personally considers him an Apostle!); the Patriarch of Antioch (who has already issued a directive to his clergy granting them permission to concelebrate with the heretical Monophysites); the Patriarch of Moscow (who has signed both the Balamand Unia and the agreement concerning the Monophysites, and who has even initiated a dialogue with the Jews "on the highest possible level").[8]

I have been given the opportunity to acquaint myself with several letters written by one of the bishops of Metropolitan Cyprian's group. From these it is quite evident that he and his fellow bishops confess their own personal, and in no wise Orthodox, doctrine concerning the possibility of the grace-filled activity of the Holy Spirit within churches which have become manifestly heretical. *ALL the New Calendarists—without the least exception—are likewise very active ecumenists.*[9] The Old Style Churches (Russian and Serbian) have for a long time now also confessed this very same heresy.

But behold, this hierarch of Metropolitan Cyprian's group insists on the opinion that, so he says, "the New Calendarists, besieged by the heresy of ecumenism and innovation, have not been deprived of grace,[10] or at any rate, it is not within our competency to make such a pronouncement on our part . . . we are not speaking of union with Belial, but (only) with those ailing in faith, several of whom are in need of spiritual treatment . . . in view of this, we do not totally break off communion with them."[11] In another letter the same hierarch expresses the thought—totally unacceptable and absurd from a dogmatic point of view and from that of the holy Fathers—that his group, while recognizing that the ecumenists have grace, is only "walling itself off from their errors."

In pronouncing its Decision concerning communion with Metropolitan Cyprian's group, our Sobor, unfortunately, did not also call to mind the text of that Decision taken formerly, under

---

[8] *Editors' Note:* From this argumentation offered by Metropolitan Cyprian, it would appear that we must wait until the Patriarchates of Constantinople, Jerusalem, Alexandria, Antioch, and the others gather in a council to condemn themselves.

[9] Bishop Gregory's emphasis.

[10] *Editors' Note:* How is it possible to speak of the New Calendarists being "besieged" by the heresy of Ecumenism and innovation, when all the facts indicate that they are completely voluntary and willing participants and perpetrators of these violations, and in some instances, even originators? What tyrannical force is "besieging" them?

[11] *Translator's Note:* Not being a party to this correspondence, we are forced here to render it back into English according to the Russian translation.

the presidency of Metropolitan Philaret, anathematizing the heresy of Ecumenism. Among others it contains such words as these: *"Therefore, to those who knowingly have communion with these aforementioned heretics, or who advocate, disseminate, or defend their new heresy of Ecumenism: Anathema."*[12]

Indeed, by not investigating the matter seriously and by forgetting about this previously confirmed anathematizing of the New Calendarists/Ecumenists (or perhaps not venturing to abrogate this resolution), our Sobor, as frightful as it may be to admit, has fallen under its own anathema. Had it probed the net spread before it more carefully, it would never have issued such a contradictory Decision.

Our previous Bishops' Sobors never raised the particular question concerning whether or not the New Calendarists have grace. But the fact that formerly concelebrations with them were never permitted already testifies with sufficient clarity that the Church Abroad considered them to be without grace.

Must we consider that our Synod has entered upon the path of betrayal of the traditions of the holy Fathers, or did it merely commit an error owing to poor judgment which it is still not too late to correct at the next session of the Sobor to be held in November in France?[13]

☦ Bishop Gregory

EDITORS' NOTE *On the Phrase: "The ordination is from God"*

During the iconoclastic period, many defected to this heresy and accepted ordination from the iconoclasts. When some of these men petitioned to return to the Church, the Fathers of the Seventh Ecumenical Council asked whether the iconoclast clergy should be received as clergy, or should the ordination they received from the heretics be rejected?

---

[12] Bishop Gregory's emphasis. For the full text of this anathema and a sobering commentary on the Russian Church Abroad's Sobor of 1983 by the then Archbishop Vitaly see *Pravoslavnaya Rus*, No. 10, 1983, pp. 3–4. For an English translation, see *Orthodox Christian Witness*, Vol. 18, No. 1, pp. 2–6.

[13] *Editors' Note:* The hierarchy of the Russian Church Abroad did not retract this decision.

The expression "the ordination is from God" is taken from the Acts of the Seventh Ecumenical Council and was uttered by Saint Tarasius, who was Patriarch of Constantinople when the Seventh Ecumenical Council was convoked (787). It was used in reference to Saint Anatolius, Patriarch of Constantinople (449-458), who had been consecrated bishop by the heretic Dioscurus in a liturgy in which the archimandrite Eutyches, also a heretic, had concelebrated. Saint Tarasius's view—that is, that the ordination performed by the heretical Dioscurus was "from God"—appears, at first sight, to agree with the view that the ordinations (and, consequently, all the sacraments of the heterodox) are sanctified and valid, like the Mysteries of the Church. Hence, heretics who return to the Church's bosom must be considered as having a valid ordination that is "from God."

Nonetheless, it is well known that, according to the Church's teaching, heretics do not have a priesthood, do not have Mysteries, and that their ordinations and all their other rituals are without substance, without sanctifying grace.

Not only do the heterodox not have Mysteries, but even the canonically ordained Orthodox lose their priesthood when they fall into heresy, without there being any need for a conciliar decision to declare this.

For example, the Fourth Ecumenical Council refers to the Archimandrites Carosus and Dorotheus simply as monks because their confession of faith was faulty; yet, they had not yet been officially deposed.

Saint Hypatius of Rufinianae declared that Nestorius "was not a bishop" even before he had been deposed by the Third Ecumenical Council. Also, the 15th Canon of the First-Second Council says that bishops who teach heresy are "pseudo-bishops."

If one considers that Nestorius and the bishops referred to in the First-Second Council *had been consecrated bishops within the Church*, but later fell away into heresy, lost the grace of the priesthood, and became pseudo-bishops—that is, laymen—one will understand that they who were ordained *within heresy* are by all means deprived of valid ordination.

Also, regarding the office of an Orthodox bishop, Saint Symeon of Thessalonica says that "by his divine consecration, the grace of God ceases not to work through him, unless only he err regarding the Faith" (*Vlatadon* 165. 220). That is, when a bishop who is Orthodox and canonically ordained errs in matters of the Faith, grace ceases to work through him.

The Mysteries of the Heterodox

If the mysteries of the heterodox are "from God," then why does the 46th Apostolic Canon depose those who accept these "mysteries" ("We ordain that those who accept the baptism or the sacrifice of heretics be deposed.")?

When Pope Saint Leo of Rome wrote to Saint Anatolius, Patriarch of Constantinople (*Epistle 106:1*) and counseled him "to make good use of a bad beginning" (*Post Nicene Fathers*, 77B), should he have not been esteemed blasphemous in calling an ordination that was "from God" a "bad beginning"?

"Let no one be deceived; whosoever is not within the altar is deprived of the Bread of God" (Saint Ignatius the God-bearer, *Letter to the Ephesians* 5:2).

In the very Acts of the Seventh Ecumenical Council, reference is made to Saint Basil's words: "I acknowledge no bishop, nor would I number among the priests of God one who had been advanced [to the priesthood] by defiled hands for the destruction of the Faith" (*PG* 32, 897 AB).

"We know that salvation itself is a property of the One Church, and that no one can be outside of the Catholic Church and yet share in the Faith of Christ, or be saved... Neither do we offer any part of that hope to the ungodly heretics, but we place them entirely outside that hope; indeed, they have not the least participation in Christ, but vainly assume for themselves that saving Name" (Saint John Chrysostom, *PG* 59: 725). "[The clergy] who broke away [from the Church] and became laity are no longer able to impart the grace of the Holy Spirit from which they themselves fell away. Hence, they who were baptized by them were commanded to come into the Church like ones baptized by laymen and to be cleansed again by the true Baptism of the Church" (Saint Basil the Great, *Epistle 188:1*).

"The Jews no longer offer sacrifice; their hands are full of blood, for they have not accepted the Word, through Whom men offer sacrifice to God. The same is true of all the assemblies of the heretics..." (Saint Irenaeus, *Ad. Haer.* IV, 18, 4).

"Since it is impossible that there should be two baptisms, he that concedes that the heretics have baptism deprives himself of baptism" (Local Council of Carthage, under Saint Cyprian, *Mansi* I, 980).

"It is not meet to receive the blessings of heretics, for they are rather foolishness than blessings" (Laodicea, canon 32—In Greek, there is a play on the words *eulogia*—"blessing"—and *alogia*—"foolishness").

"No heretic grants sanctification through his mysteries" (Pope Saint Leo of Rome, *Epistle 159, to Nicetas*).

"*For they are not priests* . . . nor are they that are baptized by them initiated, but rather *they are defiled;* nor have they received the forgiveness of sins, but rather the bonds of ungodliness..." (*Apostolic Constitutions*, 6:15).

Heretics Regain Grace When They Return to the Church

"The sacrifices of heretics can never be acceptable to God, unless they are offered in their behalf by the hands of the universal Church; ... these [sacrifices of the heretics] are not united to the perfection of sevenfold grace, except by [the heterodox] returning" (Saint Gregory the Great of Rome, *Interpretation of Job*, Prologue 17, p. 28).

Concerning Saint Anatolius, the Patriarch of Constantinople mentioned above, Pope Saint Leo of Rome writes, "On account of the fact that Anatolius was united to the Orthodox Faith, we left the matters of his consecration unexamined" (*Letter to Emperor Marcian, PG* 140: 785 B,C).[14]

---

[14] Cf. also Metropolitan Philaret's "not as ones possessing grace, but as ones receiving it by the very act of union," p. 208 above.

Consequently, if Saint Tarasius's opinion in this particular matter does not express the consensus of the Fathers, then we must follow the consensus of the Fathers and not a particular view. It is not permissible to use an isolated and disputed viewpoint in order to support an ecclesiology which comes into contradiction with the Fathers, and with the mind and practice of the Church.

However, it may be that there is also a correct interpretation of this phrase "from God." This indeed seems to be the case, because it seems improbable that Saint Tarasius, the president of the Seventh Ecumenical Council and one of the great Fathers, would err in such a basic matter regarding the Church's sacramental integrity and boundaries. An ancient historian has shed light on this subject and expressed the true meaning of the words "the ordination is from God." This historian writes that Dioscurus, the Patriarch of Alexandria, consecrated Anatolius, his *apocrisiarios* in Constantinople, because he believed that, as Patriarch, Anatolius would promote Dioscurus's heretical ideas ("he assumed that he would uphold his own [Dioscurus's] doctrines"). Then, the same historian continues, "yet even in this, God arranged matters to the contrary." That is, God arranged that something good would come out of this matter (*Select Readings from Church History*, by the Reader Theodore,[15] Vol. I, p. 351).

Truly, "ordination is from God," and it is He Who chooses and sanctifies whom He will. The ordination of Saint Anatolius was accepted and validated by the Church and confirmed by God, whereupon it exists and is valid beyond any legalistic quibblings, because it has been given content in and by the Church. But this particular instance does not allow for a general acceptance of the sacraments of those who stubbornly teach doctrines and implement practices that have been condemned and anathematized by the Church's Local, Ecumenical, and Pan-Orthodox Councils.

---

[15] Theodore the Reader served in the Church of the Holy Wisdom in Constantinople in the sixth century. In the year 530, at the urging of Bishop Procopius of Gangra in Paphlagonia, he composed a Church History covering the years 323-439. This History, known as *Historia Tripartita*, is an abbreviation of the older histories compiled by Socrates, Sozomen, and Theodoret.

APPENDIX K

A Letter to Stephen

Apodosis of Holy Pascha
18/31 May, 1995

Dear Stephen,

I pray that this message finds you well and with the peace of our Saviour. Amen.

Your e-mail message would have been answered much earlier than this were it not for the fact that I have been travelling for the entire month of May.

You asked: "How does your jurisdiction view the sacraments of the other jurisdictions, such as the Russian Church Abroad or the New Calendarist jurisdictions?"

Your question is not difficult to answer. In order to answer it, we must turn, as always, to the Holy Fathers. The First Canon of Saint Basil the Great offers us the guidelines we need in order to address this issue. In this canon, the Saint shows us how the Church may employ either strictness or *economia* in this matter, depending on the teaching of the religious groups with which we are dealing.

Oftentimes, a visiting new calendar clergyman will ask us: "Do you recognize my priesthood?" To which we respond by asking in turn, "Do you recognize our priesthood?" So far, they have always replied, "Yes, I do." And we always candidly replied, "Your hierarchy, however, does not recognize our priestly orders or our sacraments—but they do recognize the sacraments of the non-Orthodox. So where does that leave you?" Usually, at this point, the clergyman (using a way of thinking that is so typical of Protestants and many of today's Orthodox) will reply, "Well, I don't agree with my bishops on that." And, to this, we must respond, "But your personal opinion does not change your hierarchy's official position. However much it may displease you, your bishops recognize the sacraments of the non-Orthodox, but not those of the traditional Orthodox Christians. And that official—and heretical—teaching of your bishops will determine to a certain extent how we must view your own mysteries." I believe that the articles which accompany this letter will shed more light on this matter.

I hope this material will be of assistance to you, Stephen.

With love and blessings in Christ,
✠ Ephraim, Bishop of Boston

Enclosed:

1. The First Canon of Saint Basil the Great [Appendix L].

2. "'Sectarian' Orthodox Christians" (*Orthodox Christian Witness*, June 10/23, 1991) [Appendix M].

3. "'Uncanonical' Orthodox Christians" (*Orthodox Christian Witness*, June 24/July 7, 1991) [Appendix N].

4. "New Calendar Donatism?" (*Orthodox Christian Witness*, March 14/27, 1994) [Appendix O].

APPENDIX L

The First Canon of Saint Basil the Great, and Its Interpretation[1]

As to your enquiry about the Cathari, a statement has already been made, and you have properly reminded me that it is right to follow the custom prevailing in each region, because those who at the time rendered a decision on these points, held different opinions concerning their baptism. But the baptism of the Pepuzeni[2] seems to me to have no authority; and I am astonished at how this can have escaped Dionysius, acquainted as he was with the canons. The old authorities decreed to accept that Baptism which in nowise errs from the Faith. Thus they employed the categories of "heresies" [αἱρέσεις], "schisms" [σχίσματα], and "unlawful assemblies" [παρασυναγωγάς]. By *heresies* they meant those who were

---

[1] Taken from Saint Basil's *Letter to Amphilochius, Concerning the Canons* (Letter 188), written c. 346. The reader should note how Saint Basil uses both strictness and *economia* in dealing with the non-Orthodox.

[2] The Pepuzeni, or Pepuzenes, were a sect of the Montanists. Saint Basil later elaborates on this second century heresy of Montanus and his two women disciples. The name Pepuzeni is derived from Pepuza, a town in Western Phrygia in Asia Minor, which was the center of the Montanist heresy.

altogether broken off and alienated in matters relating to the actual Faith; by *schisms,* they signified those who had separated for some ecclesiastical reasons and questions capable of mutual solution; by *unlawful assemblies,* they meant gatherings held by disorderly presbyters or bishops or by uninstructed laymen. As, for instance, if a man were convicted of a crime, and prohibited from discharging his ministry, and then were to refuse to submit to the canons, but rather arrogated to himself episcopal and ministerial rights, and persons leave the Catholic Church and join him, this is unlawful assembly. To disagree with members of the Church about repentance, is *schism.* Instances of *heresy* are those of the Manichaeans, Valentinians, Marcionites, and the aforementioned Pepuzenes; for their disagreement directly concerns the actual Faith in God. So it seemed good to the ancient authorities to reject the baptism of heretics altogether, but to admit that of schismatics, on the ground that they still belonged to the Church.

As to those who assembled in unlawful assemblies, their decision was to join them again to the Church, after they had been brought to a better state by proper repentance and rebuke, so that, in many cases, when men in orders had rebelled with the disorderly, they were received, on their repentance, into the same rank. Now the Pepuzeni are plainly heretical, for by unlawfully and shamefully applying to Montanus and Priscilla the title of the Comforter, they have blasphemed against the Holy Spirit. They are, therefore, to be condemned either for ascribing divinity to men, or for outraging the Holy Spirit by comparing Him to men. They are thus also liable to eternal damnation, inasmuch as blasphemy against the Holy Spirit admits of no forgiveness. What ground is there, then, for the acceptance of the baptism of men who baptize into the Father and the Son and Montanus or Priscilla? For those who have not been baptized into the names delivered to us have not been baptized at all. So that, although this escaped the vigilance of the great Dionysius, we must by no means imitate his error. The absurdity of the position is immediately obvious and evident to all who are gifted with even a small share of reasoning capacity.

The Cathari are schismatics; but it seemed good to the ancient authorities, I mean Cyprian and our own Firmilian, to reject all these—Cathari, Encratites, and Hydroparastatae[3]—by one common condemnation; for although the origin of separation arose through schism, they who had apostatized from the Church had no longer on them the grace of the Holy Spirit, for it ceased to be imparted when the continuity was broken. The first separatists had received their ordination from the Fathers, and possessed the spiritual gift by the laying-on of their hands. But they who were broken off had become laymen, and because they are no longer able to confer on others that grace of the Holy Spirit from which they themselves are fallen away, they had no authority either to baptize or to ordain. And therefore those who were baptized by them, when they came to the Church, were ordered, as though baptized by laymen, to be purified by the Church's true Baptism.

Nevertheless, since it has seemed to some of those of Asia that, for the sake of economy for the many, their baptism should be accepted, let it be accepted. We must, however, perceive the iniquitous action of the Encratites, who, in order to shut themselves out from being received back by the Church, have endeavored for the future to anticipate readmission by a peculiar baptism of their own, violating, in this manner, even their own special practice. My opinion, therefore, is that nothing being distinctly laid down concerning them, it is our duty to reject their baptism, and that in the case of any one who has received baptism from them, we should, on his coming to the Church, baptize him. If, however, there is any likelihood of this being detrimental to general discipline, we must fall back upon custom, and follow the Fathers who have ordered what course we are to pursue. For I am under some apprehension lest our counsel concerning Baptism make them reluctant and we, through the severity of our decision, be a hindrance to those who are being saved. If they accept our Baptism, do not allow this to distress us. We are by no means bound to return them the same favor, but only strictly to obey the canons. On every ground let it be enjoined that those who come to us from their baptism be anointed by the faithful, and only on these terms approach the Mysteries. I am aware that we have received into episcopal rank Izois and Saturninus from the

[3] See the Interpretation below.

Encratite following. We are precluded therefore from separating from the Church those who have been united to their company, inasmuch as, through our acceptance of the bishops, we have promulgated a kind of canon of communion with them.

INTERPRETATION

After his preface, the Saint responds regarding those matters concerning which Amphilochius asked him. In addressing the subject of the baptism of the schismatic Cathari (i.e., the Novatians)[4] and the heretical Pepuzenes (i.e., the Montanists), the Saint proceeds step by step, and in more general terms refers to those distinctions made by ancient writers, according to whom some groupings are called heresies, others are referred to as schisms, and yet others as unlawful assemblies.

Unlawful assemblies are comprised of disobedient presbyters and bishops who fell into misdemeanors and were canonically deposed from the priesthood. They were not willing to submit to the authority of the canons, and they themselves absolved themselves, and of themselves continued to perform the office of the episcopacy and priesthood. Others followed them and left the Catholic Church.

Schismatics are they who differ with the Catholic Church not over teachings of the Faith, but over certain ecclesiastical matters that are easily healed.

Heretics are they who openly and directly are at variance [with the Church] in matters of faith in God, that is, they are separated from the Orthodox and have utterly distanced themselves over matters of faith and doctrine.[5]

---

[4] The Cathari, or Novatians, rejected those who had contracted a second marriage; also, they taught that the repentance of one who had sinned after Baptism was unacceptable to God.

[5] Thus, George Scholarius, in his treatise against simony, says that a heretic is one who, directly or indirectly, is led astray as regards any article of the Faith. And the imperial law states, "He that deviates even a little from the right Faith is a heretic and subject to the laws that pertain to heretics." In the First Act of the Seventh Ecumenical Council, [Saint] Tarasius says, "It is the same whether one err either a little or greatly in doctrine; for in either case, the law of God is set at nought." And [Saint] Photius, writing to Nicholas of Rome, writes, "For it is necessary to preserve all that is common to all, and especially, above all else the

Hence, they that have formed unlawful assemblies are joined again to the Church only by their returning and by their earnest repentance, and the priests and clergy among them who return accept the same order and rank that they had before.[6]

As for the heretics, like the Manichaeans,[7] Valentinians,[8] Marcionites,[9] Pepuzenes and all the others, when they return to Orthodoxy, they are baptized like the heathen; for the ancient Fathers determined that only one Baptism was acceptable: that which in no way deviated from the Faith. As for the baptism of the heretics, they determined that it was to be rejected utterly since it was outside the true Faith. Likewise, since the Pepuzenes do not baptize according to the traditional order—that is, in the Name of the Father, and of the Son, and of the Holy Spirit—but in the name of the Father, Son, and Montanus and Priscilla, they thereby blaspheme against the Holy Spirit (which is a blasphemy that cannot be forgiven) and attach the Name of the Comforter Him-

---

things that pertain to the Faith. Even if we deviate a little in this, we commit a sin that is unto death. The heretics differ from the unbelieving in that the heretics do not believe correctly the teachings of the Christians. The unbelievers, on the other hand, completely reject the economy of God the Word's incarnation" (See Meletius's *Ecclesiastical History*, p. 71 [In Greek]).

[6] See the 13th Canon of the First–Second Council.

[7] The Manichaeans, who were basically a Gnostic sect, taught that there are two principles in the world: one of the light and one of darkness. They declared that the sun and moon had divine powers, and that the devil was the ruler of all material things. Marriage, for them, was of the devil's law, since the birth of children only continuously imprisoned souls in new bodies. They believed that the Lord had taken upon Himself nothing human in the incarnation, and that His crucifixion, death and resurrection never actually took place. In time, the teachings of the Manichaeans underwent many revisions and took innumerable forms. The sect's teachings reached even India and China.

[8] The Valentinians believed that our bodies of flesh would not be resurrected. They rejected the Old Testament, although they read the prophets, interpreting them according to their own opinions. They taught that the flesh of Christ descended from Heaven and came through the Theotokos as it were through a conduit.

[9] The Marcionites (or Messalians), who first appeared in the second century, were another Gnostic sect that taught disdain for anything that was of this creation. Marriage was an "abomination," and God was the creator of evil.

self to mortal human beings, and they deify men. Hence, they are clearly heretics and must be baptized when they convert. Even though Dionysius (of Alexandria) says that they should not be baptized, he has erred in this matter and we should not follow him on this point.

Concerning schismatics, there are two opinions.

On the one hand, both Saint Cyprian and the two Councils that took place with him in Africa (see the Synodical and Canonical Epistle of the Local Council of Carthage, which convened in 256), and also the Council at Iconium under Saint Firmilian, observed exactness in this matter and enjoined that the Cathari, the Encratites[10] and Apotactites (see footnote for the 45th Canon of the Sixth Ecumenical Council), and the Hydroparastites[11] (see footnote for the 32nd Canon of the Sixth Ecumenical Council), and simply, all schismatics who return to the Catholic Church should be baptized. [This practice should be observed, said the above-mentioned Fathers] because, although the first clergymen among the schismatics had received from the Church the gift to ordain and to baptize, yet, once they had torn themselves from the Body of the Church, they lost this gift and could no longer baptize or ordain others, or impart grace, which they lost through their schism.[12] Hence, they that have been baptized by them are accounted to have been baptized by laymen, and thus they are in need of baptism.

On the other hand, some bishops in Asia accepted [the schismatics'] baptism out of economy and condescension, and not by exactness, as though the schismatics were still members of the

---

[10] The Encratites rejected marriage, saying that it was of Satan; also they would not partake of the flesh of any animal.

[11] The Hydroparastites used water instead of wine in their communion and taught that marriage was fornication.

[12] For, even as a bodily member straightway dies when it is severed from the body because it no longer receives vivifying strength, in like manner, once they have been separated from the Body of the Church, schismatics die straightway and lose the spiritual grace and power of the Holy Spirit, since it is no longer imparted to them through the spiritual sinews, nerves and tendons, that is, through the unity that is according to the Spirit.

Church; thus, said they, let it be accepted. According to the exactness of the Canons, however, the schismatic Encratites in particular should be baptized on their return to the Church, because they deviated from the Church's tradition in the matter of baptism and devised their own form of baptism,[13] and because no distinct and clear decision was made as to how they should be received. And though they do not rebaptize Orthodox who go to them, this should not impress us to the extent that we should not baptize those of them that come to us. However, if the fact that we baptize them becomes an obstacle in regard to the common condescension and economy that the Fathers showed toward all schismatics, let us also follow [the Fathers] in this matter, lest by the strictness of this rule we make them reluctant to receive baptism, and supposedly, cause them to be ashamed because they are being baptized as though they were complete infidels, and we thereby place an obstacle to their salvation. To put it briefly, they that have been baptized by them and return to Orthodoxy must absolutely be chrismated with holy Chrism by the faithful clergy and thus partake of the holy Mysteries.

And since we have received bishops from among the Encratites—as well as their ordinations—we have formed a rule, as it were, by this practice, and shown that they are no longer separated from the Catholic Church. See also the Interpretation of the 46th Apostolic Canon, and of the 8th Canon of the First Ecumenical Council, and of the 7th Canon of the Second Ecumenical Council.[14]

Translator's Note: The Interpretation given here is found in *The Rudder*, and is a synopsis of the commentaries made by the Church's acknowledged canon law experts: Zonaras, Balsamon, and Aristenos.

---

[13] Indeed, if, according to Saint Basil, these schismatics should be baptized, because they had devised some baptismal custom of their own, how much more should the Latins be baptized, since they have not simply strayed from the Church's tradition in the matter of baptism, but have completely corrupted it, and are not only schismatics, but clearly in heresy?

[14] It should be noted that Saint Basil's First Canon is cited in the First Act of the Seventh Ecumenical Council.

APPENDIX M

"Sectarian" Orthodox Christians[1]

Since we now live in the "Age of Information," we have also become increasingly aware of how information can be manipulated in order to shape people's opinions. Advertising is a form of information, as is propaganda. We all know about "misinformation;" in the past couple of decades, the word "disinformation" has also entered our vocabulary. Then, too, there are instances when information is withheld for some ulterior motive. Since our society is always coming up with neologisms—"new words"—we ask our readers to allow us the liberty of creating a new word—"uninformation"—to describe this stratagem of leaving out important facts for the purpose of misleading others.

An example of "uninformation" could well occur, for example, if we were to allow the military and political leaders of the Axis Powers (Nazi Germany, Fascist Italy, and Imperialist Japan) to give us their version of the history of the Second World War. "Basically," they might well say, "the history of the Second World War may be summed up in one sentence: America and her allies purposely targeted, bombed, and even 'nuked' our cities, and maimed and killed hundreds of thousands of innocent men, women and children."

We know this statement is true. We also know, however, that some vital facts are left out. First of all, the Axis historians neglect to tell us that their side started the war. Then, no mention is made of the Axis' highly effective *blitzkrieg*, the rape of Poland, Czechoslovakia, the Netherlands, France, Greece, and many other countries of Europe, the "super-race" theory, Pearl Harbor, the death marches, the holocaust, the laboratory (i.e., torture chamber) experiments on living human beings, the gas chambers, and the wholesale extermination of entire villages and towns.

Naturally, leaving out such important facets of history changes the whole picture. This constitutes "uninformation"—an ugly word, to be sure, but then, its motives and ultimate purposes are not so pretty either.

[1] *Orthodox Christian Witness*, June 10/23, 1991.

Instances of uninformation appear occasionally in articles or publications of a religious nature as well. One remarkable example of uninformation appears in Anne Freemantle's popular book, *A Treasury of Early Christianity*. In this book, Freemantle, a devoted Roman Catholic, has a chapter on the various Creeds that were used in antiquity by Christians. When she comes to the Nicene Creed, she quotes the entire text, with, however, one small alteration. That is to say, at the point where the original Nicene Creed reads:

> And in the Holy Spirit, the Lord, the Giver of life; Who proceedeth from the Father

Freemantle adds the phrase *"and from the Son,"* and, in a footnote, she explains, "These words are *omitted* [emphasis ours] by the Orthodox Church."[2]

As our readers will perceive, this must certainly rank as a remarkable example of uninformation.

Unfortunately, some new calendar Orthodox writers have begun resorting to the same sort of uncommendable methods.

In a feature article entitled "Religious Question Box" (*Hellenic Chronicle*, Feb. 28, 1991), Father Stanley Harakas deals briefly with the "old calendar" question. Father Stanley writes, "It is important to note that the Old Calendar movement has nearly all the marks of a sect." He ascribes the "I am holier than you" mentality to the "old calendarists" and then goes on to describe some of the splits that have occurred within the ranks of those who adhere to the traditional ecclesiastical calendar, noting that "sectarian movements are notoriously unstable." He also declares the "old calendarists" to be schismatics.

Having a new calendar clergyman describe the history of those who follow the Julian calendar is, in many ways, similar to allowing an Axis military commander to tell us the history of the Second World War. A lot of information falls by the wayside. Many facts become "collateral damage."

---

[2] Anne Freemantle, *A Treasury of Early Christianity*, Mentor Books, 1953, p. 256.

To begin with, it would be erroneous for us to say that *this* calendar is Orthodox and *that* one is heretical. Yet, it must be pointed out that, in this particular instance, the anathemas which Ecumenical Patriarch Jeremias II pronounced against the new calendar (and which Father Stanley omits to mention) were aimed primarily at stemming the tide of Uniatism that was seeping into the Orthodox communities in Italy and Austria. That this concern over Uniatism was entirely justified was confirmed by the Encyclical issued by the Ecumenical Patriarchate in 1920. This Encyclical—which addresses the Protestant and Roman Catholic denominations as "fellow heirs of God"—opened the flood-gates of Ecumenism when it listed what steps should be taken in order to achieve the union of "the Churches of Christ, wheresoever they might be," as it addressed the various heterodox bodies. The very first step that the Encyclical mentions is "the adoption by all the churches of one single calendar so that the great Christian feasts may be everywhere celebrated simultaneously." This attempt to establish a simultaneous celebration of the Church's feasts with the heterodox (regardless of what their doctrines are) is precisely why the new calendar was strictly condemned by *eleven* Church Councils and Holy Synods.[3]

This is a very large amount of information that Father Stanley fails to mention.

Who, then, is the sectarian? The one who obeys the decrees of Church Councils, or the one who defies them?

Also, Father Stanley also does not tell us that Archbishop Chrysostom Papadopoulos of Athens—the very man who was instrumental in having the Greek Church adopt the new calendar—prepared a report about the new calendar just one year before he himself pushed through the change. This is what he wrote:

[3] The Pan-Orthodox Councils held in Constantinople in 1583, 1587 and 1593; the Holy Synod of the Great Church in 1902 and 1904; the Holy Synods of Russia, of Jerusalem, of Greece, and of Romania, each independently, in 1903; the Holy Synod of Greece again in 1919, and the Holy Synod of the Patriarchate of Alexandria in 1924; not to mention the condemnations of the new calendar issued by Patriarch Dositheos of Jerusalem (1670), Ecumenical Patriarch Agathangelos (1827), and Ecumenical Patriarch Anthimos IV (1895).

No Orthodox autocephalous Church can separate itself from the rest and accept the new calendar without becoming schismatic in the eyes of the others.

(Report to the Committee of the Department of Religion, January 16, 1923)

Now, then, who is "creating schisms"?

But there is much more that Father Stanley does not tell us.

Father Stanley writes that the old calendarists are divided among themselves, but he does not mention the many overlapping new calendar jurisdictions that exist in North and South America, Europe, Australia and elsewhere. Also he does not tell us that, at the present, there are two, or perhaps three, sets of new calendar bishops in Greece—the "pre-junta" bishops, the "junta" bishops, and the "post-junta" bishops. Some of the pre-junta bishops were displaced by the junta bishops, some of whom, in turn, were themselves displaced by the post-junta bishops. Currently, a number of these new calendar bishops are in the courts, fighting over which of them are the legal hierarchs of the various dioceses of Greece. So far, the courts have come out in favor of the pre-junta and junta bishops, but the post-junta bishops (the ones currently in power) are trying to circumvent this decision (e.g., by the creation of seven new dioceses on a provisional and temporary basis).

Yet, we must admit that divisions do exist among the traditional Orthodox Christians also, and that these divisions are sometimes due to human weakness. However, it is equally true that many of the divisions that exist among us are due to the new calendarists. How so?

When the calendar change was first implemented in the early 1920's, the bishops of the new calendar Church in Greece (and also in Romania) unleashed a terrible persecution against those clergy and faithful who refused to follow them in this innovation. The innovating bishops ordered the police to break up any church services held according to the traditional ecclesiastical reckoning. Hence, the police, swinging their clubs, forcibly entered the churches during the services. Heads were smashed, people were killed, priests were pulled out of the sanctuary by gendarmes who walked right through the Royal Doors; Holy Communion was spilled, chalices broken in half. Priests were stripped of their rassa, shaved, dressed in dirty and ragged secular clothing and pushed out into the street. Nuns had their habits ripped off and then they too were pushed out into the street. Churches and monasteries and convents built by the True Orthodox Christians were confiscated or bulldozed.[4]

At the same time this was happening, these Orthodox Christians were told by the new calendarist bishops that their children were unbaptized, that the marriages performed by "old calendarist" priests were invalid, and that their children were illegitimate and had no inheritance rights. Yet the True Orthodox Christians saw that the new calendar bishops in Europe and America *accepted* the validity of the baptisms, weddings, and ordinations performed by Roman Catholics, Anglicans, and others—even though these people have been separated from the Church for almost one thousand years, and in the meantime have espoused additional errors and heresies (and, if one were to judge from newspaper reports, seem to be inventing new heresies and blasphemous policies all the while).

Now, how should a traditional Orthodox Christian assess this situation? How should he have responded to this vicious persecution on the part of the new calendarists, and to the fact that his Mysteries were considered invalid (although he had not changed any doctrine of the Church), and to the fact that, simultaneously, the new calendar hierarchy recognized the validity of the sacraments of those who openly taught and continue to teach heresy without any remorse whatsoever?

[4] In 1936, the new calendar Metropolitan of Phokis, Joachim, entered the "old calendar" church in Desphini of Phokis during the time of the Divine Liturgy while Father Hieromonk Theonas was serving. Metropolitan Joachim grabbed the holy chalice out of the hands of Father Theonas, threw it to the ground, and trampled it with his feet until it was completely flattened; then he seized Father Theonas, tore out his beard with his bare hands, pushed him to the ground and began kicking him mercilessly. A short time later, Father Theonas died from his wounds. Despite this homicidal act, Metropolitan Joachim was later rewarded with advancement to a larger diocese, the Metropoly of Demetrias. (*Dialogue of an Old Calendarist with a New Calendarist*, by Monk Spyridon, Birmingham, England.)

What happened was that the True Orthodox Christians became divided. Some said that the innovating hierarchy had initiated a true schism, and therefore that the canons regarding schism should be applied. They believed that there was no way that the new calendar church could in any way be the Church of Christ, since it was doing all these terrible and sacrilegious things against the faithful; others said that we should await a synodal decision before making a final judgment (although, actually, the calendar change had been condemned already by many Councils, as we have already mentioned); yet others said that the people who followed the new calendar did not really know what was going on, and that it was solely the responsibility of the new calendar bishops. And so on. Thus, this became a major cause for the True Orthodox Christians to become divided.

So, from all these facts that Father Stanley left out, we can see that it is not actually a matter of sectarianism or schism on the part of the True Orthodox Christians, but of innovation, heresy, and sacrilegious and bloody persecution on the part of those who inaugurated the innovation. In other words, it is a matter of confession of the Orthodox Christian Faith in the face of ecumenism and syncretism.

Towards the end of his article, Father Stanley writes: "They [the "old calendarists"] keep themselves out of communion with the canonical Orthodox Church. For this, we are genuinely sorry."

We also are sincerely grieved that this separation exists. However, we do not agree with Father Stanley's personal assessment of what constitutes a "canonical Orthodox Church." In this particular case, our Saviour's words come to mind: "Out of thine own mouth will I judge thee" (Luke 19:22). However, this important question will be dealt with in a subsequent article.

APPENDIX N

"Uncanonical" Orthodox Christians[1]

In response to what he may perceive as a growing threat, Father Stanley Harakas of the new calendar Greek Archdiocese has dedicated some of his recent articles to the question of the "old calendarists." In a previous article, "'Sectarian' Orthodox Christians" (*Orthodox Christian Witness*, 10/23 June, 1991), we examined how Father Stanley suppressed many important facts about the traditional Orthodox Christians, and how he omitted to mention, for example, the terrible persecutions that the new calendarists unleashed against the Orthodox faithful.

In the "Religious Question Box" of the *Hellenic Chronicle* of Feb. 28, 1991, Father Stanley wrote that "the calendar isolates [the traditional Orthodox Christians] from the rest of society and from the canonical Orthodox Church." Furthermore, he adds, the traditional Orthodox believers "deprive Orthodoxy of a constructive witness" to society and the world in general.

Orthodox Christians who have chosen to remain faithful to the Church's Tradition and its conciliar decrees find Father Stanley's statements amazing. "The calendar isolates them from the rest of society," he writes. Now, if by "isolation" he means that we prefer to observe Christmas without the help of Rudolph the Red-Nosed Reindeer and blatant commercialism, then he is 100% correct. If he associates the celebration of the Nativity of Christ with "I'm Dreaming of a White Christmas," then we'll let "the rest of society" in Australia (which celebrates that holiday in the midst of torrid summer heat) reply to him!

His assertion that the canonical church calendar "deprives Orthodoxy of a constructive witness" to society will also come as news to all of our many converts to Orthodoxy. Thanks be to God, in our monastic establishments and in many of our parishes, seventy to eighty percent of the members are converts to Orthodoxy. In some parishes, one hundred percent are converts.

[1] *Orthodox Christian Witness*, June 24 / July 7, 1991.

We wonder how many new calendar parishes have those kind of percentages?

Who, then, is "isolationist"? Those who emphasize ethnicity, or those who are earnest in bringing souls to Orthodoxy?

Perhaps Father Stanley feels that the traditional Orthodox Christians do not bear a "constructive witness" to Orthodoxy in our society because we are not members of the World Council of Churches (WCC). In *The Illuminator* (March–April, 1991), the official newspaper of the new calendar Greek diocese of Pittsburgh, Bishop Maximos, in fact, says this in so many words. In the feature column "Our Readers Ask," one subscriber poses the question: "Should our Holy Orthodox Church continue to be involved in the 'ecumenical movement'?" Bishop Maximos replies: "The answer to your question is YES. Our Church should continue to be involved with the 'ecumenical movement,' in spite of the risks that we incur by so doing." Bishop Maximos then adds some derogatory references to those who do not participate in Ecumenism:

> Our place is in the ecumenical movement, if we should continue to bear witness to the truth entrusted to Holy Orthodoxy, giving reasons for the hope which is in us!
>
> It is very correctly stated that the more well-rooted one is in his own tradition, the more flexible, compassionate, and understanding one is toward others; and the more uncertain and insecure one is with regard to his faith and church, the more impatient, nervous, and intolerant one is in the presence of others and with regard to others.

Since Bishop Maximos affirms that only the "uncertain" and "insecure" would be reluctant to discuss their Orthodox Faith with others, let us examine what the confident, secure, knowledgeable and "well-rooted" new calendar Orthodox representatives are doing in the WCC.

A cursory examination of "new style Orthodoxy's" role in the WCC will demonstrate how deficient their witness really is. A few examples:

1) At the WCC General Assembly in Uppsala in 1968, the delegates—including the Orthodox—opened the session with the prayer: "O God, Father, You can make all things new . . . Your love is stretched out upon all men, to seek the Truth, *which we have not known.*"

This is a constructive and well-rooted witness to Orthodoxy?

2) At the WCC General Assembly at Nairobi in 1975, the Orthodox delegates made this astounding statement: "The Orthodox do not expect the other Christians to be converted to Orthodoxy in its historic and cultural reality of the past and the present and to become members of the Orthodox Church." How wonderful! "We do not expect you to be converted to Orthodoxy."

This is a constructive and well-rooted witness to Orthodoxy?

3) At an official meeting of a WCC committee that met in Barr, Switzerland, from January 9-15, 1990, some twenty-one Orthodox, Protestant, and Roman Catholic representatives drafted a 2,500 word statement on "Religious Plurality: Theological Perspectives and Affirmations." These twenty-one official representatives of their respective church groups cited the need for "a more adequate theology of religions" (what the Church has taught for centuries about false belief and idolatry is apparently not sufficient), and, in the section on Christology the participants affirmed

> "that in Jesus Christ, the incarnate Word, the entire human family has been united to God in an irrevocable bond and covenant. The saving presence of God's activity in all creation and human history comes to its focal point in the event of Christ." But, they add, "because we have seen and experienced goodness, truth and holiness among followers of other paths and ways than that of Jesus Christ . . . , *we find ourselves recognizing a need to move beyond a theology which confines salvation to the explicit personal commitment to Jesus Christ.*"
> (*Ecumenical Press Service*, 16-31 Jan., 1990)

This is also a constructive and well-rooted witness to Orthodoxy?

Who, then, is depriving Orthodoxy of a constructive and true witness to society? Those who have embraced these Ecumenistic ideals, or those who refuse to participate in such compromises?

In yet another article on the "old calendarists" (*Hellenic Chronicle*, April 18, 1991), Father Stanley Harakas writes that a mark of canonicity is recognition by a canonical Orthodox Church. This is very true. A key to recognizing what group is a "canonical Orthodox Church," writes Father Stanley, is "mutual episcopal recognition."

Since "mutual episcopal recognition" is the keystone in ascertaining who is in communion with a canonical Orthodox Church, then what would Father Stanley have to say about the following bishops who "mutually recognize" one another and with whom he and his jurisdiction were and still are in full communion?

1) A bishop who boasts before many of his clergy that he gives communion to both Roman Catholics and Protestants (Ecumenical Patriarch Athenagoras).
2) A bishop who openly admits that he has given communion to those who do not accept the decisions of the Seven Ecumenical Councils (Bishop Kallistos Ware).
3) A bishop who openly and publicly gave communion to Roman Catholic clergymen in Rome (Metropolitan Nikodim of Leningrad).
4) A bishop who has openly and repeatedly given communion to Roman Catholics and refused to acknowledge that he did wrong (Metropolitan Philip Saliba).
5) A bishop who declares that the future "united" Church of Christ will be neither Roman Catholic, Protestant, or Orthodox (Archbishop Iakovos of the United States).
6) A bishop who declares—with the official approval of the Ecumenical Patriarchate—that it is permitted for Roman Catholics to receive communion from Orthodox and for Orthodox to receive communion from Roman Catholics and Anglicans (Archbishop Athenagoras of Thyateira).
7) A bishop who performs pannikhidas for avowed and militant atheists (Patriarch Pimen of Moscow).
8) A bishop who declares at his enthronement that the Pope of Rome is "the first bishop of Christianity," whereas he

himself is only "the first bishop of Orthodoxy" (Ecumenical Patriarch Demetrios).
9) A bishop who declares that, if an Orthodox or Roman Catholic layperson is dying and a clergyman of either one's denomination is unavailable, the Roman Catholic may receive communion from an Orthodox priest, and the Orthodox may receive from a Roman Catholic clergyman (Ecumenical Patriarch Demetrios).
10) A bishop who has given a blessing that communion be given to those who do not accept the decisions of the Seven Ecumenical Councils (Bishop Anthony of the new calendar Greek diocese of San Francisco).
11) A bishop who promises that, as soon as he has a printing press, he will print copies of the Koran—which, of course, contains blasphemous teachings against our Saviour and the Holy Trinity (Metropolitan Pitirim of Volokolamsk, the head of the Publishing Department of the Moscow Patriarchate).
12) A bishop who publicly declares that Mohammed is a prophet and apostle of God, and that those who speak against Mohammedanism and Buddhism are not in agreement with God (Patriarch Parthenios of Alexandria).

This list could continue for some pages.

According to Holy Tradition, there is no way that these bishops could be esteemed either "canonical" or "Orthodox," no matter now much they "mutually recognize" each other!

Bishops can "mutually recognize each other" in erroneous doctrines. The Roman Catholics, and also the Episcopalians, have been doing it for centuries! A former Anglican priest, Father Athanasios Ledwich, described his pilgrimage to Orthodoxy in a striking article entitled "Cracks in the Cathedral," in the periodical *Again* (Vol. 13, No. 3). He records his growing disillusionment with the Anglican communion, "and then," he writes, "came the Durham affair of 1984." And he continues:

> David Jenkins was a professor at Leeds University who was elected to the vacant See of Durham. Following his election he appeared on television denying that he believed in the Virgin Birth and the Bodily Resurrection of Christ as historical events.

It seemed to some of us that we could not let such a radical statement pass without challenging the rightness of ordaining him to the episcopacy.

This seemed to me a test case. If the Church of England were to consecrate a man who had openly uttered such heresy in public without asking him to retract, *then it was not a single bishop who was at fault: it was the whole body which made him a bishop that could be accused of heresy* [emphasis ours]. It was a theological litmus paper which was certainly vital for me. After a petition to the Archbishop of York (the consecrating bishop), and a national furor which gripped the media for two months, the Archbishop decided that he would proceed with the consecration. The Church of England after all, he said, was a comprehensive body which tolerated all manner of belief so long as the Creed could in good conscience be said.

Following the consecration, I offered my resignation as a clergyman of the Hereford Diocese to the bishop and gave up my job as chaplain in an Anglican school.

If we are to go on the basis of traditional Orthodox Christian theology, the hierarchy of "World Orthodoxy" has repeatedly failed the "litmus test," since not *one* of them has protested over the uncanonical and unOrthodox teachings and actions of their colleagues, nor have they cut off communion with them, as the holy canons and the Church Fathers teach us to do.

When new calendar clergy begin speaking about "canonicity," they are skating on very thin ice, and we are obliged to address them with our Saviour's words: "Out of thine own mouth will I judge thee."

Some time ago, a student at a new calendar theological school asked one of his professors, a clergyman, what he thought of a nearby Orthodox monastery that observed the traditional church calendar. "They are uncanonical," replied the priest. "Forgive me, Father," replied the student, "but in view of the fact that one of our own bishops in Australia—Bishop Ezekiel of Derbe—just recently, in a newspaper interview, referred to the holy canons and *The Rudder* as 'toilet paper,' what grounds do we have for calling these people 'uncanonical'? And, what is worse," continued the student, "not *one* of our bishops censured or rebuked Bishop Ezekiel for making that remark."

What was the priest's answer? He turned around and walked away.

Now, then, who is "uncanonical"? Those who honor the holy canons and strive to the best of their ability to fulfil them, or those who call them "toilet paper"?

Such a "constructive and well-rooted witness to Orthodoxy" we certainly can do without.

We and the many with us who have converted to traditional Orthodox Christianity are very grieved over this separation from our erstwhile brothers and sisters in the Faith. But we are also very grateful to God that we did not initiate the innovation that brought about this separation and that we have no part in what they are doing now.

No, our "little flock" prefers the narrow and afflicted path that has been marked out by our Saviour and all His Saints—to which may we adhere till the end of our earthly days. Amen.

APPENDIX O

New Calendar Donatism?[1]

No, thank God, the new calendarists are not Donatists. Neither are any traditional Orthodox Christians Donatists (at least, none that we know of).[2]

Recently, a priest of a Russian jurisdiction wrote that some traditional Orthodox Christian jurisdictions (which follow the Julian calendar) are "neo-Donatists" because they do not recognize the validity of new calendar Mysteries. However, this statement is not quite accurate for two reasons:

1) The priest in question apparently does not know what

---

[1] *Orthodox Christian Witness,* March 14/27, 1994.

[2] There were two spokesmen for this heresy who were named Donatus: Donatus Magnus ("the Great"), bishop of Carthage (A.D. 315), and Donatus, bishop of Casae Nigrae, in North Africa, who also died in the early part of the fourth century. The Donatist movement continued for over a century.

Donatism is. According to historical documents, we know, first of all, that the Donatists taught that if one apostatized from the Faith, he could never be forgiven. Secondly, they believed that if a clergyman had fallen into some sin, the Mysteries performed by him had no grace, and were invalid. The position of the Donatists was that the Mysteries depended upon the personal holiness of the priest and that apostasy was unforgivable.

The Church, however, rejected these pernicious doctrines of the Donatists and declared them heretical because God, not man, effects the Mysteries, and Christ opened His arms to receive and forgive repentant sinners (of whom the Apostle Peter was a prime example, for upon his repentance he was reinstated, despite the fact that he had denied Christ three times).

Neither the new calendar jurisdictions nor traditional Orthodox Christians adhere to these blasphemous doctrines of the Donatists.

2) The priest in question apparently is unaware of the fact that it was the new calendar bishops—not the traditional Orthodox hierarchy—who were the first to maintain that the other's Mysteries were invalid.[3] The new calendar bishops maintained this position *vis-à-vis* the traditional Orthodox Christians, while at the

[3] On April 24, 1926, in the periodical *Ecclesia* (an official organ of the new calendar Archdiocese of Athens), the new calendar Synod of the Church of Greece published an Encyclical, number 2398/2203, against the traditional Orthodox Christians. This Encyclical states, in part: "They separate themselves from the Church and cut themselves off from the Body of Christ, drawing upon themselves condemnation and excommunication, not knowing, or perhaps forgetting, that he who does not hear the Church is 'as the heathen man and the publican' (Matt. 18:17);" and further on, *"The decisions of the Church are absolutely obligatory; he who does not obey them no longer belongs to her; he is deprived of the means of divine grace; he is separated and cut off from her, and is liable to eternal torment"* [emphasis added]. This Encyclical was issued in 1926, only two years after the traditional Orthodox Christians had separated themselves from the new calendar hierarchy because they did not wish to fall under the anathemas of the Pan-Orthodox Councils of the sixteenth century. Meanwhile, the new calendarists, beginning with the Ecumenical Patriarchate, were already recognizing the unrepentant and heterodox denominations as "fellow-heirs of God" (see the Ecumenical Patriarchate's Encyclical of 1920, p. 178 of this book). So, for new calendarists and ecumenists, the non-Orthodox bodies—not the traditional Orthodox Christians—are "fellow-heirs of God"!

same time recognizing the validity of the sacraments of the non-Orthodox denominations, calling them "Churches of Christ" and "fellow-heirs of the grace of God"! In fact, this practice continues to this very day! For example, the Antiochian Archdiocese's Metropolitan Philip Saliba (who has given communion to Roman Catholics on several occasions and refused to acknowledge that he acted wrongly) recently in a letter to one of his clergymen referred to traditional Orthodox Christians as "so-called Orthodox." Apparently, the good Metropolitan feels that if you question his authority when he tramples upon a doctrine of the Orthodox Church, you automatically become a "so-called Orthodox."

What this type of mentality led to in Greece, Romania, and Russia, until a couple of decades ago, was that the innovating bishops of those countries felt they had the "right" to destroy or confiscate the churches, spill the Holy Communion, desecrate the altars, and club the heads of the traditional Orthodox Christians, and, in Russia, even send them to die by the millions in the Gulag.

But, thank God, at least these bishops are not Donatists!

It is for all the above-mentioned reasons, and only after many pleas and appeals to the innovating bishops, and only after many years, that the traditional Orthodox Christians also, basing themselves on Saint Basil the Great's First Canon, finally took the step to pronounce the Mysteries of the innovating jurisdictions invalid—but only after they had given up hope of seeing any change of direction among those jurisdictions.

Is there any chance that the traditional Orthodox Christians might reconsider and retract this decision?

Of course!

The only thing that is necessary for this to happen is that the innovating bishops must make some retractions themselves. For example:

1) They must re-affirm and adhere once again to the decisions of the Pan-Orthodox Councils of Constantinople of 1583, 1587, and 1593 (which placed under anathema anyone who adopted the new calendar).
2) They must retract their Encyclicals against the traditional

Orthodox Christians; also the Ecumenical Patriarchate must retract its Encyclical of 1920, which referred to the non-Orthodox denominations as "Churches of Christ" and "fellow-heirs of God," especially since these denominations continue to teach many false doctrines—indeed, doctrines which are getting falser and falser with every passing day, and which, in addition, are promoting a manner of life that is more and more un-Christian.

3) Since the Papacy has not retracted any of its errors, but has added even more since 1054, the anathema against that denomination must be reinstated by the innovating bishops.

4) Since the Pope has not retracted any of his errors, among which is the new doctrine of papal infallibility, the Ecumenical Patriarch must cease commemorating him in the diptychs as though he were an Orthodox bishop.

5) The Ecumenical Patriarch must also cease commemorating "all the confessions of the East and West" in the diptychs, since they are not Orthodox in their faith.

6) The bishops of "World Orthodoxy" must issue a definitive condemnation of Freemasonry, since it is the matrix of ecumenism and syncretism.

7) The bishops of "World Orthodoxy" must abandon their membership in the National Council of Churches ("Heresy Central"), and the World Council of Churches (the "Sanhedrin of Syncretism").

8) The jurisdictions of "World Orthodoxy" must cease having joint prayers with the non-Orthodox, and cease giving communion (as the Patriarchate of Antioch does officially) to those who do not accept the authority and decisions of the Seven Ecumenical Councils.

9) They should also officially condemn the "Branch Theory," and cease referring to the non-Orthodox (including the Unitarians) as members of the Body of Christ.

and

10) Their bishops should cease referring to Mohammed as an apostle of God (Patriarch Parthenios of Alexandria), and to the holy canons as "toilet paper" (Bishop Ezekiel of

Derbe, Australia), and to traditional Orthodox Christians as "so-called Orthodox"!

Really, is this asking too much from bishops who want to be known as Orthodox?

The innovating bishops must remember and honor the oath they took at their consecration to be faithful to Christ, and to preserve the deposit of the Orthodox Faith that they had received, and to transmit it inviolate to their successors. The practical application of this oath would require their acting to correct the violations of the Orthodox Faith that have been enumerated above.

We acknowledge that, under the duress of persecution, or out of desperation, or out of mistaken judgment, or just plain human weakness, the traditional Orthodox Christians also have made some canonical mistakes, just as the new calendar and innovating bishops have quite intentionally made canonical and doctrinal errors. But all things can be corrected through charity and humility in Christ.

Is this asking too much?

The fact that neither of us are Donatists is certainly a good starting point.

APPENDIX P

Our Readers Ask....[1]

(From the May–August, 1995, issue of *The Illuminator*, the official publication of the New Calendar Greek Orthodox Diocese of Pittsburgh)

Question: We know that officially our Church receives all those baptized in the Name of the Holy Trinity by profession of faith, or, if they are not confirmed, by Holy Chrismation. How do you feel about the new practice [*sic*] of receiving anyone who is not baptized in the Orthodox Church by baptism?

B. A., York, PA

---

[1] *Orthodox Christian Witness*, July 3/16, 1995.

Answer: Your assumption that our Holy Orthodox Church receives all those baptized in the Holy Trinity and correctly professing faith in the Holy Trinity is correct. Also, as is the case of the Oriental Orthodox Churches, faithful coming from those churches are accepted by profession of faith only.

You are also correct in stating that if baptized in churches which profess faith in the Holy Trinity but who do not have a true sacrament of confirmation (or Chrismation), as they do not have true ("valid") priesthood, they are accepted by Chrismation.

Non-Trinitarians, or Anti-Trinitarian sects in the United States, including those who profess a kind of Christian mythology by their belief in a "material" God, are catechized and baptized, because their "baptism" is a "baptism of water," but not of the Spirit.

However, to treat Trinitarian Christians as unbaptized heathens is an injustice committed against Christian baptism, and eventually a blasphemy against God's Holy Spirit Who is at work at any Christian baptism.

When we profess faith in *one* Christian baptism for the forgiveness of sins, we do not mean by that Orthodox baptism, but any Christian baptism which is the doing of the Christian faith in the Holy Trinity. The one faith of the Church is at work, through God's Holy Spirit whose work cannot be limited by human canonical boundaries we have established for our own convenience. We cannot bind the Spirit, and not allow Him to work with all the other Christians, just because some of us have so decided.

The famous recent book entitled *I Confess One Baptism*, which continues to limit the Spirit within the canonical boundaries of Holy Orthodoxy, does a great injustice: Holy Orthodoxy has greater discernment than this. Also, to say that the Roman Church left the Church and left the Spirit (and, consequently, the Spirit left her) at the Eighth Ecumenical Council (A.D. 879-880) is historically inaccurate and fallacious.

Actually, the Eighth Council restored the unity between the Eastern and the Western Churches. The representatives of both Churches had agreed that the Roman primacy had to be exercised in the "West" (that is, in its own jurisdictional territory, whatever that was) and the primacy of the Church of Constantinople had to continue to function within its own territory of the East (that is, the Eastern part of the Byzantine Empire), without interference from the Church of Rome.

Also, the *Filioque* clause (the procession of the Spirit *and from the Son*) was rejected by that Council as inauthentic and erroneous, and so was the teaching behind it (this teaching takes its origin in Saint Augustine's teaching).

The problem of the West is that later it alienated itself from the teaching and the authority of this Eighth Council.

Obviously, when the West will return to the teaching of this commonly accepted Council by both East and West, Rome and Constantinople alike, the "Western," Roman Catholic Church will basically become Orthodox again. We hope and pray that this day will come soon. Just look at the editorial in the other column on this same page of this *Illuminator* issue, regarding the opening of a window toward unity by the present Roman Pontiff. In his recent encyclical on Ecumenism, Pope John Paul II indicated that he would allow his primacy to be exercised "in a new situation," that is, in respect of the traditionally established primacy of the Church of Constantinople (Canons 3 of the Second Ecumenical Council in 381; 28 of the Fourth Ecumenical Council in 451; and the Eighth Council, in 879–880). This "new situation" is actually the traditional Orthodox situation.

No matter what this "new situation" in the relationship with the Roman Church might be, our Holy Orthodox Church has never formally rejected the Roman Church as a Christian Church, as some of our fanatics may believe. True, a temporary rejection of the Roman baptism by the Great Church of Constantinople for pastoral reasons has taken place. But this was corrected and re-addressed, as soon as the cause of this rejection disappeared.

This means that in spite of the division between the Eastern and Western Church, Orthodoxy and Roman Catholicism, the two "sister churches" of old, continue to recognize one another's baptism, as well as the other sacraments celebrated in these churches. The Balamand Statement invented nothing new in stating this.

It reaffirmed the main tradition and mainline theology and practice of the Holy Eastern Orthodox Church, unbiased by narrow-mindedness, fanaticism, and bigotry, which "inspires" the re-baptism of baptized Christians.

BISHOP MAXIMOS
Bishop of Pittsburgh

EDITORIAL NOTE *of the Orthodox Christian Witness*

Now let's take just a peek at what some "narrow-minded and fanatical bigots" have to say about all this:

The Traditional Teaching of the Holy Orthodox Church

"We ordain that any bishop or presbyter who has admitted the baptism or sacrifice of heretics be deposed. For what concord hath Christ with Belial, or what part hath a believer with an infidel?"

(46th Apostolic Canon)

"Let a bishop or presbyter who shall baptize again anyone who has rightly received baptism, or who shall not baptize one who has been polluted by the ungodly [i.e., those in heresy] be deposed, as despising the Cross and death of the Lord, and not making a distinction between the true priests and the false."

(47th Apostolic Canon)

"Those baptized by heretics shall be baptized with the one true baptism in order to be admitted to the Church."

(Canon 1 of the Local Council of Carthage)

"We have cut the Latins off from us for no other reason than that they are not only schismatics, but also heretics. For this reason it is wholly improper to unite with them."

(Saint Mark of Ephesus)

"The division of the churches which transpired during the time of Saint Photius the Great was rather for the better, since the Church was in danger of falling away from the One Catholic and Apostolic Church (Orthodox) and becoming Roman, or rather Papal, which preaches not any longer those things of the Holy Apostles, but the dogmas of the Popes."

(Saint Nectarios of Pentapolis)

"Who is the antichrist? ... The one is the pope and the other is he who is on our head" [i.e., the Ottoman Moslem rulers].

(Saint Cosmas of Aitolia)

In the limited space of this article, only one official document is sufficient in order to fully demonstrate to the reader what the Orthodox Church has officially declared concerning Papism.

In 1583, the Pope of Rome, Gregory XIII, who changed the Julian calendar, repeatedly pressured the Patriarch of Constantinople, Jeremias II, who was called "the Illustrious," to follow him in the calendar innovation. The Patriarch repeatedly refused with letters, and finally the same year he convened a Council in Constantinople at which, besides himself, were present the Patriarch of Alexandria, Sylvester; the Patriarch of Jerusalem, Sophronios; and many other bishops. This Council issued a *Sigillion* which was sent to all the regional Orthodox churches and which enumerates the principal heresies of the Papacy and anathematizes (that is, proclaims as being out of the Church) all those who profess them. Here is the entire text of the *Sigillion:*

> To all genuine Christian children of the Holy, Catholic, and Apostolic Church of Christ of the East in Trigovyst and in all places, be grace and peace and mercy from Almighty God.
>
> Not a little distress took possession of the Ark of old, when, storm-tossed, it was borne upon the waters; and if the Lord God, remembering Noah, had not in His good will calmed the water, there would have been no hope of salvation in it. In a like manner with the new Ark of our Church, the heretics have raised up a relentless war against us, and we have deemed it well to leave behind the present tome against them so that with the things written in it you may be able more surely to defend your Orthodoxy. But in order that the document may not be burdensome to simpler people, we have decided to set forth the entire subject to you in simple speech as follows:
>
> From old Rome have come certain persons who learned there to think like Latins; and the bad thing is that from being Byzantine (that is, Greeks), born and bred in our own parts, they not only have changed their faith, but they also battle the Orthodox and true dogmas of the Eastern Church which Christ

Himself and the divine Apostles and the Holy Councils of the Holy Fathers delivered to us. Whereupon, having cut them off as rotten members, we order:

I) Whosoever does not confess with heart and mouth that he is a child of the Eastern Church baptized in an Orthodox manner, and that the Holy Spirit proceeds only from the Father, essentially and hypostatically, as Christ says in the Gospel, although He proceeds from Father and Son in time, let such a one be out of our Church and let him be anathematized.

II) Whosoever does not confess that in the Mystery of Holy Communion laymen should commune from the two kinds, both of the precious Body and Blood, but says that it is enough to receive only the Body, for the Blood is also there, even though Christ has spoken and has given each one separately, and they do not keep it, let such be anathematized.

III) Whosoever says that our Lord Jesus Christ at the Mystical Last Supper used unleavened bread as do the Hebrews and not leavened bread, that is, raised bread, let him be far from us and under the anathema as one who thinks like a Jew and as one who introduces the doctrines of Apollinarius and of the Armenians into our Church, on which account let him be anathematized a second time.

IV) Whosoever says that when our Christ and God comes to judge He does not come to judge the souls together with the bodies, but comes in order to decide only for the body, anathema to him.

V) Whosoever says that when they die the souls of the Christians who repented in this life but did not do their penance go to Purgatory—which is a Greek myth—where fire and torment purify them, and they think that there is no eternal torment, as did Origen, and give cause by this to sin freely, let such a one have the anathema.

VI) Whosoever says that the Pope, and not Christ, is the head of the Church, and that he has authority to admit into Paradise with his letters and can forgive as many sins as will be committed by one who with money receives an indulgence from him, let such a one have the anathema.

VII) Whosoever does not follow the customs of the Church which the Seven Holy Ecumenical Councils have decreed, and the Holy Pascha and calendar which they enacted well for us to follow, but wants to follow the newly-invented Paschalion [the method of fixing the date of Pascha] and the new calendar of the atheist astronomers of the Pope; and, opposing them, wishes to overthrow and destroy the doctrines and customs of the Church which we have inherited from our Fathers, let any such have the anathema and let him be outside of the Church and the Assembly of the Faithful.

VIII) We exhort all pious and Orthodox Christians: remain in these things which you learned and in which you were born and bred, and when the time and circumstances call for it, shed your very blood in order both to keep the Faith given us by our Fathers and to keep your confession. Beware of such people and take care, that our Lord Jesus Christ help you. May the blessing of our humility be with you all. Amen.

The 1,583rd year from the birth of the God-man, Indiction 12, November 20th.

☩ Jeremias, of Constantinople
☩ Sylvester, of Alexandria
☩ Sophronios, of Jerusalem
(and the rest of the Bishops of
the Synod who were present)

This *Sigillion* is found in manuscript Codex 772, in the Sacred Monastery of Saint Panteleimon on the Holy Mountain, and manuscript Codex No. 285 of the cell "The Akathist Hymn" of the Sacred Skete of Kafsokalyvia on the Holy Mountain. It was first published in 1881, in the periodical *The Romanian Orthodox Church* in Bucharest (12th issue), by the Russian Archimandrite Porphyry Uspensky, who copied it from a manuscript codex of the great library of Mount Sinai.

Is a clearer or more eloquent condemnation of Papism needed than this one? Certainly not. Nonetheless, modern "Orthodox" ecumenists within themselves will scorn it, as they have scorned so many other Patristic declarations.

Another eloquent refutation of Bishop Maximos's position is the *Tome of the Holy Church of Christ, Upholding the Holy Baptism Given by God, and Condemning the Variously Performed Baptisms of* the Heretics (see *Against False Union,* Alexander Kalomiros, Saint Nectarios Press, Seattle, 1990, pp. 98-100). This *Tome,* composed in 1756, was signed by Ecumenical Patriarch Cyril, Patriarch Matthew of Alexandria, Patriarch Parthenios of Jerusalem, and endorsed also by Patriarch Sylvester of Antioch.

Evidently—for Bishop Maximos of Pittsburgh—Saint Mark of Ephesus, Saint Cosmas of Aitolia, Saint Nectarios of Pentapolis, and the above-mentioned Orthodox Patriarchs do not belong within "mainline Orthodoxy"!

APPENDIX Q

Letter to Anastasia[1]

Holy Martyr Laurence, Archdeacon of Rome
10/23 August 1995

Dear Anastasia,

I pray that this letter finds you well and with the peace of our Saviour. Amen.

Thank you for your kind note. It is always a great pleasure for me to communicate with people who love our Saviour and strive to live the Christian life in the midst of a society which—as one editorial in the *Wall Street Journal* recently observed—"is suffering from sickness, coarseness and lack of spirituality." (Please note, I do *not* subscribe to the *Wall Street Journal;* a copy of this was sent to me.)

You write that you are saddened about the conflicts within the Orthodox Church, and that you wish you understood these matters more clearly.

Everyone who loves the holy Orthodox Faith is saddened over these conflicts, Anastasia. And unfortunately, the things that divide us are becoming more and more distinct and clear with every passing day. Allow me to explain as briefly as possible:

The 10th Apostolic Canon, which was ratified and accepted by subsequent Ecumenical Councils, states the following:

---

[1] *Orthodox Christian Witness,* August 14/27, 1995.

Whoever is in communion with one who is excommunicated is himself to be excommunicated, as one who brings confusion into the order of the Church.

Saint Mark of Ephesus says:

All the teachers of the Church, all the Councils, and all the Divine Scriptures, exhort us to flee those who uphold other doctrines and to separate from communion with them.

(*Confession of Faith*, XIII, 304)

Canon 15 of the First–Second Council of Constantinople commends those who separate themselves from false bishops *"because of some heresy condemned by the Holy Councils or Fathers."*

What does all of the above have to do with the present day conflicts within Orthodoxy?

The heresy of Monophysitism was officially and solemnly condemned by the last four Holy Ecumenical Councils. Yet, in spite of this, the Patriarchate of Antioch officially and synodically entered into communion with the Monophysites on July 22, 1991—despite the fact that the Monophysites refuse to accept the authority of the last four Ecumenical Councils.

This means that the Patriarchate of Antioch—and all those in communion with it—now come under the solemn condemnations and anathemas of those last four Ecumenical Councils.

Likewise, the teachings of the Roman Catholic denomination have been condemned repeatedly by Local and Pan-Orthodox Councils, and by Saints and Fathers of the Orthodox Church. This brings us to the next point.

On January 25, 1994, the Monophysite Patriarchate of Syria (which, as we just noted above, is now in communion with the Patriarchate of Antioch) entered into full communion with the Roman Catholic Church.

What does this mean?

The answer is not complex at all. It is, alas, all too clear: "World Orthodoxy" (which includes the Greek Archdiocese of North and South America) is in communion with the Patriarchate of Antioch, which is in communion with the Monophysite Patriarchate of Syria, which is in communion with the Roman Catholic Church.

This means that the bishops of "World Orthodoxy," by not cutting off communion with Antioch, have now come under the anathemas of the Holy Ecumenical and Pan-Orthodox Councils.

I wish this were not true, but it is.

This, basically, is what the "conflict" is all about. We, on our part, do not desire to come under the condemnations of the Saints and the holy Councils. Your bishops, on their part, don't seem to be overly concerned about these matters.

This is the crux of the matter. I pray that this answers your concerns.

You are always in our prayers.

In Christ,
✢ Bishop Ephraim

APPENDIX R

Obituary: Elder Sabbas, Monk

From the Cell of Saint Nicholas, Kapsala, Karyes, Mount Athos.

The respected Elder, Father Sabbas, had followed the policy of the nineteen ruling monasteries of Mount Athos, which believed, as do many people, that we must make certain concessions and accommodations in matters of Faith for a period of time.

Since he was virtuous, with a sincere and good intention, the fathers who have only recently come to Mount Athos—the so-called New Holy Mountain Fathers—who hold communion with Ecumenists and commemorate the Ecumenical Patriarchate, would visit the Elder frequently. They would hold him up as an example to their disciples and would say that if the zealot dissent and protest were good, would not the virtuous Father Sabbas belong to it?

However, when the Ecumenical Patriarch Demetrios concelebrated with the Pope of Rome in December of 1987, the Elder roused himself; his soul could not bear to be found in such a blatantly Ecumenistic Church. Along with other ascetics, he protested and separated himself from all the other fathers of Mount Athos who followed the nineteen monasteries. He would not go to church in any of those nineteen or in any of the cells or dependencies which followed them.

All the commemorators were in an uproar; from monastery and cell, many ran to persuade the Elder. But the frequent visits, which became burdensome, were to no avail.

Finally, the Elder was obliged to answer in writing one monk who troubled him frequently, thereby answering all the others troubling him, for they were well-organized and committed to using every means to draw the Elder out of Orthodoxy into the embrace of Ecumenism.

Below is the text of the Elder's letter.

The Cell of Saint Nicholas, Kapsala
August 13, 1991

Dear Father Nicodemos,

Bless!

During your visit to our cell a few days ago, you repeated your un-Orthodox dogmatic pronouncements that we are outside the Church because we do not commemorate Patriarch Demetrios. You also made some other statements as well, for which cause we feel constrained to write the following for your fuller instruction, since the evidence and refutations we tendered during our conversation destroyed your peace and made you angry.

In the *Sayings of the Desert Fathers* it is written that when Abba Agatho was asked if he were proud, a fornicator, and a heretic, he answered that he confirmed the first two accusations, for it was profitable for his soul to do so, but not that he was a heretic, for that signifies separation from God.[1]

According to you (and according to all the monasteries of Mount Athos as well, except for the Monastery of Esphigmenou, the Skete of Prophet Elias, and many zealot Fathers), we are deceived and are schismatics. You find it difficult to admit that the Patriarchate of Constantinople is preaching heresy, because you would be required to admit that your holding communion with these wolves and not shepherds is worthy of condemnation, or you would have to cease following them, according to the command of all the holy Fathers and Councils.

---

[1] Sin and heresy, as the holy Fathers teach us, differ essentially: Sin is a transgression of God's law, but heresy is an *alteration* of God's law.

The Elder Sabbas of Karyes, Mount Athos ✣ October 15/28, 1991.

You attempt to justify the Phanar, but their words and actions show you to be in error. In vain do you invoke the opinion of Father Paisios and of others who are indulgent with present conditions and make concessions, that is, they deal with it by "economy," but when the time comes (supposedly when Demetrios shall enter into communion with the Pope, as you said), you will separate yourselves from whatever is not in concord with the teachings of the holy Fathers and Councils. You greatly deceive yourselves.

As for the admonitions to which you refer—whether of Elder Paisios, or of your neighbor Papa-Isaac, or of anyone else—which maintain that Demetrios rightly divides the word of truth, how can you expect us to accept them as being pleasing to God when they are completely contrary to Orthodox teaching? Since the Truth is betrayed, should it not be called iniquity rather than economy, concession, accommodation, or indulgence? You maintain your stand because Elder Paisios said, "Demetrios is misled by the hierarchs around him to do that which he does not want," and "If we stop commemorating [the Patriarch] we will be outside the Church!" and much more, to which can be applied the words of Saint John Chrysostom, "All their words are foolishness, and the tales of foolish children." These words of theirs are the fruit of a new theology, which the Phanar used in the notorious Encyclical of 1920 by calling heretics "fellow heirs of the grace of God."

You bring forward the words of Saint John Chrysostom, "Not even the blood of martyrdom blots out schism," and of Saint Ignatius the God-bearer, "Let nothing be enacted without the bishop." You conclude that when we separate ourselves from our bishop, we are outside the Church.

The Saints made these true pronouncements, however, in a time of Orthodoxy and Church serenity. Today, when the hurricane of the Ecumenist pan-heresy sweeps away even the elect, the words of the same Saints have force. "If your bishop be heretical, flee, flee, flee as from fire and a serpent" (Saint John Chrysostom). "If thy bishop should teach anything outside of the appointed order, even if he lives in chastity, or if he work signs, or if he prophesy, let him be unto thee as a wolf in sheep's clothing, for he works the destruction of souls" (Saint Ignatius). If Demetrios rightly divided the word of truth, you would have been justified in your use of those quotations you took from the two Saints; but now you edit the Fathers' writings to your taste, in order to justify your guilt for being a fellow-traveler of Demetrios, Parthenios of Alexandria, Iakovos of America, Stylianos Harkianakis of Australia. Are all the many quotations from the holy Councils and Saints not enough for you? Or do you fear, perhaps, being cast out of the synagogue of the heretics? The fact that the other patriarchates hold communion with the Phanar is not really important. What is important is, who follows in the footsteps of the Saints and is with the truth? Parthenios, Patriarch of Alexandria, said that he recognizes Mohammed as an Apostle who worked for the Kingdom of God, and other such blasphemies which you know. There is no need for us to write again the heresies of Iakovos Koukouzis of America, and Stylianos Harkianakis of Australia. You are in communion with these men as though they supposedly rightly divided the word of truth! Who is going to condemn Iakovos Koukouzis? Parthenios? or the committee of Phanariotes under Bartholomew which has been "investigating" for two years now whether Harkianakis is a heretic?[2] Do you not understand that they do not want to pronounce a verdict?

The Phanar promised the delegation of three abbots from Mount Athos that they would retract and correct Patriarch Demetrios's statement to the United Press about receiving communion from the Latins, that they would replace Stylianos Harkianakis as president of the commission for theological dialogue, etc. Has anything been corrected to this day? Or do you believe that we have no responsibility, or guilt, and may remain in communion because Elder Paisios shamelessly says that the declarations and actions of Demetrios are not contrary to our doctrines and do not violate the truth?

History repeats itself. Saint Theodore the Studite, Saint Maximus the Confessor, and many of the other Christians who did not follow the hierarchy which at sundry times preached heresy, were all called schismatics by that hierarchy. Although Saint Gerasimus of the Jordan was served by a lion and was a wonderworker, he was in error because he would not accept the Fourth Ecumenical Council, drawing along with him thousands of monks in Palestine, until he was corrected by Saint Euthymius the Great and repented.

You ask, "Could Elder Paisios and the seventy bishops of the State Church of Greece be in error?"

[2] *Editors' Note:* Harkianakis was accused of preaching heresy by Metropolitan Augustine of Florina and the Orthodox faithful from Australia.

Do you want God to force them to confess Him? At the Iconoclast Council of 754 in the reign of Copronymus, we read in the minutes that fearsome acclamation of the 338 bishops present at the council, "Long live the King! The icons are idols and should either be destroyed or hung high so that they might not be venerated." Do you find it hard to believe that seventy bishops can be deceived today, when, as you see, so many were deceived then? Nowadays, monks desire to gain mitres, abbatial staves, while observing only a nominal confession of Faith—that is, protesting somewhat, but not stopping the commemoration of the Patriarch, and tolerating all the innovations to the Gospel introduced by Demetrios, Iakovos, Parthenios, and those like them. Saint Theodore the Studite, however, writes that the work of the monk is not to tolerate even the least innovation in the Gospel of Christ.

At the concelebration in Rome, Demetrios did not receive the host from the Pope in order to avoid hostile reactions from "conservatives." However, there in Rome, he did subscribe to the doctrine that the Latins possess the Mysteries of the Church, and he continues to do so. Is that not enough? When did the Saints and Christians of any century in which a heresy was widely preached ever react as do you, who continue to commemorate Demetrios? What precedent have you found in the history of the Church so you can say you are following it? If you are sons of the Saints (that is, imitators and followers of the Saints), "ye would have done the works of Abraham" as the Gospel says. In the time of Patriarch Beccus, the fathers of Mount Athos stopped commemorating him even though he had not been deposed by a Council; and because they remained steadfast in their adherence to the precepts of the Fathers (that is, had no communion with those who departed from the Orthodox Faith), Christ granted them the martyr's crown. As for those who concelebrated with the commemorators of the Latin-minded "official" patriarch, Beccus, their corpses are found to this day, as is well known, swollen, stinking, and undecomposed, to be an example to all.

You told us that if Demetrios does not go to confession for the things he has done, he will be damned. You are now admitting that

Cell at Karyes, Mount Athos.

you are following a man who is damning himself by what he is doing. For him to be damning himself [and indeed, for matters pertaining to the Faith and not personal and private sins] means that he is doing the work of the devil. Consequently, you yourself admit that you have the devil as a fellow-traveler.

Are you serious, Father Nicodemos, or are you jesting? If Athenagoras had "repented" and confessed his sin shortly before he died, then would he be saved?[3] Show me even one patristic witness which justifies remaining in a church that preaches heresy, as does that of the "meek and quiet Leader of Orthodoxy, Demetrios." Would such an obedience to a hierarchy that does not rightly divide the word of truth sanctify us? If you do not wish to admit that the Monastery of Esphigmenou and so many zealot Fathers are worthy of honor—according to the Fifteenth Canon of the First-and-Second Council—at least be silent and do

---

[3] Private confession suffices for the forgiveness of personal and private sins, but for public sins against the Faith, a public repentance and correction must also be made according to our Saviour's words: "Whosoever, therefore, shall confess Me before men, him will I confess before My Father which is in Heaven. But whosoever shall deny Me before men, him will I deny before My Father which is in Heaven."

not blaspheme by saying that they are schismatics and outside the Church. You ignore the existence of the Testament of Saint Mark Eugenicus of Ephesus, who did not want the Latin-minded even to come to his funeral.

First study and then make pronouncements. According to your way of thinking, Saint Mark of Ephesus, Saint Maximus the Confessor, and hosts of others who did not hold communion with heretics are outside the Church!

Do you see where your "new theology" leads? Who would ever have thought that fathers of the Holy Mountain would have as their bible the book *The Two Extremes* by Father Epiphanios Theodoropoulos? You recommend making protests like those recommended on pages 19 and 22 of that book, protests over—according to the Ecumenists—"sacred canons which are not applicable in our times because they are lacking in love." He also describes Athenagoras as "having a demonic love." Nevertheless, he remained in communion with those who have "a demonic love." Marvellous consistency!

We saw similar protests on the occasion when the representative of the Monastery of Grigoriou asked that it be recorded in the decisions of the Sacred Community that if the chief secretary were sent to Australia, he would not concelebrate there. The chief secretary finally did not go; but Father Basil, Abbot of Stavronikita, ignoring the decision of all the other monasteries, sent Father Tychon to "help" Archbishop Stylianos Harkianakis. When Father Tychon returned, he was sent to the festival of the Cell of Bourazeri. There the representative of the Monastery of Grigoriou (Father Athanasios) concelebrated with Father Tychon and the rest. No commentary is needed.

Father Epiphanios Theodoropoulos was silenced when they refuted his errors some twenty years ago. But you, with the same untheological arguments, want to justify your communion with patriarchs who preach heresies "with bared head," having a demonic love for heretics while persecuting the genuinely Orthodox, and so emulating Patriarch Beccus, the Emperor Copronymus, and all those like them. When you chant them many years and commemorate them, it is the same as if you said, "You are sound in the Faith, and obedience, honor, and commemoration are due to you." You do not help them understand that they are walking upon an evil path; whereas if you had broken communion with them, mayhap they would have had pangs of conscience and would search for the truth. Your guilt for your reprehensible silence—which Saint Gregory Palamas calls a third kind of atheism—grows day by day, in spite of your so-called protests.

When the Latin-minded were coming here during the patriarchate of Beccus to enforce the union with the Latins, our Lady, the Virgin Mother, the Guardian of the Holy Mountain Athos, spoke herself, saying, "The enemies of my Son and of me are coming."

Last year, when the successor of Beccus—Demetrios (the "Leader of Orthodoxy"!)—arrived, he found the Holy Mountain swathed in black from two weeks of continuous fires.[4] He that hath ears to hear, heareth the voice of the All-holy Mother of God.

May you find the path of good disagreement, as Saint Nicodemos of the Holy Mountain teaches in his Interpretation of the Fourteen Epistles of Saint Paul, saying, "If he [the abbot or bishop] is evil in Faith, that is, he believes heretical and blasphemous doctrines, flee from him, though he be an angel from Heaven."

Elder Sabbas,
an un-monastic, but Orthodox, monk

The ever-memorable Elder remained staunch in his good confession until his repose in October of 1991, despite the many efforts of the "new Holy Mountain Fathers" to persuade him to come over to their views. His worthy disciple and heir, Father Alypios, remembering the Will and Testament of Saint Mark of Ephesus, and following his example, would not permit the commemorators to hold memorial services at the grave of the Elder.

We pray that the example of the Elder Sabbas will find imitators.

Editors' Note: Translated from the periodical *Saint Agathangelos of Esphigmenou*, November–December, 1991 (in Greek).

---

[4] *Editors' Note:* The fire lasted from the first of August to the fifteenth, that is, the whole of the fast of the Theotokos.

Icon of the Righteous Martyrs of Mount Athos, who preferred death to union with the papists under Ecumenical Patriarch John Beccus.

APPENDIX S

Selective Blindness

Orthodox Ecclesiology and New Calendar "Conservatism"

An article in the Greek religious newspaper *Orthodoxos Typos* (September 4, 1987, Athens, Greece) comments on an interview of the Ecumenical Patriarch Demetrios by the Greek newspaper *Kathimerini*, August 6, 1987. The author of the article, Athanasios K. Sakarellos, quotes the Patriarch's response to the question if in special circumstances an Orthodox Christian can receive communion in a Roman Catholic church if there is no Greek Orthodox church nearby. The Patriarch is reported to have answered, "By an extreme economy, it can be done, and by all means if it concerns one who is dying." The author waxes wroth with the Patriarch and claims that "not even Athenagoras dared this" and that Demetrios "is worse than Athenagoras."

We can sympathize with Mr. Sakarellos's indignation but are somewhat surprised by it. Without examining the question whether Patriarch Demetrios is worse than Patriarch Athenagoras, whose statements can almost form a dictionary of heresies, it is an undeniable fact that Patriarch Demetrios in his enthronement speech vowed to follow the policy of Ecumenism formulated by Athenagoras; and he has been faithful to his vow. When he sent greetings to the Roman Pope, he called himself "the Primate of Orthodoxy" and called the Pope "the Primate of Christendom." He greeted the leader of the all-embracing whole in his own capacity as the leader of a segment, thus affirming his unity with the Pope in a secondary and inferior position. Little more would be needed for one to understand that the Patriarch has departed from Orthodoxy, yet more statements abounded, both by him and by "Orthodox theological commissions" under his aegis. These statements affirmed both directly and indirectly that the same baptism exists in both churches, and the same priesthood and sacraments also. The only things remaining to be settled were some canonical quibbles over territory and authority, holdovers from the dark ages of the past. In faith, however, we were already

Pope John Paul II and Patriarch Demetrios in joint public prayer.

one. This policy has been the same from 1948 when Athenagoras acceded to the Patriarchal Throne. It certainly did not alter even one instant after 1972 when Demetrios succeeded him.

One can only suppose that Mr. Sakarellos has been overlooking these facts out of an understandable but irrational hope and confidence in the hierarchy of his church. Since he finally can no longer whitewash them or repress the facts, he openly condemns Patriarch Demetrios as a heretic; and even more, a traitor. In the last paragraph of his article he states, "All this increases a suspicion that we had within us these recent years. We fear that the Phanar and the Vatican have already agreed and signed a Union, and they reveal it to us slowly in order to nullify the opposition of the faithful, who will one day fall asleep Orthodox and awaken Franks."

As we have said, Patriarch Demetrios has maintained the same policy, although so-called "conservative" Orthodox, such as *Orthodoxos Typos* and Mr. Sakarellos, have up to now blinkered themselves to this fact. Recent statements from the Patriarchate and the Patriarchal visit to Rome, however, also prompted a letter from the Sacred Community of Athos to the Ecumenical Patriarch (*Orthodoxos Typos*, Jan. 15, 1988). In this letter, the fathers of the

Holy Mountain, Athos, refer to the aforementioned statement of the Patriarch concerning intercommunion and challenge it by mentioning the letter addressed to them, dated December 28, 1983, protocol number 649, in which the synodical decision prohibiting intercommunion is renewed and which was later distributed as an encyclical to all the hierarchs and to the Patriarchates of Antioch and Russia. They also mentioned and quote from the sermon of Archbishop Stylianos of Australia, the Orthodox Co-chairman of the Mixed Commission for theological dialogue with the Roman Catholics, at the Divine Liturgy in the Church of Saint Nicholas, Bari, Italy, on June 14, 1987. He said, "Who can deny that in Roman Catholic worship the Lord Jesus Himself is present? And who can deny that the Spirit, Who is all-powerful in operation, is He Who perfects all of the priestly offices and sacraments in the church of both of the churches represented here?" Additionally, the fathers in their letter quote a portion of the common statement by the Pope and Patriarch on his visit to Rome in the beginning of December 1987, which says, "The two churches possess and serve the same sacred sacraments." However, the crowning scandal referred to in the letter of the fathers was the Patriarch's concelebration with the Pope in Saint Peter's on December 6, 1987. Although the Patriarch did not actually take communion from the Pope's hands, he did everything that he would have done if he were attending and presiding at an Orthodox service, indeed, even more than is customary. His two attendant deacons were vested, said petitions, and read the Gospel. The Creed and the Our Father were recited by the Patriarch, and he exchanged the kiss of peace with the Pope. All these words and actions had disturbed the Holy Mountain Athos and "the Orthodox people" and prompted this letter from the fathers. They assure the Patriarch and state that they have "not the least doubt" of his Orthodoxy or that of the other hierarchs of the Synod, but they question the wisdom of his actions. They beg him humbly to clarify the stand of the Patriarchate on these "serious and dogmatic questions in order to avoid new inter-Orthodox divisions."

Other Orthodox added their protest to that of the Sacred Community. The fathers of Saint Anne's Skete also sent a letter dated January 20, 1988. Other open letters appeared also in many periodicals from December 1987 on. Again all of these protests from "conservative" Orthodox in communion with the State Church of Greece were addressed respectfully to the Patriarch and assured him that they considered him to be Orthodox but ill-advised.

An answer from the Ecumenical Patriarch was slow in coming. Finally, an answer dated March 4, 1988 was sent to the Sacred Community of Athos. A copy was sent at the same time to *Orthodoxos Typos* with a covering letter dated April 16, 1988, which requested that the Patriarch's answer be published by them, one supposes, as a general answer to all the protests. It was published in their issue number 788, May 6, 1988.

The Patriarch's response is quite short when compared with the letters of protest. He assures the fathers that "our Mother Church ever remains firm, unshaken, and unchanged upon the rock of the Faith and the Apostolic Tradition" and is an "unsleeping guard, witness, and minister of Orthodoxy." He attributes the disturbance caused among the fathers of Mount Athos to "misinformation and a mistaken evaluation by some men of the contacts and relations of our Mother, the Holy Great Church of Christ, with the heterodox in recent years."

He congratulates the Holy Mountain for its dogmatic sensitivity and preservation of Orthodoxy and states that the Mother Church "hears the voice of the desert calling" the Church to gather its strength "for the service of the holy purpose of unity in Christ and the peace of the whole Christian world."

"However," he continues, "the Holy Mother, the Great Church of Christ, hears another voice also, which proceeds from her position as the Church of the Primatial Throne, responsible for the unity of the local Orthodox Churches and for the sound advancement of Christian unity desired by the whole Christian world."

The Patriarch did not in any way address the issues raised by the fathers except in passing at the conclusion of the letter where he says, "We admonish you paternally to consider the things mentioned above and to study them, to remain 'steadfast and unmoveable,' not 'tossed to and fro and carried about,' stretching a listening ear to strange voices, of which many arise from the powers of darkness and the devices of the evil one. In addition, we furthermore declare that the Mother Church experiences great bitterness and sorrow whenever she sees the Sacred Community of the Holy Mountain meddling in her work and responsibilities, as well as in the responsibilities of other sister Churches, who have expressed their dismay and grievance at such interference by you." In other words, mind your own business and keep your nose out of ours.

Orthodoxos Typos printed its reply to the Patriarchal letter in the same issue. This somewhat prolix and diffuse letter points out that the Holy Mountain fathers were not misinformed, nor did they submit "certain thoughts and disquiet" to the Patriarch; rather they protested against clear-cut canonical violations and against completely un-Orthodox statements by ecclesiastical figures. The letter also affirms that no local church can alone be responsible for universal unity, no matter how respected its primacy; Orthodoxy does not have in the Phanar a sort of Vatican. The letter states that "the Holy Mountain fathers nowhere recommend that ecumenistic dialogue be severed" but that we must urgently tend to the needs of our own house first.

Although the letter of *Orthodoxos Typos* protests the Patriarch's answer to the Holy Mountain fathers and defends them, the issues raised by the fathers are not discussed in particular. In fact, the letter addresses the Patriarch with fulsome language and ends with the statement that there can be no doubt of the Patriarch's Orthodoxy. He has only been ill-advised by some of the clergy around him.

Such a statement—that there can be no doubt of Patriarch Demetrios's Orthodoxy—certainly disregards the history of the last sixteen years. Patriarch Demetrios has swerved not a whit from the road opened by Patriarch Athenagoras. *Orthodoxos Typos* in its answer quotes the history of the Church in the patristic period in detail, yet apparently cannot remember the history of the last sixteen years; indeed, not even of the last few issues of their own newspaper, which published the article mentioned above written by their correspondent Mr. Sakarellos.

Perhaps one might think that *Orthodoxos Typos* wishes to allow the Patriarch an opportunity to retreat gracefully and correct himself while preserving his dignity. It is for this reason, perhaps, that they do not impugn the Orthodoxy of the Patriarch. Certainly, in view of the past history of the Patriarch and his statements—all reported and commented upon in *Orthodoxos Typos* itself—it would be the utmost naiveté to think that the personal beliefs of the Patriarch are different from his own words, pronouncements, and deeds and from the whole policy of the Patriarchate. In any case, the Patriarch—and every Christian—will be judged for his open avowals and public confession, not for some supposed Orthodoxy in his heart. "Whosoever shall confess Me before men, him will I confess before My Father and His angels." The sacred canons simply repeat and codify this truth pronounced by our Saviour.

Another factor may explain this selective blindness which characterizes not only the "conservative" Orthodox of *Orthodoxos Typos*, but of the State Church of Greece and of almost all "World Orthodoxy" during the last forty years of the Patriarchates of both Athenagoras and Demetrios. If Patriarch Demetrios is openly and formally condemned as a heretic, a further step is required if the new calendar conservatives are to remain consistent. They must break off communion with the Patriarch and with all those in communion with him. All the canons, Fathers, and Saints—that is, that very tradition which they call to witness—requires it. If they do not break off communion, they declare by their actions that communion with heretics is permissible. In this way, their whole "conservative" approach is undermined. If communion with one heretic or heresy is permissible, why not with others? What is wrong, then, in holding communion with Roman Catholics, Protestants, or even Moslems? Tradition is no longer determinative.

The editors of *Orthodoxos Typos* and the "conservative" faction of World Orthodoxy are certainly intelligent enough to understand the consequences arising from declaring Demetrios a heretic. To deny tradition is intolerable to them, yet because of pressure from the state, or from fear of disorder, or from fear of becoming "the little flock," or from whatever reason which the Lord alone knows, they cannot follow the dictates of tradition. The only way they can escape this dilemma is by being willfully blind and by imputing all of the "most Orthodox" Patriarch's actions and words to his advisors and associates. This gambit does not arise out of charity for Patriarch Demetrios in order that he might save face; rather it is a desperate, face-saving tactic of the "conservatives" for their own survival.

Such a tactic, however, is superficial and obviates the problem in appearance only. If in reality the ground has been cut out from underneath the "conservatives," how long can the pretence maintain itself? Even our modern television-bred generation, whose attention span is ephemeral, cannot fail to register this history of repeated violations of Orthodoxy and to perceive the hypocrisy of being willfully blind—blind to the fact that Patriarch Demetrios is such a convinced adherent of Ecumenism that he is no longer Orthodox.

On his visit to Rome, the Patriarch stood beside the Pope and blessed together with him when the Pope gave his blessing *urbi et orbi* from the Balcony of Benedictions of Saint Peter's. This event is unique and unheard of, for this blessing *urbi et orbi* is a papal prerogative. Immediately after his election, the Pope appears before the people to give this blessing and to be acclaimed. It sets the seal on the election and is the first official, public action of the Pope. To allow Patriarch Demetrios to share in this papal prerogative indicates at the least that the Roman Catholics are very convinced of his adherence to Ecumenism, leaving aside the suspicions mentioned by Mr. Sakarellos.

In issue number 792, June 3, 1988, of *Orthodoxos Typos,* correspondent Mr. Kostas Sardelis reports on the commission sent to the Ecumenical Patriarch by the Sacred Community of Mount Athos to inquire of the issues raised in their letter. He reports that "the delegation of the Holy Mountain returned satisfied." The delegation met with both the Patriarch and the special synodical committee and was assured by them that their tactics in ecumenical dialogue are "absolutely Orthodox." "The misunderstanding has vanished" which existed recently between the Holy Mountain and the Patriarchate. Everything was discussed and explained to the delegation's satisfaction, although no details are mentioned nor what issues were discussed. We were never told and we have never seen published anywhere those answers of the Patriarchate which so satisfied the delegation. In other words, business as usual.

Holy Transfiguration Monastery, Brookline, Mass.

APPENDIX T
The New Martyr Catherine of Attica[1]

The crown of martyrdom didst thou receive, O Catherine, by struggling steadfastly for the tradition of our Fathers; and thou didst surrender thy soul to Jesus the Bridegroom, when, on the festival of the Archangels at Mandra of Megaris, thou didst sincerely proclaim the dogmas of the Faith of the Scriptures.

The True Orthodox Christians were tried just as gold is purified in the furnace, because they preciously guarded the Orthodox Faith, received from the holy Fathers, as a priceless treasure. In depicting briefly the essential part of the New Martyr Catherine's witness, we are fulfilling an imperative duty. The triumph of our Orthodox Faith must be made known; the sacrifice of this faithful ewe-lamb of our Lord's flock, full of the flame of faith and the love of Christ, must be proclaimed.

The New Martyr Catherine was born in Mandra in Attica in 1900 to poor but pious parents, the ever-memorable John and Maria Peppas. Wherever necessary, Catherine, the youngest of the family, offered her services cheerfully and was hardworking.

At the age of twenty-two she married Constantine Routis from the same village. God gave them two children, Christos and Irene. The devout Routis family joined the resistance of the True Orthodox Christians, participating in all the services and public

---

[1] *The Struggler*, Vol. 2, No. 3 (October–November 1993).

demonstrations for their Faith, even when this was perilous—all for the sacred defense of the traditions of the holy Fathers.

It was in fact at the end of the Divine Liturgy on November 8, 1927, that Catherine was to sacrifice herself, thus receiving the unfading crown of martyrdom.

But let us leave it to the writer of *Ta Patria* to explain:

Mandra in Attica, a place of heroic and tragic events, is also the place which offers as an example to our materialistic age a heroine for the Faith, the young New Martyr Catherine Routis.

Every Christian has heard that rivers of blood have been shed to make steadfast the True Faith in Christ, but who would have foreseen that the blood of martyrs is still necessary to save the Church from heretical influences and innovation? Come, Christians, you that bear patiently the contempt of the crowds who call you "Old Calendarists." Come, and learn the way our fathers and brothers, who lived during the first years after the schism, contested; how they glorified the Church of the True Orthodox Christians, that you might live in all freedom and honor and adore God.

Let us follow the thread of the bloody events at Mandra, which started during the All-night Vigil and the Liturgy in honor of the Holy Archangels, at dawn on November 8, 1927, and which ended tragically in the church at that place.

On the eve of the festival of the Heavenly Orders, some pious women from Mandra, together with the brave Catherine, had cleaned the church and prepared it, so that nothing was lacking for the awaited festival. They had also done everything they could to find an Orthodox priest, faithful to the calendar of the Fathers, for at that time such clergymen were literally overwhelmed by the demands of the faithful. The faithful at Mandra had therefore welcomed the ever-memorable Father Christopher Psallidas with enthusiasm. The whole population greeted him with joy, whilst the bells of all the churches rang out merrily—so greatly esteemed and loved were faithful priests, those first fighters in the sacred struggle of the True Orthodox Christians, which was then just beginning.

Vespers started quietly, in peace. The Vigil could have started and ended in the same atmosphere, if the police, who were not

Icon of the New Martyr Catherine Routis.

welcome on such an evening, had not appeared and, with evil intent, surrounded the church. It is reasonable to inquire the reasons for this state of siege. Neither malefactors nor gangsters were hidden in the church. The church was "occupied" only by decorous guardians of Patristic Orthodox Tradition, who, in a fitting manner, had gathered to celebrate their guardian saints. What was it, then, that the police so insistently wanted? They were only obeying the orders of the schismatic Archbishop of Athens, namely to arrest the priest and scatter the "mob" of the Faithful.

The police had received their orders, but the Christians of Mandra also had to obey an order, the God-given order not to permit the celebration to be disrupted. Thus the door of the church was closed, and the Liturgy proceeded with even more compunction because of the ever-present threat of arms. The police then struck the doors with their rifle butts, trying to knock them down. They broke the window panes. And yet we are in the twentieth century, in the middle of an era of progress, an era of religious liberty! What a terrible example from the motherland of the Hellenes, from the motherland of Orthodox Christians!

The faithful continued to pray inside the church, quietly, piously, whilst outside the schismatic forces were moving about shouting insults. Inside the faithful were asking for the Lord's support, that they might patiently bear the unjust persecution.

Outside, the police called for reinforcements so that they might attain their impious goal. But did they need reinforcements? Did they need so much to arrest one pious, quiet, and brave priest? But how were they to break the resistance of the faithful people, if not by arms?

It was nearly dawn. Inside the church most of the faithful received Communion and were waiting for the blessing of the priest to end the service, so that they could take him out safely and give him an opportunity to rest in a neighboring house. But how could they do this, when the praetorians of the schismatics were on guard outside? But they had just received the only strength they needed: they had just communed the Body and Blood of Christ! Nothing was frightening for them any more. They advanced; the door opened; the faithful started to go out. A living wall of pious women from Mandra surrounded the endangered priest. From the shadows, the schismatic forces sprang in front of them like rapacious wolves, and demanded that the people surrender the priest into their hands.

But why? the faithful wondered with good reason. Has he committed a crime? Has he done wrong? No, nothing like that. But still they demanded the priest. Who would go and hand him over to them? Among the faithful there were no Judases.

"You will arrest our priest only over our dead bodies!" Such were the noble words that came from the mouth of one woman. It was the voice of Catherine Routis, who, having made sure her husband and children were safely hidden at home, came back to rejoin the priest.

The parents of the New Martyr Catherine have attested to the fact that after Vespers her husband had suggested that they go home because he feared an incident. But it was impossible for Catherine to stay home. So when her sister told her of the dangers that the faithful were facing in the church, besieged by the police, she left the house and rushed in among the combatants. She ran to her martyrdom!

The police, failing to break through the human cordon, started to shoot with their rifles to frighten the people. They only succeeded to a degree. A few faithful moved away, but the human wall stayed intact around the priest. They were taken aback by the savagery of the police attack. A bullet struck the ever-memorable Angeliki Katsarellis in the temple. To the end of her life, Angeliki proudly showed the "mark of the Lord" on her forehead, which had been inscribed there by a murderous police bullet on that night.

Meanwhile, Catherine Routis did not flinch. She went on courageously denouncing the praetorian forces of the schismatics, until she saw a policeman raise his rifle butt to strike the priest. As soon as she realized his evil intention, with courage and complete self-sacrifice she covered the priest with her body and received the mortal blow to the back of her head. Catherine fell, staining the floor of the church with the blood of martyrdom. One could just hear her whisper for the last time, "Most Holy Mother of God ..."

The anxious, weeping women took up her bloodied body, and, having informed her husband Constantine, took her to the Annunciation Hospital in Athens. The pious Angeliki, who had been injured by the bullet, was also taken there at the same time as Catherine, but she came out after a few days.

Catherine, motionless on her bed, suffered enormously for seven days. Unable to speak, she gestured for a paper and pencil to write a note to her husband, to commend to his care their two little children, one four years old and the other only a few months old.

On November 15, 1927, according to the Orthodox Calendar, on the first day of the Nativity Fast at 4 a.m., Catherine gave her martyric soul into the hands of Christ, Who crowned her.

The church council of the parish of the True Orthodox Christians then mobilized all the faithful they could contact. Hers was no funeral, but a procession of the relics of a martyr. Thousands of faithful people followed the procession, some with flowers, some with candles, and others with palm branches.

Christians! Take strength from the example given by a young mother, a woman of twenty-seven, who gave her life for the sacred Faith! The New Martyr Catherine is "the honor, the glory, and the pride" of the Church of the True Orthodox Christians, and she will be remembered as an example of faith and love, and a witness filled with self-denial and sacrifice for the traditions of the Fathers.

"Catherine, in our times, there were no swords, stakes, or spears. They had only the butts of their guns to try to frighten you. What a miserable weapon to make you deny your Faith! But you gave your life for it. May your mediation support us, and may your prayers protect the Body of our Orthodox Church from every malicious arrow of the enemy. Amen."

The Church of the True Orthodox Christians believes and proclaims that Catherine contested unto blood, and that she belongs to the choir of the Holy Martyrs. November 15/28, the day of her death, is the anniversary festival of the New Martyr Catherine.

The article above was translated from the French, as published in Foi Transmise et Sainte Tradition, *July 1987. This is the French-language magazine of the Mission of the True Orthodox Christians in France. We are indebted to Mrs. S.C. Phillips for the translation into English.*

Chronology

1582 Pope Gregory XIII changes the calendar.

1583 Pan-Orthodox Council in Constantinople condemns and places the new calendar under anathema.

1587 Pan-Orthodox Council in Constantinople condemns and places the new calendar under anathema.

1593 Pan-Orthodox Council in Constantinople condemns and places the new calendar under anathema.

1670 Patriarch Dositheos of Jerusalem and his Holy Synod condemn the new calendar.

1827 Ecumenical Patriarch Agathangelos and his Holy Synod condemn the new calendar.

1895 Ecumenical Patriarch Anthimos VII and his Holy Synod condemn the new calendar.

1902 Ecumenical Patriarch Joachim III and his Holy Synod condemn the new calendar.

1903 Patriarch Damianos of Jerusalem and his Holy Synod condemn the new calendar.

1903 Holy Synod of the Church of Russia condemns the new calendar.

1903 Holy Synod of the Church of Romania condemns the new calendar.

1903 Holy Synod of the Church of Greece condemns the new calendar.

1904 Ecumenical Patriarch Joachim III and his Holy Synod again condemn the new calendar.

1910 The modern Ecumenical Movement is born at the World Missionary Conference in Edinburgh.

1914-1918 World War I.

1919 Holy Synod of the Church of Greece again condemns the new calendar.

1919 Meletios Metaxakis becomes Archbishop of Athens.

1920 Metropolitan Dorotheos of Prusa, *locum tenens* of the throne of the Ecumenical Patriarchate, issues the Encyclical entitled, "To the Churches of Christ Wheresoever They Might Be," thereby indicating for the first time Constantinople's willingness to enter into ecumenical discussions.

1921 In December, Meletios Metaxakis is deposed as Archbishop of Athens for canonical infractions and for causing schism.

1922 In January, with the support of the Greek Ministry of Foreign Affairs, but without being canonically elected, and though deposed by the Holy Synod of the Church of Greece, Meletios Metaxakis is enthroned as Ecumenical Patriarch. Under intense political pressure from the government of Greece, his defrockment as Archbishop of Athens is lifted in September.

1922 Ecumenical Patriarch Meletios Metaxakis recognizes the validity of Anglican orders.

1922 Meletios Metaxakis establishes the Greek Archdiocese in the United States and places it under the jurisdiction of the Ecumenical Patriarchate.

1923 In January, in a Report to the Committee of the Department of Religion in Greece, Chrysostom Papadopoulos (the future Archbishop of Athens) writes: "No Orthodox autocephalous Church can separate itself from the rest and accept the New Calendar without becoming schismatic in the eyes of the others."

1923 In February, the Revolutionary Greek government of Colonel Plastiras finds Archbishop Theokletos of Athens "unsuitable" and appoints Chrysostom Papadopoulos as his replacement.

1923 Ecumenical Patriarch Meletios Metaxakis recognizes the Communist-sponsored Living Church in Russia.

1923 Meletios Metaxakis convenes the Pan-Orthodox Congress in May and June. At this "Pan-Orthodox" assembly, only the Orthodox Churches of Greece, Romania, and Serbia and the Anglican Church are represented.

1923 In July, outraged Orthodox Christians of Constantinople physically expel Metaxakis from the premises of the Patriarchate. Metaxakis officially resigns as Ecumenical Patriarch in September, citing "reasons of health."

1924 Pressured by the Greek Ministry of Foreign Affairs, the Ecumenical Patriarchate and the State Church of Greece adopt the new calendar on March 10/23, 1924.

1924 In Romania, Metropolitan Myron Christea accepts the new calendar. Shortly thereafter, working in close conjunction with the Uniate prime minister of Romania, Julius Manius, he unilaterally adopts the Western Paschalion as well. Riots break out in the streets over this issue, and the adoption of the Western Paschalion is retracted.

1924 In unanimity with Patriarch Gregory of Antioch, Patriarch Damianos of Jerusalem, and Archbishop Cyril of Cyprus, Patriarch Photios of Alexandria and his Holy Synod condemn the introduction of the new calendar.

1925 On September 14 (o.s.), the Feast of the Exaltation of the Precious Cross, the Cross appears in the heavens over the Church of Saint John the Theologian on Mount Hymettos, outside of Athens, where two thousand faithful had gathered to celebrate the Vigil. The police, who were sent by Archbishop Chrysostom Papadopoulos of Athens to break up the service and arrest the priest, are converted.

1925-1935 Some 800 communities of those who follow the traditional Orthodox calendar are established. Memoranda from bishops of the State Church and from the traditional Orthodox Christians pour into the offices of the Greek government and the State Church. Intimidated, a few government officials allow some accommodation for the believers, but the State Church under Chrysostom Papadopoulos insists on persecuting and exiling the traditional Orthodox clergy and faithful.

1926 The State Church of Greece issues an encyclical declaring the Mysteries (sacraments) of the traditional Orthodox Christians "bereft of divine grace."

1926 Meletios Metaxakis, under the auspices of the Greek government and the British Mandate government in Egypt, becomes Patriarch of Alexandria. The Patriarchate of Alexandria adopts the new calendar.

1927 The Churches of Constantinople, Alexandria, Jerusalem,

Greece, Cyprus, Serbia, Bulgaria, Poland, and Romania participate in the (Protestant) Faith and Order Conference in Lausanne.

1929 In July, Archbishop Chrysostom Papadopoulos of the State Church of Greece convokes a meeting of his Holy Synod in an effort to legitimatize the adoption of the new calendar and to condemn all those who remain faithful to the traditional Church calendar. Of the forty-four bishops present, thirteen depart from the Synod meeting, twenty-seven refuse to endorse this decree; only four sign.

1931 An Orthodox delegation under the leadership of Meletios Metaxakis attends the Anglican Lambeth Conference.

1935 In May, seeing that nothing avails in convincing Archbishop Chrysostom Papadopoulos to reject his innovation, three Metropolitans of the State Church—Germanos of Demetrias, Chrysostom of Florina, and Chrysostom of Zakynthos—renounce the innovation and take up the leadership of the traditional Orthodox Christians. Four new traditionalist bishops are consecrated by them: Germanos of the Cyclades Islands, Christopher of Megaris, Polycarp of Diavlia, and Matthew of Bresthena. In an encyclical to the faithful, the three Metropolitans who first left the State Church declare that body to be schismatic and under the condemnation of the Pan-Orthodox Councils of 1583, 1587, and 1593.

1935 In June, the State Church holds a spiritual court and condemns the above-mentioned traditional Orthodox hierarchs. All are "deposed"; of these, three are banished and exiled, while Matthew of Bresthena is confined to his monastery. Chrysostom of Zakynthos, Polycarp of Diavlia, and Christopher of Megaris recant and return to the State Church.

1935 In July, Meletios Metaxakis dies in Zurich and is buried in Cairo. Anglican churches throughout Egypt and the Sudan pray for him.

1937 In Edinburgh, the Churches of Constantinople, Alexandria, Antioch, Jerusalem, Greece, Cyprus, Bulgaria, Poland, and Albania participate for a second time in the Faith and Order Conference.

1937 Metropolitans Chrysostom of Florina and Germanos of Demetrias disagree with Metropolitans Germanos of the Cyclades Islands and Matthew of Bresthena over whether the State Church is in true schism or not. The traditional Orthodox Christians become divided into two factions—the "Florinites" and the "Matthewites."

1939-1945 World War II.

1943 Metropolitan Germanos of Demetrias reposes, leaving Metropolitan Chrysostom of Florina briefly by himself.

1944 Christopher of Christianopolis (formerly of Megaris) and Polycarp of Diavlia leave the State Church of Greece, and rejoin Metropolitan Chrysostom of Florina.

1948 In violation of the Apostolic Canons, Matthew of Bresthena consecrates new bishops by himself. As a result, many clergy and faithful leave his jurisdiction and join Metropolitan Chrysostom of Florina.

1948 The Faith and Order Conference fuses with the "Life and Work Movement" in Amsterdam to become the "World Council of Churches" (WCC). The Churches of Constantinople, Alexandria, Antioch, Jerusalem, Greece, and Romania participate.

1948 Ecumenical Patriarch Maximos is declared "mentally unfit" and forcibly retired; Archbishop Athenagoras of North and South America arrives in Constantinople on an aircraft of the United States State Department and becomes Ecumenical Patriarch. The Western religious and secular media report on the political overtones and illegality of Athenagoras's election.

1949 Metropolitan Germanos of the Cyclades Islands returns to the Holy Synod of Metropolitan Chrysostom of Florina.

1950 Seeing no sign of repentance from the State Church of Greece, the Holy Synod under Metropolitan Chrysostom of Florina issues an encyclical declaring the State Church schismatic and its mysteries void of grace.

1950-1955 Archbishop Spyridon of the State Church of Greece initiates and maintains a period of fierce persecutions against the traditional Orthodox Christians, accusing them of being pro-Slavic, pro-Communist, and traitors to Greece.

1950 Bishop Matthew of Bresthena reposes.

1951 Metropolitan Germanos of the Cyclades Islands reposes. The State Church does not permit funeral rites for him. Metropolitan Chrysostom of Florina is arrested and sent into exile for a year and a half.

1952 Constantinople, Antioch, Cyprus, and the American Metropolia (later, OCA) participate in the Faith and Order Conference in Lund.

1952 Intimidated by the persecutions, Polycarp of Diavlia and Christopher (now of Christianopolis) return to the State Church.

1954 At the Evanston assembly of the WCC, in a statement prepared and inspired primarily by Father Georges Florovsky, the Orthodox delegates declare, "We are bound to declare our profound conviction that the Holy Orthodox Church alone has preserved in full and intact the Faith once delivered unto the saints."

1955 Metropolitan Chrysostom of Florina reposes, leaving no successor. Patriarch Christopher of Alexandria presides over a full memorial service for Metropolitan Chrysostom in Alexandria.

1957 At the WCC's conference in Oberlin, Ohio, in response to the Protestants' conference theme, "The Unity We Seek," the Orthodox delegates, again, at the inspiration of Father Georges Florovsky, respond that this "Unity has never been lost.... For us, this Unity is embodied in the Orthodox Church."

1959 Archbishop Iakovos is enthroned as head of the Greek Archdiocese in the Americas. The secular press reports on the irregularities in his election to this position.

1960 Archbishop Seraphim of Chicago and Bishop Theophilus of Detroit (both of the Russian Church Abroad) secretly consecrate Archimandrite Akakios Pappas as Bishop of Talantion for the Florinite jurisdiction.

1961 At the order of Ecumenical Patriarch Athenagoras, conveyed through his exarch, Archbishop Iakovos of North and South America, the Orthodox delegates at the WCC assembly in New Delhi are "to refrain" henceforth from issuing "separate statements" at WCC conferences. The Moscow Patriarchate joins the WCC, followed quickly by Poland, Romania, and Bulgaria.

1962 Archbishop Leonty of Chile and Peru (Russian Church Abroad) and Akakios of Talantion consecrate three more bishops for Greece: Parthenios of the Cyclades Islands, Auxentius of Gardikion, and Chrysostom of Magnesia. Later, Akakios of Diavlia and Gerontios of Salamis are also consecrated.

1963 In April, in an address to members of a WCC gathering in Buck Hills Falls, Pennsylvania, Archbishop Iakovos states: "It would be utterly foolish for the true believers to pretend or to insist that the whole truth has been revealed only to them, and that they alone possess it. Such a claim would be both unbiblical and untheological.... Christ did not specify the date nor the place that the Church would suddenly take full possession of the whole truth."

1963 Akakios of Talantion reposes. Auxentius of Gardikion becomes Archbishop.

1964 Ecumenical Patriarch Athenagoras and Pope Paul VI meet and hold joint prayers in the Holy Land in January.

1965 The Patriarchate of Serbia joins the WCC. In December, Constantinople unilaterally lifts the 1054 Anathema against an unrepentant Rome. The canonist of the new calendar Greek Archdiocese of North and South America, Reverend Theodore T. Thalassinos, writes: "The removal of the mutual excommunication between the two Churches *restores canonical relations between Rome and New Rome. This restoration is a canonical necessity, since there is no possible third situation between ecclesiastical communion and its negation: ecclesiastical excommunication*" (emphasis added). In a letter to Patriarch Athenagoras, Metropolitan Philaret of the Russian Church Abroad protests this alleged lifting of the Anathema.

1966 Ecumenical Patriarch Athenagoras states that "theoretical unity [between Rome and Constantinople] already exists. But actual unity will shortly take place."

1967 In July, Pope Paul VI travels to Constantinople and holds joint prayers with Ecumenical Patriarch Athenagoras.

1967 In October, Patriarch Athenagoras travels to Rome and holds joint prayers with Pope Paul VI.

1967 In London, Patriarch Athenagoras holds joint prayers with the Archbishop of Canterbury.

1968 At the WCC assembly in Uppsala, the Protestant and Orthodox delegates open the sessions with the prayer, "O God, Father.... Your love is stretched out upon all men, to seek the Truth, which we have not known." For the first time, the Orthodox officially become "organic members" of this ecumenistic body.

1968 In his Christmas Encyclical, Ecumenical Patriarch Athenagoras announces that he has inserted Pope Paul VI's name in the diptychs (the list of canonical, Orthodox bishops whose names are commemorated during the Holy Eucharist).

1969 Metropolitan Philaret of the Russian Church Abroad writes a letter of protest to Archbishop Iakovos of North and South America; in addition, he addresses a "Sorrowful Epistle" to all the hierarchs of World Orthodoxy.

1969 The Moscow Patriarchate officially begins giving communion to Roman Catholics.

1969 The Holy Synod of the Russian Church Abroad recognizes the episcopal consecrations of the Synod of Archbishop Auxentius of Athens which had been enacted without the knowledge of the Synod of the Church Abroad.

1971 With specific conditions, the Russian Church Abroad regularizes the uncanonical consecrations of the Matthewite jurisdiction. The Russian Synod's conditions are only partially implemented by the Matthewites.

1971 Ecumenical Patriarch Athenagoras publicly proclaims that he gives communion to Roman Catholics and Protestants.

1971 Metropolitan Philaret of the Russian Church Abroad addresses his "Second Sorrowful Epistle" to the bishops of World Orthodoxy.

1972 Ecumenical Patriarch Athenagoras dies. Demetrios is enthroned in his place. In his enthronement speech, the new Patriarch addresses the Pope of Rome as the leader of Christendom, while speaking of himself as the leader of the Orthodox. He also vows to continue Athenagoras's policies.

1974 Ecumenical Patriarch Demetrios banishes thirteen Athonite monks—including three Abbots—who refuse to commemorate him because of his ecumenistic policies.

1974 The Holy Synod of Archbishop Auxentius re-confirms the 1950 encyclical of the Holy Synod of Metropolitan Chrysostom of Florina concerning the invalidity of the mysteries of the schismatic State Church of Greece and all followers of the calendar innovation.

1975 Metropolitan Athenagoras of Thyateira and Great Britain, with the written commendation and approval of the Holy Synod of the Ecumenical Patriarchate, publishes his *Thyateira Confession*, which recognizes the priesthood and the sacraments of heretical denominations, espouses the "Branch Theory," admits that Muslims deny the divinity of Christ, but nonetheless teaches that "they believe in the true God"; and finally, it permits Orthodox, in the absence of their own clergy, to have intercommunion with Roman Catholics and Anglicans. This document is never repudiated or condemned by the Ecumenical Patriarchate.

1975 At the WCC's assembly in Nairobi, the Orthodox representatives state: "The Orthodox do not expect that other Christians be converted to Orthodoxy in its historic and cultural reality of the past and present and to become members of the Orthodox Church."

1976 The Matthewites break with the Russian Church Abroad and later repudiate that Church's regularization of their consecrations in 1971.

1978 During an official audience with the newly-elected Pope John Paul I, Metropolitan Nikodim of Leningrad collapses and dies in the arms of the Pope, from whom he receives the last rites. It is later revealed that Nikodim had secretly espoused Roman Catholicism.

1979 Formation of the Kallistos Schism. Metropolitan Kallistos of Corinth (formerly of the Matthewites, but a member of the Holy Synod of Archbishop Auxentius since 1976) and Anthony of

Megaris secretly and uncanonically consecrate eight bishops. The Holy Synod of Archbishop Auxentius deposes both consecrators and the "consecrated" of the Kallistos Schism, and consecrates ten new bishops.

1979-1986 A period of disarray prevails among the various groups of traditional Orthodox jurisdictions in Greece, with the emergence of two new groups: the Kiousis Synod and the Synod of Cyprian.

1983 WCC holds assembly in Vancouver, during which shamanistic and other pagan rituals are performed.

1983 Metropolitan Philaret of the Russian Church Abroad and his Synod pronounce an anathema against the pan-heresy of Ecumenism and its adherents.

1984 Demise of the short-lived Kallistos Schism, with various re-groupings of its former bishops.

1984 In affirmation of the teaching of the *Thyateira Confession* of 1975, Bishop Kallistos Ware confirms in writing that he gives communion to Monophysites.

1985 In November, Metropolitan Philaret of the Russian Church Abroad reposes, and that jurisdiction, under the new Metropolitan, Vitaly Ustinov, initiates a change of ecclesiastical policy, with increasing joint prayers with ecumenistic clergy.

1985 Bishop Mark of Germany, of the Russian Church Abroad, visits the Holy Mountain, Athos, and commemorates Ecumenical Patriarch Demetrios.

1986 In January, the "Church Leaders' Covenant" is jointly signed by Orthodox, Protestant, and Unitarian clergy in Boston in order "to manifest more clearly the oneness of the Body of Christ."

1986 In October, the "Assisi Gathering" is convoked by Pope John Paul II. "World Orthodoxy" bishops participate, together with representatives of other religions.

1986 Archbishop Anthony of Geneva (Russian Church Abroad) gives a blessing to his clergy to concelebrate with clergy of ecumenistic jurisdictions. After protests which go unanswered over the span of a year, two monastic establishments, many parishes, and thirty-six clergy in the United States and Canada leave the Russian Church Abroad.

1986 Metropolitan Vitaly of the Russian Church Abroad, in his Nativity Epistle, re-defines the 1983 Anathema against Ecumenism.

1987 The hierarchy of the Russian Church Abroad synodically endorses the letter of priest Alexander Lebedev which permits intercommunion with ecumenistic jurisdictions.

1987 More parishes and clergy in the United States, France, and elsewhere in Europe leave the Russian Church Abroad. All these parishes and clergy are finally united with the Holy Synod of Archbishop Auxentius.

1987 Ecumenical Patriarch Demetrios states that it is permitted to receive communion from and impart communion to Roman Catholics under certain conditions. This re-affirms the teaching of the *Thyateira Confession* published in 1975 with the official approval of the Holy Synod of the Ecumenical Patriarchate.

1987 Ecumenical Patriarch Demetrios and his archdeacon participate in a papal mass in Rome.

1988 In March, Archbishop Iakovos of America states, "The unity we seek cannot be Orthodox, Roman Catholic, or Protestant. It has a wider dimension, that of Catholicity."

1988 In August, the Holy Synod of Archbishop Auxentius consecrates a bishop, Ephraim of Boston, for the traditional Orthodox Christians in North America.

1989 In September, Metropolitan Pitirim of Volokolamsk of the Moscow Patriarchate declares his intention to publish the Koran "for the disciples of the Prophet Mohammed" in Russia.

1989 In October, Patriarch Parthenios of Alexandria declares that "Mohammed is a prophet of God," and that anyone who "speaks against Islam or Buddhism speaks against God."

1989 In October, the Holy Synod of Archbishop Auxentius consecrates a bishop, Photios of Lyons, for the traditional Orthodox Christians in France.

1990 Metropolitan Bartholomew (future Ecumenical Patriarch) of the Patriarchate of Constantinople, during a visit to

San Francisco in company with Ecumenical Patriarch Demetrios, expresses views tolerant of abortion.

1990 The WCC's Barr Statement, with the participation of Protestant, Roman Catholic, and Orthodox theologians, "affirms the need to move beyond a theology which confines salvation to the explicit personal commitment to Jesus Christ."

1991 The Holy Synod of Archbishop Auxentius consecrates a bishop, Makarios of Toronto, for the traditional Orthodox Christians in Canada.

1991 At the WCC's assembly in Canberra, Protestant and Orthodox delegates participate in pagan purification rites.

1991 The Holy Synod of Archbishop Auxentius consecrates a bishop, Gury of Kazan, for the traditional Orthodox Christians in Russia.

1991 "Agreed Statement" of the Patriarchate of Antioch with Monophysites (Jacobites), allowing joint prayers and intercommunion, though the Monophysites do not accept the Seven Ecumenical Councils.

1991 Ecumenical Patriarch Demetrios dies. Metropolitan Bartholomew of Chalcedon replaces him.

1992 In their "Summit Message," the heads of the autocephalous Churches of "World Orthodoxy"—including Patriarchs Diodoros of Jerusalem and Paul of Serbia—condemn attempts to convert non-Orthodox "Christians" to the Orthodox Faith.

1992 In October, Patriarch Paul of Serbia is received by Archbishop Anthony of San Francisco (Russian Church Abroad) in the Russian Synodal Cathedral with full patriarchal honors and the chanting of *"Eis polla eti, Despota."*

1993 The "Balamand Agreed Statement," signed by representatives of the Churches of Constantinople, Alexandria, Antioch, Russia, Romania, Cyprus, Poland, Albania, and Finland, accepts the Roman Catholic denomination as a "Sister Church," with fully valid sacraments.

1994 Repose of Archbishop Auxentius. At his funeral, many of his former adversaries (including bishops) come to pay their last respects to him and tearfully ask his forgiveness.

Bibliography

Books or articles printed in bold are recommended for further reading.

SOURCES IN ENGLISH

Acker, J.W., *Strange Altars—A Scriptural Appraisal of the Lodge*, Concordia Publishing House, Saint Louis, Missouri, 1965.

Athenagoras, Archbishop of Thyateira and Great Britain, *The Thyateira Confession*, The Faith Press, Leighton Buzzard, Beds., 1975.

Azkoul, Father Michael, *Anti-Christianity, the New Atheism*, Monastery Press, Montreal, 1984.

_____, *The "Sorrowful Epistle" of Metropolitan Philaret—A Rejoinder to Father Alexander Schmemann*, Saint Nectarios Educational Series #53, Saint Nectarios Press, Seattle, Washington.

_____, *What is Secularism?*, Saint Nicholas Educational Series, Roslindale, Massachusetts, 1978.

Basil, Priest-monk of Holy Transfiguration, Monastery, Boston, **A Letter to Bishop Kallinikos on Why the North American Parishes Did Not Join the Kiousis Jurisdiction**, July 17, 1990.

Cavarnos, Constantine, *Father Georges Florovsky on Ecumenism*, Saint Gregory Palamas Monastery, Etna, California.

Dunlop, John, *Recent Activities of the Moscow Patriarchate Abroad and in the U.S.S.R.*, Saint Nectarios Press, Seattle, Washington, 1974.

Grabbe, Father George, *The Canonical and Legal Position of the Moscow Patriarchate*, The Russian Ecclesiastical Mission in Jerusalem, 1971.

_____, *Did Saint Cyprian Change the Doctrine of the Church?*, Saint Nectarios Educational Series #28, Saint Nectarios Press, Seattle, Washington.

_____, *The Dogma of the Church in the Modern World*, Holy Trinity Monastery, Jordanville, New York, 1976.

_____, *The Unity and Uniqueness of the Church*, Saint Nectarios Educational Series #29, Saint Nectarios Press, Seattle, Washington.

Guettée, Abbé, D.D., *The Papacy*, reprinted from the English edition of May, 1866, by Minos Publishing Co., New York City.

The Holy Orthodox Church in North America, *Sister Churches—Five Hundred Years After Florence*, Boston, Massachusetts, 1994.

Holy Transfiguration Monastery, Boston, *A Reply to Athenagoras*, The Monastery Press, Montreal, 1978.

John, Bishop of Amorion, "Patriarch Meletios Metaxakis: A True Visionary," *Hellenic Chronicle*, Sept.–Oct., 1994 (in four installments).

Johnson, Father Seraphim, "The People of God," in *Orthodox Light*, editor Father P. Carras, Willowdale, Ontario.

Kalomiros, Alexander, *Against False Union*, Saint Nectarios Press, Seattle, Washington, 1990.

_____, *The Touchstone* (Τό Σύγκριμα), published by the Convent of the Annunciation, Oinoussae, Chios, 1976; published with the author's permission in serialized form in English by Saint Nectarios Press in Volumes 14 and 18 of the *Orthodox Christian Witness*, 1981 and 1984.

Kitsikis, Dimitri, *The Old Calendarists and the Rise of Religious Conservatism in Greece*, Saint Gregory Palamas Monastery, Etna, California.

The Life of Our Holy Father Maximus the Confessor, translated by Father Christopher Birchall, Holy Transfiguration Monastery, Boston, 1982.

Macris, Father George, *The Orthodox Church and the Ecumenical Movement During the Period 1920–1969*, Saint Nectarios Press, Seattle, Washington, 1986.

Nicene and Post Nicene Fathers of the Christian Church, Vol. XIV, "The Seven Ecumenical Councils," Henry R. Percival, Editor, Hendrickson Publishers, Peabody, Massachusetts, 1994.

Orthodox Christian Witness:

The Orthodox Christian Witness *holds a very special place in the struggle against Ecumenism. Indeed, it may be said that its pages record the history and development of this pan-heresy over the past thirty years. The listing that follows includes some of the more prominent articles that have appeared in the* Witness *regarding this subject:*

"The 1983 Sobor of Bishops," Aug. 20/Sept. 2, 1984.

"All the News That's Fit to Print," Jan. 15/28, 1990.

"The Case of Hans Kung," Father George Metalinos, April 14/27, 1980.

"Church Council: Selective Indignation," Don Feder, March 2/15, 1992.

"'Dear. . . .' —A Letter to a Methodist Minister," Sept. 15/28, 1980.

"Delete Cheesefare Sunday," Apr. 29/May 12, 1985.

"Ecumenism Down Under," Aug. 5/18, 1991.

"The Faith of the Apostles," April 15/28, 1985.

"Father Abbacum the Barefoot," Sept. 2/15, 1985.

"The Heretic and His Heresy," Aug. 17/30, 1981.

"A Letter to One of Our Readers," Sept. 25/Oct. 8, 1989.

"Monophysitism and the Orthodox Church," June 6/19, 1992 (See Appendix F).

"New Calendar Donatism?," March 14/27, 1994 (See Appendix O).

"New Calendar Holy Days," Nov. 26/Dec. 9, 1984.

"Orthodoxy and 'Orthodoxy'," Oct. 14/27, 1985.

"Pope Defends Papal Primacy," June 13/26, 1988.

"A Question of Integrity," Dec. 9/22, 1985.

"Reflections on Metropolitan Vitaly's Nativity Epistle," Feb. 16/March 1, 1987 (See Appendix E).

"The Religion of the Future," Feb. 4/17, 1985.

"'Sectarian' Orthodox Christians," June 10/23, 1991 (See Appendix M).

"A Sequel to 'Worse Than Any Heresy,'" April 19/May 2, 1982.

Orthodox Christian Witness/[cont.]:
"The Spiritual Testament of Patriarch Athenagoras," Dec. 17/30, 1979.
"Stolen Doctrines—Concerning Restless Minds and Itching Ears," March 17/30, 1986.
"True Orthodoxy," Archbishop Averky, Jan. 10/23, 1983.
"'Uncanonical' Orthodox Christians," June 24/July 7, 1991 (See Appendix N).
"The Universal Patriarch," Aug. 3/16, 1981 and Nov. 25/Dec. 8, 1991.
"Worse Than Any Heresy," March 8/21, 1982.

Orthodox Life:
"The Announcement of the Extraordinary Joint Conference of the Sacred Community of the Holy Mount Athos," Sept.–Oct., 1980, p. 8.
"Are the Terms 'Christian' and 'Orthodox' Accurate In Our Times?," Archbishop Averky, May–June, 1975, p. 4.
"The Challenge of Ecumenism—The Rise of Sectarianism Among the Orthodox," Father Michael Azkoul, Nov.–Dec., 1973, p. 22.
"Humanistic Ecumenism," Father Justin Popovich, Jan.-Feb., 1979, p. 26.
"The Julian Calendar—A Thousand-Year Icon of Time in Russia," Ludmilla Perepiolkina, Sept.–Oct., 1995, pp. 7-37.
"Roman Catholic Ecumenism in Relation to the Orthodox Church," Protopresbyter George Grabbe, July–Aug., 1973, p. 20.
"The Seventieth Anniversary of the Pan-Orthodox Congress in Constantinople," Bishop Photios of Triaditsa, Part One, Jan.–Feb., 1994, pp. 36-45; Part Two, March–April, 1994, pp. 36-48.

The Orthodox Word:
"The Decline of the Patriarchate of Constantinople," Archbishop John Maximovitch, July–Aug., 1972, p. 166.

"A Desperate Appeal to the Ecumenical Patriarch," Father Philotheos Zervakos, Jan.–Feb., 1968, p. 4.

"The Ecumenical Patriarchate," Father Theokletos, Jan.–March, 1966, p. 31.

"Ecumenism," Archbishop Vitaly of Montreal, July–Aug., 1969, p. 145.

Epistles of St. Cyril of Kazan, July-Aug., 1977, pp. 175-189.

"The 'Great Synod' of Patriarch Athenagoras: The Response of Genuine Orthodoxy," Nov.–Dec., 1968, p. 259.

"The Orthodox Mission Today: Saint Nectarios Orthodox Church in Seattle," Father Neketas Palassis, Sept.–Oct., 1969, p. 183.

"The Sunday of Orthodoxy," Father Sebastian Dabovich, Jan.–March, 1966, p. 20.

"Two More Greek Priests Leave the Greek Archdiocese for the Russian Synod," Nov.–Dec., 1969, p. 232.

"A Voice of Conscience in the Greek Archdiocese," Jan.–Feb., 1968, p. 37.

"The Zealots of Mount Athos: Leaven of True Orthodoxy Today," Sept.–Oct., 1972, p. 219.

Ostroumoff, Ivan N., *The History of the Council of Florence*, translated by Basil Popoff, Holy Transfiguration Monastery, Boston, Massachusetts, 1971.

Papa-Nicholas Planas—the Simple Shepherd of the Simple Sheep, translated and published by Holy Transfiguration Monastery, Boston, Massachusetts, 1981.

Philaret, Metropolitan, (Russian Church Abroad):

Epistle to Athenagoras, Patriarch of Constantinople, 1965, see *History of the Council of Florence*, pp. 192-199.

Epistle to Athenagoras, Patriarch of Constantinople, 1968, see *History of the Council of Florence*, pp. 200-207.

Epistle to Iakovos, Archbishop of North and South America, 1969, see *History of the Council of Florence*, pp. 208-214.

On the Thyateira Confession, Orthodox Life, March–April, 1976, Jordanville, New York, pp. 21-25.

Philaret, Metropolitan, (Russian Church Abroad)/[cont.]:
A Sorrowful Epistle to the Primates of the Holy Orthodox Churches, 1969, see *History of the Council of Florence*, pp. 215-235.

A Second Sorrowful Epistle to the Primates of the Holy Orthodox Churches, 1972, Saint Nectarios Educational Series #61, Saint Nectarios Press, Seattle, Washington.

Recent Efforts for Unity Between the Two Families of the Orthodox Church, [i.e., the Orthodox Church and the Monophysites], unpublished manuscript, undated.

Saint Cyprian of Carthage, "**On the Unity of the Church**," *Ante-Nicene Fathers*, Vol. V, Fathers of the Third Century, pp. 421-429. Alexander Roberts, D.D. and James Donaldson, LL.D., Editors, Hendrickson Publishers, Peabody, Massachusetts, 1994.

Saint Gregory Palamas Monastery, *The Balamand Union—A Victory of Vatican Diplomacy*, Etna, California.

_____, *The Non-Chalcedonian Heretics*, Etna, California.

_____, (Bishops Chrysostomos and Auxentios, with Hieromonk Ambrosios), *The Old Calendar Orthodox Church of Greece*, Etna, California, 1991. (This book is reviewed in *The True Vine*, No. 20, p. 56.)

Saint Nectarios Educational Series:
Declaration of the Ninth Congress of the Diocese of Western Europe of the Russian Orthodox Church Outside of Russia, translated by Holy Transfiguration Monastery, Boston, Massachusetts, published in Saint Nectarios Educational Series #26, Saint Nectarios Press, Seattle, Washington.

Latest Developments in the Church of the Genuine Orthodox Christians of Greece—the Schism of the "Kallistos" Group, Saint Nectarios Educational Series #93, SNP, Seattle, Washington.

An Open Letter to the "Logos," Holy Transfiguration Monastery, Boston, Massachusetts, published in Saint Nectarios Educational Series #1, SNP, Seattle, Washington, 1970.

A Second Open Letter to the "Logos," Holy Transfiguration Monastery, Boston, Massachusetts, published in Saint Nectarios Educational Series #3, SNP, Seattle, Washington, 1970.

Sakkas, Father Basile, *The Calendar Question*, translated by Holy Transfiguration Monastery, published by Holy Trinity Monastery, Jordanville, New York, 1973.

The True Vine:
Becoming Orthodox, a book review, No. 5, p. 64.
"Becoming Orthodox—the Sequel," No. 12, p. 5.
Biography of Archbishop Auxentius of Athens, No. 23, pp. 13-46.
Biography of Bishop Gury of Kazan, No. 11, pp. 21-37.
Broken, Yet Never Sundered, a book review, No. 1, p. 80.
"The Creed," Father Michael Gelsinger, No. 15, p. 42.
"Encyclical Concerning Holy Baptism," Bishop Ephraim of Boston, No. 2, p. 2.
"Fern-Seed and Elephants," C.S. Lewis, No. 18, p. 64.
"The Form of Holy Baptism," Bishop Ephraim of Boston, No. 2, p. 8.
The Orthodox Study Bible: New Testament and Psalms, a book review, No. 18, p. 20.
"A Pastoral Encyclical on Freemasonry," Bishops Ephraim of Boston and Makarios of Toronto, No. 21, p. 48.
"A Pastoral Encyclical on the Primary Reason for the Existence of an Orthodox Christian Parish," Bishop Ephraim of Boston, No. 13, p. 9.
"A Pastoral Encyclical on the True Homeland of Orthodox Christians," Bishop Ephraim of Boston, No. 1, p. 21.
"On the Reception of the Tennessee Faithful," Archbishop Auxentius of Athens, No. 12, p. 18.

Troitsky, Ilarion, of Solovki, Archbishop and Hieromartyr, *Christianity or the Church?*, translated by Lev Puhalo and Vasili Navokshonoff, Holy Trinity Monastery, Jordanville, New York, 1971.

_____, *The Unity of the Church and the World Conference of Christian Communities*, translated by Margaret Jerenic, Monastery Press, Montreal, 1975.

SOURCES IN GREEK

Akakios, Metropolitan of Diavlia and Gabriel, Metropolitan of the Cyclades Islands, *Λύσις Σιωπῆς* [*An End to Silence*], Athens, 1986.

Chrysostom, Metropolitan of Florina, *Ἀκριβὴς Θέσις τοῦ Ἡμερολογιακοῦ Ζητήματος* [*The Precise Position of the Calendar Question*], Athens, 1950.

_____, *Τὸ Ἐκκλησιαστικὸν Ἡμερολόγιον ὡς Κριτήριον τῆς Ὀρθοδοξίας* [*The Ecclesiastical Calendar as a Criterion of Orthodoxy*], Athens, 1945.

_____, *Ὑπόμνημα* [*Memorandum*] of Kyr Chrysostom, formerly Metropolitan of Florina, (subtitled: *A defense in behalf of the restoration of the Ecclesiastical Calendar of the Fathers, and in behalf of the revoking of the essentially invalid deposition supposedly imposed upon him by the Autocephalous Orthodox Church of Greece because of this [his defense of the traditional usage], and also concerning the Pan-Orthodox Council which will assemble in the future to unite all the Orthodox Churches in the celebration of the Christian feasts and in the observances of the fasts and the other rites*), 1945 (title page missing).

Saints Cyprian and Justina, Sacred Monastery of, *Αἱ Ἐκκλησιολογικαὶ Θέσεις Μας* [*Our Ecclesiological Position*], Attica, Greece, Nov. 1984.

_____, *Ὀρθόδοξος Ἔνστασις καὶ Μαρτυρία* [*Orthodox Resistance and Witness*], Attica, Jan.-Mar. 1987.

_____, *Ὀφειλομένη Ἀπάντησις εἰς Δεινὴν Συκοφαντίαν—Εἶναι οἱ «Παλαιοημερολογῖται» Ἐκτὸς τῆς Ἐκκλησίας*; [*A Necessary Response to a Grievous Slander—Are the "Old Calendarists" Outside the Church?*], Athens, 1972.

Epiphanios, Metropolitan of Kition [Matthewite Synod], *Μία Διασάφησις Σύντομος περὶ τοῦ Ὑπομνήματός μου, τῆς Ἐκκλήσεως καὶ τῆς Ὁμολογίας· Διατὶ Ἐξεδόθησαν*; [*A Short Clarification concerning My Memorandum, Summons, and Confession: Why Were They Published?*], 1977.

Epiphaniou, Archimandrite Euthymios, *Τὸ Παλαιοημερολογι-*

τικὸν ἀπὸ Ἀπόψεως Κανονικῆς [*The Old Calendar Issue from a Canonical Point of View*], Athens, 1977.

Φύλακες τῆς Ὀρθοδοξίας [*Guardians of Orthodoxy*], a publication of the short-lived "Kallistos Schism", 1979-1984.

Germanos of Demetrias, Chrysostom of Florina, and Chrysostom of Zakynthos, Most Reverend Metropolitans of the Autocephalous Church of Greece, **Διασάφησις περὶ τοῦ Ζητήματος τοῦ Ἐκκλησιαστικοῦ Ἡμερολογίου** [*Clarification concerning the Matter of the Ecclesiastical Calendar*], Athens, 1935.

_____, Διαμαρτυρία πρὸς τὰς Ὀρθοδόξους Ἐκκλησίας ἐπὶ τῇ Μονομερεῖ καὶ Ἀντικανονικῇ Εἰσαγωγῇ τοῦ Νέου Ἡμερολογίου [***A Protest to the Orthodox Churches over the Unilateral and Anticanonical Introduction of the New Calendar***] reprinted by the periodical *Saint Agathangelos of Esphigmenou*, Athens (the original was published in 1935).

_____, Προκήρυξις πρὸς τὸν Ἐφημεριακὸν Κλῆρον καὶ τοὺς Μοναχοὺς τῆς Ὀρθοδόξου Ἑλληνικῆς Ἐκκλησίας περὶ τοῦ Ζητήματος τοῦ Ἐκκλησιαστικοῦ Ἡμερολογίου [*A Proclamation to the Parish Clergy and Monastics of the Orthodox Greek Church concerning the Matter of the Ecclesiastical Calendar*], reprinted by the periodical *Saint Agathangelos of Esphigmenou*, undated (the original was most likely published in 1935).

Giannakoulopoulos, Bishop Kalliopios, Τὸ Μωρὸν Ἅλας [*The Salt That Has Lost Its Savour*], Piraeus, 1991.

_____, **Τὰ Πάτρια** [idiomatically: *The Traditions and Institutions of Our Fathers and Ancestors*], Piraeus.

Haniotes, Monk Mark, Τὸ Ἡμερολογιακὸν Σχίσμα [*The Calendar Schism*], Athens, 1975.

Karamitsos, Stavros, Ἡ Ἀγωνία ἐν τῷ Κήπῳ τῆς Γεθσημανῆ [*The Agony in the Garden of Gethsemane*], Athens, 1961.

_____, Ὁ Σύγχρονος Ὁμολογητὴς τῆς Ὀρθοδοξίας [*The Contemporary Confessor of Orthodoxy*], Athens, 1990.

Klimatianos, Monk Polycarp, Σωσίβιον Ναυαγῶν Ψυχῶν [*A Lifesaver for Shipwrecked Souls*], Athens, undated.

Koutsoumbas, Archimandrite Cyprian, Πῶς Ἐγνώρισα τὸ Πάτριον Ἡμερολόγιον καὶ Ἐπέστρεψα εἰς Αὐτό [*How I Came to*

Know the Traditional Calendar and Returned to It], Fili, Attica, 1968.

Ktenas, Lambros, Πίσω Ἀπ' Ὅ, τι Φαίνεται Στὸ Ἡμερολογιακό [*What Lies Hidden Behind the Calendar Issue*], Patras, 1989.

Lahanas, Monk Cyprian, Ποία ἡ Διαφορὰ Μεταξὺ Παλαιοῦ καὶ Νέου Ἡμερολογίου [*The Difference Between the Old and New Calendar*], Athens, 1972.

Macris, Metropolitan Kallistos (Matthewite Synod), Ἡ Ἱστορία τῶν Ἱερῶν Μονῶν Ἁγίων Ταξιαρχῶν Μιχαὴλ καὶ Γαβριὴλ, καὶ Εὐαγγελισμοῦ τῆς Θεοτόκου [*A History of the Sacred Convents of the Holy Supreme Commanders Michael and Gabriel, and of the Annunciation of the Theotokos*], Corinth, 1972.

Magdalene, Nun, Ἡ Αἱματοπότιστος Ἄμπελος [*The Blood-drenched Vineyard*], Athens, 1970.

Οὕτω Φρονοῦμεν, Οὕτω Λαλοῦμεν [***Thus Do We Believe, Thus Do We Speak***], published by the Church of the True Orthodox Christians of Greece (Synod of Archbishop Auxentius), Athens, 1974.

Papadopoulos, Archbishop Chrysostom of Athens, Ἡ Διόρθωσις τοῦ Ἰουλιανοῦ Ἡμερολογίου ἐν τῇ Ἐκκλησίᾳ τῆς Ἑλλάδος [*The Correction of the Julian Calendar in the Church of Greece*], Athens, 1933.

Paul, Monk of Cyprus, Νεοημερολογιτισμός—Οἰκουμενισμός [*New Calendarism—Ecumenism*], Athens, 1982.

Polycarp, Bishop of Diavlia, **Ἡ Ἡμερολογιακὴ Μεταρρύθμισις** [*The Calendar Change*], Athens, 1947.

Ἡ Πραγματικὴ Ἀλήθεια περὶ τοῦ Ἐκκλησιαστικοῦ Ἡμερολογίου [*The Real Truth about the Ecclesiastical Calendar*], a reprint of a series of articles in the newspaper «Σκριπ» (*Script*), Athens, 1929. Third edition [by the Matthewite Synod], Athens, 1977.

Savvopoulos, Father Michael, Ἄμυνα Ὀρθοδόξου Πίστεως [*Defense of the Orthodox Faith*], Drama, 1951.

Tambouras, Priest-monk Amphilochios, Αἴτια καὶ Ἀφορμαὶ τοῦ Διαχωρισμοῦ τῶν Γ.Ο.Χ. εἰς Παρατάξεις [*The Causes and Reasons for the Separation of the True Orthodox Christians into Separate Jurisdictions*], Larisa, 1975.

Theodoretos, Monk of the Holy Mountain, Κανονικὴ Θεώρησις τοῦ Ἡμερολογιακοῦ Σχίσματος [*A Canonical Review of the Calendar Schism*], Athens, 1976.

Vasileiades, Nicholas, Ὁ Ἅγιος Μάρκος ὁ Εὐγενικὸς καὶ ἡ Ἕνωσις τῶν Ἐκκλησιῶν [*Saint Mark Eugenicus and the Union of the Churches*], Athens, 1993 (4th edition).

Vokos, John, Ἡ Διάσπασις τῆς Ὀρθοδοξίας (Παλαιὸν καὶ Νέον Ἡμερολόγιον) [*The Sundering of Orthodoxy (Old and New Calendar)*], Athens, 1977.

Xeni, Nun, Τὸ Πάτριον Ἑορτολόγιον [*The Festal Calendar of the Fathers*], Petroupolis, 1977.

Zealot Fathers of the Holy Mountain, Φωνὴ ἐξ Ἁγίου Ὄρους [*A Voice from the Holy Mountain*], Holy Mountain, Athos, 1973.

Zervakos, Archimandrite Philotheos, Τὸ Νέον Παπικὸν Ἡμερολόγιον καὶ οἱ Καρποὶ Αὐτοῦ [*The New, Papal Calendar and Its Fruits*], Thessalonica, undated.

Index

Page numbers in italic indicate an illustration.

Abortion, tolerance of by future Patriarch Bartholomew, 163, 321-22
Afanasy, Archbishop of Buenos Aires and Argentina-Paraguay, 133
Agathangelos, Ecumenical Patriarch, 34, 265, 311
Agatho, Abba, 289
Agreed Statement with Monophysites, 118, 159, 163, 216-19, 322
Akakios, Metropolitan of Diavlia, 80, *81*, 100, 141-42, 317
Akakios Douskos, Metropolitan of Montreal and All Canada, 100, 127
Akakios Pappas, Archbishop of Talantion, 79-81, *80*, *81*, 82, 83-86, 90, 93, 162, 316, 317
Albania, Church of, 164, 232, 314, 322
Alexandria, Church of, 33, 34, 38, 164, 232, 265, 313, 314, 315, 322
Alexis I, Patriarch of Moscow, 206
Alexis II (Ridiger), Patriarch of Moscow, 203, 248-49
Alipy, Bishop of Cleveland, 133, 139
Alypios, Fr., 296
Ambrose of Milan, St, 119, 223
Ambrose, Archimandrite of the French Orthodox Mission, 146, 148
Amphilochius of Iconium, St, 119, 256, 259
Anastasy, Metropolitan, 79, 135, 136, 188, 191, 203, 208-9, 242
Testament of, 136, 203, 208-9
Anathema, 141, 143-45, 146, 147, 153, 164, 212
against Gregorian Calendar, 58, 118, 158, 167, 265, 276, 277, 285, 311
against papal teachings (*Sigillion* of 1583), 283-85
as used by St Paul, 212, 241
defined by St Nicodemos, 144, 147, 212, 240-41
of 1054 against Rome, "lifting" of, 130, 159, 278, 317
of 1983, against Ecumenism, 132-34, 137, 138, 139, 143-44, 145, 147-48, 151-52, 196, 211-16, 240, 250, 320, 321
of Patriarch Tikhon and All-Russian Church Sobor, against Communists, 200-1
of Russian Catacomb Church, against Soviet Church, 202
of Seventh Council, 59-60, 119, 159
Anatolius, Patriarch of Constantinople, St, 251, 252, 253, 254
Andrew, Bishop of Patras, then Archbishop of Matthewites, 64, 101
Andrew, Bishop of Rockland, 83
Anglicans. *See* England, Church of.
Anthimos, Ecumenical Patriarch, 34, 158, 265, 311
Anthony, Archbishop of Geneva and Western Europe, 126, 127, 133, 137, 139, 140, 142, 143, 145, 146, 147, 154, 184, 192, 194, 210, 320
Anthony, Archbishop of Los Angeles and Texas, 83, 133
Anthony, Archbishop of Western America and San Francisco, 83, 133, 322
Anthony, Greek Archdiocese Bishop of San Francisco, 273
Anthony, Metropolitan of Megaris, 100, 103, 104, 106, 108, 111, 120, 319-20

334

INDEX 335

Anthony, Metropolitan of Patras, 46
Anthony (Khrapovitsky), Metropolitan, 135, 149, 188, 191, 192, 193, 194, 195, 207, 208, 242, 246
Antichrist, 145, 197, 199, 204, 283
Antioch, Patriarchate of, 34, 38, 119, 164, 218, 219, 232, 278, 287, 288, 300, 314, 315, 316, 322
Antiochian Archdiocese, 213, 239
Apollinarius, 284
Apostolic Constitutions, 91-92, 253
Apotactites, 261
Aristenos, 94, 262
Arius, Arians, 16, 189-90, 223
Assisi Gathering of 1986, 320
Association of the Orthodox, 39, 42-44
Ataturk, Kemal, 38
Athanasios, Metropolitan of Acharnae, 109
Athanasios, Metropolitan of Larisa, 109, 121
Athanasios, Metropolitan of Syros, 46
Athanasios Haralambidis, Metropolitan of Grevena, 104, 105, 106
Athanasios Postalas, Metropolitan of Platamon, 104, 105, 106
Athanasius the Great, St, 12, 119, 239, 240
Athenagoras, Archbishop of Thyateira and Great Britain, 33, 272, 319
Athenagoras, Ecumenical Patriarch, *28*, 130, 136, 159, 272, 294, 295, 298, 299, 302, 303, 315, 316, 317, 318, 319
Athos, Mount, 39, 69, 79, 126, 138, 232, 236, 237, 248, 285, 288-97, 299, 300, 301, 304, 319, 320
See also Sacred Union of Zealot Monks.
Augustine, Bishop of Hippo, 281
Augustine, Metropolitan of Florina, 170, 292
Auxentian Synod, 65, 86, 89, 97, 103, 113, 115, 122, 125-62, 164, 319, 321, 322
appeals to and is received by Russian Church Abroad, 82, 318
consecrates bishops for North America and for France, 160
consecrates Catacomb Bishop Gury of Kazan, 162, 322
declares Tsakos consecration null and void, 121
deposes members of Kallistos Schism, 103-9, 122, 320
Encyclical of 1974, 98-100, 113, 115, 319
and Free Serbian Church, 127
perceived by Catacomb Christians of Russia to be canonical Church of Greece, 161-62
receives back repentant members of Kallistos Schism, 110
receives French Mission, 148
status in 1973, 86
Auxentius, Archbishop of Athens and All Greece, 65, *81*, 82, *86*, 90, 95, 100, 103, 104, 105, 107, 109, 110, 111, 122, *124*, *128*, *129*, 157, 159, 160, 162, *166*
approves consecration of Bishop Gury of Kazan, 162
as Bishop of Gardikion, 80, *81*, 317
character of, 125
consecrates bishops for North America and for France, 160, 321
Declaration of the Clergy under, 157, 158-59
elected Archbishop, 81, 317
injured by police in 1935, 51, *52*
mistakes of, 125-29
queries Russian Church Abroad on reception of Matthewite clergy, 89
receives French clergy and faithful, 148
receives North American clergy and faithful, 142
repose of, *128*, 129, *129*, 322
tried and "deposed" by his own bishops, 120-21
Averky, Archbishop of Syracuse and Trinity, 83, 87, 149, 216

Balamand Agreed Statement, 159, 164, 231-38, 249, 281-82, 322

Balsamon, 262
Baptism, 68, 69, 94, 99, 100, 112, 126, 127, 132, 133, 149, 186, 189, 208, 210, 213, 221, 226, 234, 252, 253, 256-62, 267, 279-82, 284, 285, 298
Baptism, Tome of 1756, 285-86
Barr Statement of 1990, 163-64, 181, 271, 322
Bartholomew, Ecumenical Patriarch, 123, 163, 232, 237, 248, 292, 321, 322
Basil the Great, St, 12, 14, 22, 50, 55, 67, 93, 94, 98, 99, 107, 116, 187, 207, 252, 253, 255, 256-59, 262, 277
Basil, Metropolitan of Anchialos, 29
Basil, Metropolitan of Drama, 46
Basil, Metropolitan of Dryinopolis, 46
Beccus. *See* John Beccus.
Belden, Fr. David, 238-42
Berdyaev, Nicholas, 198-99
Bishop, to be consecrated by more than one bishop, 64, 84, 91-93, 95
Bobich, Archimandrite Seraphim, 138
Branch Theory, 132, 133, 137, 159, 226-28, 278, 319
British Mandate, 32, 313
Brothers Karamazov, The, 221
Buddhism, 163, 224, 273, 321
Bulgakov, Fr. Sergius, 198-99
Bulgaria, Church of, 165, 244, 314, 317

Canterbury, Archbishop of, 139, 318
Carras, Fr. Panagiotes, 241, 242
Carter, President James, 197
Carthage, 275
   13th Council in, 107
   Canon 79 of, 95
   Church of, 94
   Local Council of, under St Cyprian, 253, 261, 282
Catacomb Church of Russia, 18, 160-62, 199, 200, 202, 203, 204-5, 207, 208
Cathari (Novatians), 94, 95, 256-59, 261
Chambesy, Geneva, 216, 218
Cheirothesia (laying-on of hands), 46, 89, 94, 95, 97, 98, 258

Cheirothetoúmenoi, 94
Cheirotonía, 94
Chekists, 204
Chiliasm, 245
Chrismation, 59, 67, 68, 94, 98, 99, 113, 126, 240, 262, 279, 280
Christopher, Metropolitan of Leontopolis, later Patriarch of Alexandria, 21, 38, 45-46, *45*, 74, 79, 91, 316
Christopher, Metropolitan of Megaris, then Christianopolis, 46, 53, 63, *64*, *66*, 67, 69, 73, 90, 314, 315, 316
Chrysostom, Bishop of Magnesia, 80, *81*, 317
Chrysostom, Bishop of Thessalonica, 100
Chrysostom, Metropolitan of Florina, 47, 56, *56*, 57, *58*, 61, 62, 63, *64*, *66*, 67, 69, *72*, *73*, *75*, *78*, 79, 87-88, 90, 162
   attempts of, to meet Bishop Matthew, 65-66
   brought to trial with fellow bishops and banished, 1935, 50-51, 314
   convictions of, in issuing Encyclical of 1950, 113-14
   declaration of May, 1935, 47-50
   declines to consecrate bishops for the Matthewites, 87-88, 102
   declines to consecrate new bishops in last years, 73-74
   Encyclical of 1950, 61, 67-69, 98, 110, 113-14, 115, 315, 319
   exiled, 1951, *72*, 73, 114, 316
   forms Synod of True Orthodox Christians of Greece and consecrates bishops for them, 46-47, 314
   forsaken by Germanos of the Cyclades and Matthew of Bresthena, 62, 315
   initial hopes of, that innovations will be corrected, 48, 57-59, 60-61, 63
   Letter of 1937 to Germanos of the Cyclades on "potential schism," 57, 59-60, 61, 68, 110, 113
   Pastoral Encyclical of June, 1935, 53-55, 67, 68, 69, 113, 114, 115, 314

INDEX

337

rejoined by Germanos of the Cyclades, 63, 65
repose and funeral of, 74, 75, 316
sole bishop in 1943, 63
sole bishop 1954-55, 73, 90
See also Florinites.
Chrysostom, Metropolitan of Zakynthos, 46, 47, 50, 53, 90, 314
Chrysostom Gonzalez, Bishop of Etna, 103, 116, 245
Chrysostom Kiousis, Metropolitan, 120-23, 142, 155, 244, 320
Chrysostom Papadopoulos, Archbishop of Athens, 29, 32, 34, 35, 36, 37, 37, 39, 40, 47, 48, 51, 53, 59, 99, 115, 118, 169, 265-66, 308, 312, 313, 314
Chrysostom, St. *See* John Chrysostom.
Church Leaders' Covenant, 163, 223-24, 320
Churchill, Winston, 13
Communism, 18, 69, 136, 197, 200-1, 205
Concelebration/joint prayer, 116, 137, 139, 140, 143, 145, 146, 150-51, 172, 193, 214-16, 248, 250, 251, 288, 293, 295, 300, 304
of Antioch with Monophysite Syrian Patriarchate, 218-19
of Athonites with Latins, 293
of Ecumenist Orthodox and Papists, 163, 172
of Ecumenist Orthodox and Protestants, Papists, and pagans, 320, 322
of Kiousis Synod and Jerusalem Patriarchate, 123
of Patriarch Athenagoras with Archbishop of Canterbury, 318
of Patriarch Athenagoras with Pope Paul VI, 159, 317, 318
of Patriarch Demetrios with Pope John Paul II, 299, 300-5, 321
of Russian Church Abroad with Ecumenistic jurisdictions, 139, 140, 143, 145, 146, 150-51, 214
of Russian Church Abroad with Serbian Patriarchate, 138, 239, 322

Congress of 1923, 32, 33-34, 36, 38, 312
"Conservative" new calendarists, 293, 298-305
Constantine, Bishop of Brisbane, later of Richmond and Britain, 96, 97, 133
Constantine, King of Greece, 26, 60
Constantinople, Church of (Ecumenical Patriarchate), 23, 32, 34, 58, 150, 151, 164, 180, 183, 198, 219, 231, 232, 240, 243, 254, 265, 281, 283, 288, 289-96, 311, 312, 313, 314, 315, 316, 317, 322
Copronymus, Emperor (Constantine), 293, 295
Cosmas of Aitolia, St, 283, 286
Council:
Ecumenical Councils (Seven), 35, 48, 50, 54, 118, 147, 237, 272, 273, 278, 284, 286, 288, 322
Ecumenical Councils (last four), 119, 163, 217-18, 287
First Ecumenical, 13, 16, 49, 58, 77, 92, 93, 94, 95, 167-68, 262
First-and-Second, 116, 117, 247, 251, 260, 287, 294
Second Ecumenical, 17, 93, 187, 262, 281
Third Ecumenical, 168, 251
Fourth Ecumenical, 107, 251, 281, 292
Sixth Ecumenical, 91-92, 192, 261
Seventh Ecumenical, 59-60, 61, 92, 94, 95, 159, 206, 246, 250, 251, 252, 254, 259, 262
"Eighth Ecumenical," 280, 281
of 754, Iconoclast, 293
of 1583, 1587, and 1593, Pan-Orthodox, 34, 35, 41, 54, 58, 62, 118, 158, 167, 265, 268, 277, 287, 311, 314
of 1848, under Patriarch Anthimos, 158
of Gangra, 107
of Iconium, 261
of Laodicea, 253
Quinisext, 107
of Sardica, 107
in Trullo, 92
See also under Carthage.

Cross, appearance of, above Mount Hymettos outside of Athens in 1925, 22, 41-44, *43*, 56, 313
Cyprian of Carthage, St, 158, 188, 253, 257, 261
Cyprian, Metropolitan of Oropos and Fili, 102, 103, 106, 108, 111-20, 122, 155, 156, 243-50, 320
Cyprus, Church of, 164, 232, 314, 316, 322
Cyril, Archbishop of Cyprus, 38, 313
Cyril, Ecumenical Patriarch, 286
Cyril, Patriarch of Alexandria, St, 119

Damianos, Patriarch of Jerusalem, 29, 38, 313
Daniel, Bishop, 245
Declaration of the Clergy. *See under* Auxentius, Archbishop of Athens.
Demetrios, Bishop of Thessalonica, 64
Demetrios, Ecumenical Patriarch, 138, 163, 273, 288-96, 298-305, *299*, 318-19, 320, 321, 322
Dimitry, Bishop of Hailar, 188-89
Diodoros, Patriarch of Jerusalem, 248, 322
Dionisije, Founder of Free Serbian Church, 127
Dionysius of Alexandria, St, 256, 257, 261
Dioscurus, Patriarch of Alexandria, 251, 254
Diptychs, commemoration of Pope in Orthodox, 278, 318
See also under Concelebration/joint prayer.
Donatists, 94-95, 275-79
Dorotheos, Metropolitan of Prusa, 23, 180, 312
Dositheos, Patriarch of Jerusalem, 34, 265, 311
Dostoyevksy, Fyodor, 221
Dudko, Fr. Dimitry, 196-210
Durham Affair, 273-74
Dutch Church, 128-29

Economy, *economia*, 48, 81, 88, 90-91, 93-94, 95, 128-29, 134, 141, 145, 146, 150, 153-54, 207-8, 211-16, 255, 256, 258, 261-62, 290, 298
Ecumenical Council. *See under* Council.
Ecumenical Movement. *See* Ecumenism.
Ecumenical Patriarchate. *See* Constantinople, Church of.
Ecumenism, 18, 23, 98, 119, 122, 130-32, 135, 137, 139, 140, 150, 157, 159, 160, 162, 165, 166, 196, 211-16, 224, 227, 236, 243, 248, 265, 278, 291, 311
Encratites, 258-59, 261-62
Encyclical of 1920 (Ecumenical Patriarchate), 23-25, 34, 57, 158, 171, 172, 174, 177-81, 265, 276, 278, 312
Encyclical of 1926 against True Orthodox Christians, 39-41, 57, 119, 276, 313
Encyclical of 1935, Encyclical of 1950. *See under* Chrysostom, Metropolitan of Florina.
Encyclical of 1974. *See under* Auxentian Synod.
End to Silence, An, 142
England, Church of, 30, 32, 33, 139, 226, 273-74, 312, 314
Ephraim the Syrian, St, 230
Ephraim, Bishop of Boston, 125, 160, 162, 219-38, 255-56, 286-88, 321
Epiphanios, Metropolitan of Kition, 87, 88, 90, 95, *96*, 97, 98
Epiphanius of Cyprus, St, 128
Episcopalian Church, 149, 153, 223, 273
Esphigmenou Monastery, 289, 294
Estonia, 165
Euthymios, Metropolitan of Thessalonica, 127
Euthymios Orphanos, Metropolitan of Stavropolis, 104, 105, 106, 109
Euthymius the Great, St, 292
Eutyches, 251
Evlogios, Metropolitan of Korytsa, 79
Evlogy, Metropolitan ("Paris Group"), 183, 188-89, 190, 198

INDEX 339

Ezekiel, Bishop of Derbe (Australia), 274-75, 278-79

Faith and Order Conference in Amsterdam, 315
Faith and Order Conferences in Lausanne, and in Edinburgh, 314
"Faith, Sacraments, and the Unity of the Church" discussed at Bari, 234
False-Autocephalites, American. See Orthodox Church in America.
Ferrara and Florence, false council of, 235, 240
Fifteenth Canon of First-and-Second Council, 117, 247, 287, 294
Filioque, 17, 168, 235, 264, 281, 284
Finland, Church of, 58, 150, 164, 232, 322
Firmillian, Bishop of Caesarea in Cappadocia, St, 257, 261
First Apostolic Canon, 64, 84, 92, 95
Florence. *See* Ferrara and Florence.
Florinites, 63, 65, 79, 82, 98, 130, 315
 See also Auxentian Synod; Chrysostom, Metropolitan of Florina; *and* True Orthodox Christians of Greece.
Florovsky, Fr. Georges, 316
France, True Orthodox Christians of (French Mission), 140, 141, 142-48, 321
Free Serbian Church, 127
Freemantle, Anne, 264
Freemasonry, 29, 33, 83, 127, 218, 278

Gabriel, Bishop of Zarna, as example of one bishop consecrating others, 91
Gabriel, Metropolitan of the Cyclades, 100, 141-42
Gavalas, Fr. Anthony, 133
George Scholarius, 259-60
Gerasimos, Metropolitan of Boeotia, 120, 121-22
Gerasimos Vrakas, Metropolitan of Talantion, 104, 105, 106, 109

Gerasimus of the Jordan, St, 292
German, Patriarch of Serbia, 138
Germanos, Metropolitan of Aeolia, 121
Germanos, Metropolitan of the Cyclades, 46, 51, 55, 56, *56*, 57, 59, 60, 62, *62*, 63, *64*, 65, 67, 69, 73, *74*, 87, 90, 314, 315, 316
Germanos, Metropolitan of Demetrias, 46, *47*, 50, 51, 55, 56, *56*, *61*, 63, 90, 314, 315
Germanos (Athanasiou), Metropolitan, 103, 106, 108, 110
Germanos (Karavangeis), Metropolitan of the Holy Synod of Greece, 30-31
Gerontios, Metropolitan of Piraeus and Salamis, 80, *81*, 100, 104, 105, 317
Gore, Charles, Bishop of Oxford, 33
Gorny, Soviet Convent, 138
Grabbe, Fr. George. *See* Gregory (Grabbe), Bishop of Washington and Florida.
Greece, Holy Synod of Church of, 30, 34, 35, 154, 265, 311, 312
Greece, State Church of, 37, 39-41, 46, 54-55, 57-58, 69, 73, 74, 77, 79, 85, 98, 100, 118-19, 122, 125, 172, 292, 303, 312, 313, 314, 315, 319
 See also Revolutionary Government of Greece.
Greek Archdiocese of North and South America, 213, 222, 223, 232-33, 239, 269, 279, 287, 312, 316, 317
Gregorian Calendar. *See* New Calendar.
Gregory the Great, St, Pope, 253
Gregory Palamas, St, 17, 227, 238, 296
Gregory the Theologian, St, 12, 22, 186-87
Gregory, Patriarch of Antioch, 38, 313
Gregory, Patriarch of Constantinople, 36, 37
Gregory (Grabbe), Bishop of Washington and Florida, 133, 149, 151, 154, 193, 201, 208, 210, 242, 243-50, *244*
Gregory XIII, Pope, 167, 283, 311
Grigoriou Monastery, 295
Gury, Bishop of Kazan, 160-62, *161*, 322

Harakas, Fr. Stanley, 264-75
Haralampos, Hieromonk, 97
Heresy, as distinguished from sin, 289
Heresy, schism, and unlawful assemblies, defined by St Basil, 256-57, 259-60
Hilandar Monastery, Athos, 138
Hilarion, Bishop, of Russian Church Abroad, 138, 152, 155, 156
Hilarion Troitsky of Solovki, Archbishop, New Martyr, 149, 216
Hilary of Poitiers, St, 13
Historia Tripartita, 254
Holy Cross Seminary, Jerusalem, 29
Holy Cross Theological School, Brookline, Mass., 232, 233
Holy Mountain. *See* Athos, Mount.
Holy Orthodox Church in North America, 160
  percentage of converts in, 269
Holy Transfiguration Monastery, Brookline, Mass., 11, 87, 89, *96*, 97, 109, *131*, 141, 149, 150, 160, 184-85, *185*, 298-305
Holy Trinity Monastery, Jordanville, N.Y., 87, 154, 155, 184, 199, 238
Hydroparastatae, 258, 261
Hypatius of Rufinianae, St, 251

I Confess One Baptism, 280
Iakovos, Archbishop of North and South America, 228, 272, 291, 292, 293, 316, 317, 318, 321
Iconoclasm, 250, 293
Ignatius the God-bearer, St, 187-88, 252, 291
Ignatius IV, Patriarch of Antioch, 218, 248
Indulgences, 284
Ioasaph, Bishop of Alaska, 91
Irenaeos, Metropolitan of Cassandria, 46
Irenaeus of Lyons, St, 253
Irinej, Bishop of Free Serbian Church, 127
Islam, 163, 224, 319, 321

James the Brother of God, St, 15
Jenkins, Bishop David, 273-74
Jeremias II, "the Illustrious," Ecumenical Patriarch, 17, 35, 167, 169, 265, 283-85
Jerusalem, Church of, 15, 34, 37-38, 120, 123, 139, 150, 163, 226, 265, 313, 314, 315
Jews, dialogue with, 249
Joachim III, Ecumenical Patriarch, 311
Joachim, Metropolitan of Phokis, 267
John Beccus, Ecumenical Patriarch, 293, 295, 296, 297
John Chrysostom, St, 128, 187-88, 189, 194, 227, 228, 252, 291
John Maximovitch, Archbishop of San Francisco, St, 128-29, 190
John Paul I, Pope, 319
John Paul II, Pope, 281, *299*, 300, 320
John Rosha, Bishop of Portugal, 126-27
John, Bishop of Sardinia, 112
John, Bishop of Smolensk, 94
Johnson, Fr. Seraphim, 149-57
Joint prayer. *See* Concelebration.
Joseph, Hieromonk, later Photios, Bishop of Lyons. *See* Photios, Bishop of Lyons.
"Junta," "pre-junta," and "post-junta" bishops with State Church in Greece, 266
Justin Kulutouros, Metropolitan of Marathon and Euboea, 105, 106, 109

Kallinikos, Metropolitan of Phthiotis and Thavmakos, 100, 104, 105
Kallinikos (Karaphylakis), Metropolitan, 103, 106, 108, 110
Kallinikos (Sarantopoulos), Metropolitan of Achaia, 103, 106, 108, 111, 121
Kalliopios (Giannakoulopoulos), Metropolitan, 97, 103, 106, 108, 109-11, 121
Kallistos, Metropolitan of Corinth, 64, 87, 88, 90, 95, *96*, 97, 98, 101, 103,

INDEX 341

104, 106, 107, 108, 109-11, *111*, 114-15, 120, *244*, 319
Kallistos Schism, 102-12, 319
Kallistos Ware, Bishop, 272, 320
Karamitsos, Stavros, 63, 65, 125
Karmiris, John, 25, 221
Keratea, Matthewite Convent, 65
KGB, 123, 160, 200
Kiousis Synod. *See* Chrysostom Kiousis.
Kochergin, Fr. George, 140, 160
Kondylis, George, Prime Minister of Greece, 55-56
Koran, 273, 321

Lambeth Conference, 314
Lardas, Fr. George, 11, 36, 38, 39, 41, 62, 71, 86
Latins. *See* Roman Catholics.
Laurus, Bishop of Manhattan, then Archbishop of Syracuse and Trinity, 83, 97, 133, 139, 152, 156, 245
Laying-on of hands. *See Cheirothesia.*
Lebedev, Fr. Alexander, 134, 152-54, 156, 321
Ledwich, Fr. Athanasios, 273-74
Leo, St, Pope of Rome, 119, 252, 253
Leonty, Archbishop of Chile and Peru, 80, 85, 317
Lesna Convent, 143, 182
Lewis, Fr. John, 213
Living Church, 33, 312
Lumière du Thabor, La, 147

Macedonius, 17
Magdalena, Abbess of Lesna, 182-96, 208
Makarios, Bishop of Toronto, 160, 162, 322
Makrakis, Apostolos, 154
Manicheans, 257, 260
Marcionites, 257, 260
Mariam, Abbess of Keratea, 66
Mark Eugenicus of Ephesus, St, 145, 218, 238, 239-40, 282, 286, 287, 295, 296

Mark, Bishop of Berlin and Germany, 133, 138, 320
Mary, the Mother of God, 296
Masons, Masonry. *See* Freemasonry.
Matthew, Bishop of Bresthena, 47, 51-53, 56, 59, 62, 64-65, 65-66, 79, 81, 87, 90, 95, *102*, 115, 314, 315, 316
Matthew, Patriarch of Alexandria, 286
Matthew Langis, Metropolitan, 103, 106, 108, 109-11
Matthewites, 63, 64, 65, 79, 81, 87, 93, 95, 97-98, 101-2, 130, 315, 318
  agree to Russian Church Abroad's conditions for *cheirothesia* but do not fully comply with them in deed, 97-98
  defend icons of the God the Father, 101
  not to be compared to Donatists or Novatians, but single consecrations by Matthew uncanonical, 95
  petition Russian Church Abroad to regularize their consecrations, 87-88
  repudiate regularizations by Russian Church Abroad, 98, 102, 319
  sever ties with Russian Church Abroad, 98
  teach that State Church lost all grace in 1924, 59, 101-2, 114
Mavros, Fr. Theodoretos, 59, 112
Maxim, Bishop of Serpukhov, St, 202
Maximos, Bishop of Pittsburgh, 233, 237-38, 270, 279-82, 285-86
Maximos, Ecumenical Patriarch, 315
Maximos (Tsitsimbakos), Metropolitan, 103, 106, 108, 110
Maximos (Vallianatos), Metropolitan of Cephalonia and the Seven Islands, 105, 106, 109, 120-21, 162
Maximus the Confessor, St, 164, 227, 231, 238, 239-40, 292, 295
Maximus the Cynic, 93
Melehov, Fr. Victor, 140, 162
Meletios Metaxakis, Archbishop of Athens, then Ecumenical Patriarch, then Patriarch of Alexandria, 25, 26, 27, 29-33, *31*, 34, 36, 38, 130, 311, 312, 313, 314

Mercurios, Metropolitan, 103, 106, 108, 110
Messalians. *See* Marcionites.
Methodios, Bishop of Boston, 223
Methodios (Kondostanos), Metropolitan, 33
Metropolia. *See* Orthodox Church in America.
Mitrophan, Bishop, 245
Mohammed, 162-63, 191, 224, 248, 273, 278, 292, 321
Monophysites, Monophysitism, 118, 119, 155, 163, 216-19, 248, 280, 287, 320, 322
Montanus, Montanists, 256-61
Moscow Patriarchate, 112, 123, 136, 139, 145, 148, 150, 154, 160, 164, 165, 169, 196-210, 214, 232, 239, 249, 273, 300, 317, 318, 322
Moulatsiotis, Fr. Nektarios, 170-74
Mount Athos. *See* Athos, Mount.
"Mutual episcopal recognition" as criterion of canonical Orthodox church, 272
Myron (Christea), Patriarch of Romania, 58, 313
Mysteries of heterodox without grace, 251-53

Nathaniel, Archbishop of Vienna, 188
National Council of Churches, 278
Nativity Epistle of 1986. *See under* Russian Church Abroad.
Nazi occupation of Greece, 63
Nectarios of Pentapolis, St, 126, 282, 286
Nectary, Bishop of Seattle, 83, 191
Nektarios, Bishop of Kalymnos, 222
Nestor, Bishop of Kamchatka, 188
Nestorians, 112
Nestorius, 251
New Age Theology, 224
New Calendar, 18, 23, 27, 48-49, 57, 169, 170-74, 246-47, 249, 314
  adopted in Church of Greece under duress in 1924, 35, 36-37, 313
  condemned by Synods and Pan-Orthodox Councils, 34, 35, 167, 265, 284-85, 311, 313
  created schism, 50, 54, 77, 158
  devised by Pope Gregory XIII, 167, 311
  followers of declare Mysteries of the True Orthodox Christians invalid. *See* Encyclical of 1926.
  followers of recognize sacraments of heterodox, 53, 164, 218-19, 235, 255-56, 267, 280-82, 298-305, 319, 322
  initially rejected in Europe, 168
  introduced by guile, by Metaxakis, in Constantinople, 34
  introduced by Metaxakis in Alexandria, 38
  opposed in 1924 by Alexandria, Antioch, Cyprus, and Jerusalem, 38, 313
  uncanonical overlapping jurisdictions among new calendarists, 130, 165, 266
New Martyr Catherine of Attica. *See* Routis, Catherine.
Nicephorus the Confessor, St, 175
Nicholas I, Pope, 168, 259
Nicholas Milosh, Bishop, 94
Nicodemos of the Holy Mountain, St, 144, 147, 188, 212, 216, 240-41, 246-47, 296
Nikodim, Metropolitan of Leningrad, 206, 272, 319
Nikolaj Velimirovic, Serbian Bishop, 73
Nikon, Archbishop of Washington and Florida, 83
Novatians. *See* Cathari.

Old Calendarists. *See* True Orthodox Christians.
Oriental Orthodox. *See* Monophysites.
Origen, 284
Orthodox Association. *See* Association of the Orthodox.
Orthodox Church in America (OCA), former "Metropolia," 151, 154, 155, 184, 193, 194, 213, 214, 239, 240, 316

INDEX

Orthodoxos Typos, 111, 112, 163, 172, 232, 298-305

Paisios, Bishop of Euripus and Euboea, 100
Paisios, Elder (Athonite), 290-92
Paisios (Loulourgas), Metropolitan (in United States), 105, 106, 122, 123
Paisios (Phinokaliotis), Metropolitan of Aegina, 104, 105, 106
Palassis, Fr. Neketas, 134, 138-39
Pan-Orthodox Congress. *See* Congress of 1923.
Pan-Orthodox Councils. *See under* Council.
"Pan-Orthodox" Vespers, 139
Panteleimon, Archimandrite, 97, 184
Papal prerogative, 168
Papists. *See* Roman Catholics.
Parnitha Convent, 74
Parthenios, Metropolitan of the Cyclades, 80, 81, *81*, 317
Parthenios, Patriarch of Alexandria, 162-63, 224, 248, 273, 278, 291, 292, 293, 321
Parthenios, Patriarch of Jerusalem, 286
Paschalion, 16, 33, 49, 58, 77, 118, 129, 158, 167-68, 285, 313
Pastoral Encyclical of June, 1935. *See under* Chrysostom, Metropolitan of Florina.
Patric (Ranson) of France, Fr., 146, 148
Paul the Apostle, St, 53, 55, 92, 164, 226, 230, 241
Paul, Archbishop of Sydney and Australia-New Zealand, 133, 138
Paul, Patriarch of Serbia, 322
Paul VI, Pope, 159, 317, 318
Paula, Abbess of Ascension Convent, 191
Pepuzenes, 256-60
Perepiolkina, Ludmilla, 32, 34
Persecutions. *See under* True Orthodox Christians of Greece.
Peter of Alexandria, St, 189
Peter the Apostle, St, 276

Peter, Metropolitan of Astoria, 100, 122, 155
Phanar. *See* Constantinople, Church of.
Philaret, Metropolitan, 82-83, *86*, 87, 96, 130, *131*, 132-34, 135, 136, 137, 141, 142, 145, 146, 147, 148, 149, 182-210, *185*, 211, 212, 216, 240, 242, 250, 253, 317, 318, 320
Philip Saliba, Metropolitan, 272, 277
Philotheus, Archbishop of Hamburg, *96*, 97, 193
Photios, Bishop of Lyons (formerly Hieromonk Joseph), 146, 148, 160, 321
Photios, Bishop of Triaditsa, 29, 30, 32, 33, 244
Photios, Patriarch of Alexandria, 38, 313
Photius the Great, St, 17, 168, 238, 259, 282
Pimen, Patriarch of Moscow, 145, 148, 206, 272
Pitirim, Metropolitan of Volokolamsk, 273, 321
Plastiras, Colonel Nicholas, 35, 36, 312
Poland, Church of, 164, 232, 314, 317, 322
Polycarp, Metropolitan of Diavlia, 46, 53, 63, *64*, *66*, 67, 69, 73, 90, 314, 315, 316
Potapov, Fr. Victor, 138
Potential schism. *See under* Schism.
Priscilla, 257, 260
Prokopios, Archbishop of Athens, 27
Prokopios, Bishop of Andrubis, 91
Prophet Elias Skete, Athos, 138, 289
Proselytism. *See* Summit Message.
Purgatory, 235, 284

Revolutionary Government of Greece, 25, 27, 35, 36, 38, 312
Roman Catholics, 93, 126-27, 136, 163, 164, 172, 181, 191, 207-8, 214, 215, 223, 232, 234-36, 238, 247, 262, 264, 267, 271, 272, 273, 277, 280-85, 287, 292, 296, 298-305, 318, 319, 321, 322

Roman Catholics desiring Orthodoxy rejected by new calendarists, 222
Romania, Church of, 34, 38, 58, 164, 232, 265, 266, 312, 313, 314, 315, 317, 322
Romanides, Fr. John, 232, 233
Routis, New Martyr Catherine, 39, *40*, 305-10, *307*
Royalist Government, 25,
Rudder, The, 94, 144, 147, 188, 262, 274-75
Russia, Holy Synod of Church of, 34, 91, 154, 265
 uncontested jurisdiction of, in North America before 1917 Revolution, 130
 See also Moscow Patriarchate.
Russian Catacomb Church. *See* Catacomb Church of Russia.
Russian Church Abroad, 126-27, 238-42, 255-56
 accepts clergy fleeing heretical bishops without canonical release, 132, 153, 213
 accepts Synod of Archbishop Auxentius, 82-83, 85, 318
 Anglican ecclesiology espoused by, in Fr. Alexander Lebedev's *Open Letters*, 152-53
 and Archbishop Akakios Pappas, 79-81, 84-85, 316
 canonical abuses of, 138-39, 150-56
 Certificate of Incorporation, 1952, 136
 changes doctrinal position after repose of Metropolitan Philaret, 134
 claims departure of clergy and faithful in 1986 was for personal reasons, 141
 and Cyprian Synod, 120, 155, 243-50
 departure from, of 30 clergy, 25 parishes, monastery, convent, and many faithful, in 1986, 140-41, 150, 161, 241, 242, 320-21
 falls under own Anathema, 250
 forbidden to have relations with Moscow Patriarchate by Metropolitan Anastasy, 136, 203
 gives Holy Mysteries to those from Moscow Patriarchate, new calendarists, Makrakist, and Copt, 154-55
 haven of Orthodoxy for those fleeing heresy, 132, 149
 "inglorious end" of, 242
 issues Anathema of 1983 under Metropolitan Philaret, 132-34, 320
 and Kiousis Synod, 155-56
 and Matthewites, 87-98, *96*, 318
 negates Anathema of 1983 in Vitaly's Nativity Epistle of 1986, 141, 143, 147, 152-52, 153, 211-16, 240-41, 321
 New England Deanery of, sends letter to Metropolitan Vitaly, 135-40
 and Orthodox Church in America, 154-55, 184, 193-94
 perceived by Catacomb Christians of Russia to have changed its theological course, 161
 policies of imply loss of grace by new calendarists, 153, 193, 194, 213, 250
 rejects as unlawful elections of Patriarchs of Moscow from 1943 on, 206
 Report of 1969 by Archbishop Vitaly, 137, 145
 and Russian Exarchate in Paris, 183-96
 "two minds" of, 240
 See also under Concelebrations.

Sabbas of Karyes, Elder, 288-96, *290*
Sabbas, Bishop of Edmonton, 83
Sacred Union of Zealot Monks, 39, 79, 288-96
Saint Anne's Skete, Athos, 301
Saint Joseph of Arimathea Parish, 238-42
Saint Vladimir's Seminary, 239
Saints Cyprian and Justina, Monastery of, in Fili, 106, 119
Sakarellos, Athanasios, 298-305
Salvation, other than in Jesus Christ. *See* Barr Statement.
Sardelis, Kostas, 304-5
Schism, 55, 59, 187-92
 as ruinous as heresy, 189

INDEX 345

defined by Canon XV of First-and-Second Council, 117-18
defined by St Basil, 116, 256-59
"potentially and in actuality," 69
"potentially and in essence," 49
"potentially but not actually," 59-60
redefined by Synod of Cyprian, 116, 118
Seraphim, Archbishop of Athens, 170, 174
Seraphim, Archbishop of Caracas and Venezuela, 133
Seraphim, Archbishop of Chicago and Detroit, 79, 83, 85, 132, 316
Seraphim, Archbishop of Finland, 34
Serbia, Church of, 34, 120, 137, 138, 139, 150, 153, 154, 163, 226, 241, 249, 312, 314, 317
See also Free Serbian Church.
Serbian Orthodox Centre, 239
Sergianism, 135, 139, 140
Sergius, Metropolitan, 201-2, 206
Declaration of 1927, 201
Sigillion of 1583, 283-85
"Sister Churches" (Roman Catholic and Orthodox), 163, 173, 235, 281, 322
Solovki Nuns, miracle of, 203-5
Solzhenitsyn, Alexander, 209
Sophronios, Patriarch of Jerusalem, 283, 285
Sorrowful Epistles, 132, 137, 212, 216, 240, 318
Soviet Union, 136, 138, 139, 160, 196-210
Spyridon, Archbishop of Athens, 69, 315
Spyridon, Bishop of Trimythus, 64, 65
Stalin, 201
Stephanos, Bishop of Chios, *129*
Stephen Tsikouras, Bishop of Kardamyllae, 105, 106
Storozhev, Fr. John, 191
Stratigeas, Archimandrite Paul, 122-23
Stylianos, Archbishop of Australia, 291, 292, 300
Summit Message, 219-31, 322
Sylvester, Patriarch of Alexandria, 283, 285

Sylvester, Patriarch of Antioch, 286
Symeon the New Theologian, St, 143
Symeon of Thessalonica, St, 252
Synodicon of Orthodoxy, 118, 119, 134, 147

Talantov, Boris, 206
Tarasius, St, 94, 246, 251, 254, 259
Thalassinos, Fr. Theodore, 317
Theodore the Reader, 254
Theodore the Studite, St, 158, 292
Theodoropoulos, Fr. Epiphanios, 295
Theokletos, Archbishop of Athens, 35, 312
Theonas, Bishop of Thessaly, 160
Theonas, hieromonk kicked to death by new calendar bishop, 267
Theophan the Recluse, 205
Theophilos Tsirbas, Metropolitan of Christianopolis, 104, 105, 106
Theophilus Ionescu, Bishop of Detroit, 79, 84, 316
Thus Do We Believe, Thus Do We Speak, 67, 82, 98, 102
Thyateira Confession, 319, 320, 321
Tikhon, Patriarch of Moscow, St, 200-1, 202
To the Churches of Christ Wheresoever They Might Be. See Encyclical of 1920.
Tombros, Fr. Eugene, 66, 87, 88, *96*, 97
Traditional Orthodox Christians. *See* True Orthodox Christians.
True Orthodox Christians of Greece, 38, 67, *68*, 161, 241
accused of pan-Slavism and Communism, 69, 315
beginning of, 39ff, 313
clergy of shaven, Epitaphios overturned, Mysteries profaned, 70, 71, *71*, 266-67
declare State Church in schism, 53-55, 314
Decree No. 45 of Greek Government against, 71
hierarchy of, in 1963, *81*
legally recognized by State, 100

True Orthodox Christians/[cont.]
  Mysteries of declared by State Church to be without grace, 39-41, 57, 119, 173, 276-77, 313
  origin of "Florinite" – "Matthewite" divisions among, 59-63, 268, 315
  persecuted, 39, 50-51, *51*, *52*, 63, 69-73, *70*, *71*, 77, 266-67, 277, 305-10, 313, 315
  and Russian Church Abroad, 79-86, 89-97
  suspicious clergymen among, 65
  sympathy for, among new calendar bishops and clergy, 46, 57-58, 59, 60-61, 63, 74-76, 79
  Synod of, formed in 1935, 46-47, 314
  See also Auxentian Synod; Chrysostom, Metropolitan of Florina; *and* Florinites.
Tsakos, Dorotheos, 120-21
Two Extremes, The, 295

Unhealthy ecumenism," 171-73
Uniatism, 58, 167, 234, 236, 265, 313
  real reason for adopting new calendar, 34, 168, 170-74, 265
Unitarians, 163, 223-24, 226, 278, 320
Urbi et orbi blessing given by Pope and Patriarch, 304
Uspensky, Archimandrite Porphyry, 285

Valentinians, 257, 260
Varnava, Patriarch of Serbia, 188
Vasily, Serbian Bishop, 138
Vatican, the, 164, 172, 234, 299, 302
  See also Roman Catholics.
Venizelos, Eleftherios, 25, *26*, 27, *28*, 29, 30, 31
Videkanich, Fr. Chedomir, 138
Vikentios, Bishop in Astoria, 122, 123

Vitaly, Archbishop of Montreal and Canada, then Metropolitan, 83, 127, 133, 135, 141, 143, 145-46, 147, 149, 200, 203, 211-16, 240-41, 242, 243, 320
Vladimir, Great Prince of Kiev, St, 183

Willebrands, Cardinal, 234
World Council of Churches (WCC), 120, 123, 137, 138, 139, 144, 145, 159, 163, 202, 214, 218, 270-71, 278, 315, 317
  Buck Hills Falls Gathering, 1963, 317
  Canberra Assembly, 1991, 322
  Evanston Assembly, 1954, 316
  Lund Faith and Order Conference, 1952, 316
  Nairobi Assembly, 1975, 221-22, 271, 319
  New Delhi Assembly, 1961, 316-17
  Oberlin Faith and Order Conference, 1957, 225, 316
  Uppsala Assembly, 1968, 271, 318
  Vancouver Assembly, 1983, 320
  See also Barr Statement.
"World Orthodoxy," 119, 123, 130, 132, 162-65, 174, 232, 236, 237, 238, 274, 278, 287-88, 303, 318, 320, 322

Yakunin, Fr. Gleb, 197

Zaitsev, Archimandrite Constantine, 199, 200
Zealots of Mount Athos. *See* Sacred Union of Zealot Monks.
Zervakos, Fr. Philotheos, 76-78, *76*, 174
Zervoudakis, Alexander, 29
Zeses, Fr. Theodore, 233-38
Zonaras, 262

To subscribe to *The True Vine*, official diocesan periodical of the Holy Orthodox Church in North America, or to obtain back issues, please write to:

The True Vine
P.O. Box 129
Roslindale, MA 02131

To subscribe to *The Orthodox Christian Witness*, or to obtain a catalogue of the Saint Nectarios Press, which includes many Saints' Lives and books on Orthodox doctrine, history, and spirituality, please write to:

Saint Nectarios Press
10300 Ashworth Ave. North
Seattle, WA 98133

The Struggle Against Ecumenism
was typeset in Adobe Caslon
by the Holy Transfiguration Monastery
and printed in an edition of 3000 copies by
the Kingsport Press in Kingsport, Tennessee,
on Glatfelter Offset sixty pound weight paper,
an acid-free paper of proven durability.

GLORY BE TO GOD FOR ALL THINGS.
AMEN